THE PROSPECTS

OF

AMERICAN DEMOCRACY

THE PROSPECTS

OF

AMERICAN
DEMOCRACY

GEORGE S. COUNTS

THE JOHN DAY COMPANY

NEW YORK

This country, with its institutions,
belongs to the people who inhabit it.

—ABRAHAM LINCOLN.

Foreword

For many years, as I have studied the revolution-ary and counter-revolutionary movements of Europe against the background of American life and history, the conviction has grown within me that, as a people, we *need* not follow any pattern of political change developed in the Old World. This is not to say that we may not blunder upon some mad, oppressive, and sanguinary course, quite as terrifying as anything to be observed beyond the Atlantic. Nor is it to say that we can learn nothing from the experiences of other peoples. Most certainly we can learn much; and we should keep our eyes focussed continually on developments abroad. But at the same time we should resolutely choose our own road to the future, making full use of our vast, unique, and priceless heritage of liberty and democracy and refusing to wear the blinders of social doctrines and dogmas either unsuited to our situation or calculated to repudiate great popular victories won generations ago. The central purpose of the present volume is to direct attention to this heritage and to suggest how it may be employed in the task of adjusting our democracy to the conditions of the industrial age.

In the preparation of the work I am greatly indebted to my assistant, Mrs. Nucia P. Lodge, who has worked with me indefatigably from the beginning; to my colleagues, Professors John L. Childs, Merle Curti, and Jesse H. Newlon, for reading and criticising the manuscript and generally for helping me to mature my thinking about the problem; to my friends Professor William Gellermann of Northwestern University, Dr. Mordecai Grossman of the College of the City of New York, Professor Harold Hand of Stanford University, and Mr. Edward A. Shils of Teachers College for similar services; and to Mr. Nathan K.

Mendelsohn, a Teachers College student, for certain researches. I am under peculiarly heavy obligation to Dean William F. Russell of Teachers College for support and encouragement in my studies, even when he has disagreed vigorously with my conclusions. He also read and criticised the manuscript.

GEORGE S. COUNTS.

August 2, 1938.

Contents

CHAPTER *1:*

DEMOCRACY IN RETREAT

A GENERATION ago in America an order of society and government called democracy seemed triumphant. The wisdom, beneficence, and perdurance of this order were generally accepted as axiomatic. The people of the United States took pride in the characterization of their country as the "great democracy of the West" and nourished the conviction that for generations they had been leading mankind in the long struggle for popular liberty and justice. They believed firmly that the twentieth century would witness the spread of democratic ideas, values, and institutions throughout the world. To them the principle of autocracy was a barbaric survival from the dark ages, at last in full retreat before the rising tide of popular enlightenment and destined soon to be relegated to the limbo of history.

To the discerning eye, to be sure, somber clouds, presaging coming storms, appeared above the social horizon. At home, the contest between capital and labor would burst forth now and then into bloody conflict—bitter and ruthless—to reveal deep differences bearing the seed of eventual civil strife. Abroad, the great nations, engaged in a struggle for markets, raw materials, colonies, and spheres of influence, had entered upon a war of diplomatic maneuver and military armament which with every year became more strained and savage. And in all modern nations minority parties, organizations, and movements, born of industrial capitalism, were demanding profound changes in the social structure and even preaching the doctrines of violent revolution.

Shortly before his death in 1910, William Graham Sumner, seeing these portents and being aware of fundamental changes in society already far advanced, made a striking observation and prophecy. "I have lived through the best period of my country's history," he said. "The next generations are going to see war and social calamities. I am glad I don't have to live on into them." [1] Others, both scholars and men of affairs, foresaw in broad outline the coming crisis in American and world civilization; but the vast majority of people, then as in times past, stood on the threshold of great convulsions and had not the slightest inkling of the forces stirring beneath their feet—forces which within a few years would alter the whole aspect of their lives and bring pain, privation, disillusionment, desperation, and death to millions throughout the world. To the ordinary middle-class American, socialism was an annoying curiosity, communism but a word in the dictionary; while the term fascism was yet to be coined. The class struggle, the red flag, the hammer and sickle, the swastika, the totalitarian state held for him little or no social significance. He passed from election to election much as he passed from one baseball season to the next. Not that bitter political battles were unknown to him. The Civil War was vividly recalled to his mind every Memorial Day. But he felt that at last the rules of the game had been firmly established and that even the stars in their courses were fighting on the side of democracy and the democratic process. He would have agreed with the following estimate with which Professor J. B. Bury in 1913 concluded his study of the history of freedom of thought: "The struggle of reason against authority has ended in what appears now to be a decisive and permanent victory for liberty. In the most civilized and progressive countries, freedom of discussion is recognized as a fundamental principle." [2]

Today the outlook is radically changed. No friend of free institutions can view the present situation in the nation and the world with equanimity. Since the Great War one country after another has taken the road to revolution and dictatorship; and no country, not even the oldest of the democracies, has wholly escaped the virus. These new autocracies, seizing power by diverse methods, have suspended civil liberties and rule by the radio and the machine gun. Having established their special orthodoxies, they organize priesthoods of the new political faiths, forge into a single instrument all the agencies of propaganda, set up rigorous border patrols against the entrance of "dangerous ideas and persons," and seek in every way to mold the minds of their respective peoples. Where propaganda fails, they have recourse to espionage, secret police, torture, concentration camps, firing squads, sadistic orgies, and assassinations. At the same time piracy returns to the seas, powerful nations wage undeclared war on defenseless peoples, rival systems of provocation carry on a deadly struggle under the cloak of peaceful professions, and the moral foundations of international order are contemned and mocked. Only too well authenticated is the doubt, expressed by Lytton Strachey in his review of Professor Bury's book at the time of its publication, that the long struggle for liberty of thought had been crowned with final success during the reign of Queen Victoria: "Well, that is very nice, very nice indeed—if it is true. But, after all, can we be quite so sure that it *is* true? Is it really credible that the human race should have got along so far as that? That such deeply rooted instincts as the love of persecution and the hatred of heterodoxies should have been dissipated into thin air by the charms of philosophers and the common sense of that remarkable period the nineteenth century?" [8]

The attack upon democracy comes from both left and right. Under the banners of communism a dictatorship is set up, paradoxically, in the name of democracy—a "dictatorship of the proletariat" which in actual practice becomes a dictatorship first of a party that claims to represent the proletariat and then of a handful of men who claim to represent the party. The object and justification of the dictatorship, according to the theory, is the establishment ultimately of the most complete democracy in history—a society without economic classes in which the exploitation of man by man will be abolished, all races and peoples will live in peace and harmony, and mankind generally will achieve maturity and enter upon its rightful inheritance. The repudiation of democracy is said to be temporary and partial, a hard necessity forced upon the present epoch by an irreconcilable and irrepressible conflict of classes. But whatever the doctrine the fact is that free political institutions are repudiated and a regime of minority rule and strict censorship of speech and thought inaugurated.

In the case of fascism the repudiation of democracy is complete and uncompromising. The concept of equality, whether applied to races or to individuals, is scorned and rejected, not merely because it is unattainable, but because it is contrary to the spirit that rules the universe. Inequality being everywhere the law of nature, the strong are urged to mastery, even as the weak are admonished to practice submission. For the strong to refuse to exercise fully the rights attached to power would be to engage in the grossest immorality, to violate the purpose of creation, to commit the unpardonable sin of history. This theme constitutes the core of the philosophical writings of the fascist leaders and permeates the program of public education. In a guide prepared by Wilhelm Stuckhart for the German teacher of history the following doctrine is propagated repeatedly: "The experience of history and the findings of racial science teach us that Democracy has always been the political form of the racial decline of a creative people." [4]

There is of course nothing novel in the struggle between democracy and autocracy. The former has had to contend with the latter wherever and whenever it has appeared in human history. The novel and disturbing feature of the present situation is the fact that the contemporary dictator actually achieves power through an appeal to the broad masses of the population. Thus in Germany, a nation justly renowned for its cultural achievements and for the high intellectual level of its people, Hitler succeeded in building up the most powerful political party in the Reich, took over the reins of government by constitutional means, and immediately destroyed the republic. The German people seem to have abdicated deliberately in favor of a dictator who during his career had given every evidence of being arbitrary, ruthless, brutal, and mad. Democracy, having lost its *elan vital*, its desire to live, its belief in itself, presumably committed suicide. At the present juncture in world affairs it seems that a considerable proportion of men and women have neither the desire nor the will to govern themselves. They prefer to prostrate both body and soul before a leader to whom they attach divine or quasi-divine attributes and to submerge their persons in a movement which they do not understand but which they hope will prove beneficent. In any country today, if circumstances should become favorable, it would be possible to secure wide popular support for the overthrow of popular rule. The extraordinary careers of Huey Long and Father Coughlin, not to mention others, suggest that this could happen even in the greatest and most celebrated of the democracies.

The contemporary attack upon democracy is militant and inspired. It has assumed the features of a crusading faith. It has formulated an interpretation of history which provides moral support for the spirit of unabashed aggression and destroys utterly the foundations for the promotion of peace and understanding among the nations. Indeed it rejects peace as an ideal and glorifies war and conquest, raising imperialistic adventure to the level of the paramount national virtue. "For Fascism," writes Mussolini in a considered article in the *Enciclopedia Italiana*, "the growth of empire, that is to say the expansion of the nation, is an essential manifestation of vitality, and its opposite a sign of deca-

dence. Peoples who are rising, or rising again after a period
of decadence, are always imperialistic: any renunciation is a
sign of decay and death." [5] And the spirit of fascism, in both
its domestic and its international implications, is by no
means absent from the United States. During the present
period of distress there has been talk of substituting bullets
for ballots and not a little resort to violence in the settlement
of disputes.

In the face of the world-wide assault upon its ideas, values,
and institutions, democracy tends either to retreat or to assume a defensive role. As the democratically elected government of Spain fights for its life against the aggressive designs
and even invading armies of two fascist states, officially supported and blessed by the hierarchy of the most powerful
authoritarian ecclesiastical organization in the contemporary
world, the great democracies, torn by internal doubts and
conflicts, stand idly by and even acquiesce in the subversion
of international law calculated to weaken the Spanish democracy. These events lend support to the paradoxical observation of H. N. Brailsford that the democratic governments of
Western Europe, had they not been democracies, "might
have saved Democracy in Germany with comparative ease." [6]
It may later be added that, if they had not been democracies,
they might have saved democracy within their own borders
without difficulty.

In their theoretical advocacy the friends of democracy
adopt a defensive or even an apologetic tone. The best they
can say is that while democracy is not as good as it should
be, it is not as bad as it might be. Cataloguing and com-
mending its merits, conceding and lamenting its defects, and
conscientiously balancing argument against argument, they
arrive at the tentative conclusion that democracy is a trifle
superior to any rival order of society and life, as if diverse
social systems were readily commensurable. Moreover, in an
age when great choices have to be made, when positive and

determined social action has to be taken, democracy is denominated the middle way. Obviously if such a conception of democracy should prevail, its worst enemies could ask for nothing better. It would become a deceptive haven for the timid and the vacillating, while the bolder spirits would enroll under banners representing positive and challenging philosophies and programs. As a matter of fact, democracy is by no means a middle way between extremes, lacking substance of its own and defined in terms of its opponents. It is another way—unique, radical, revolutionary—the most adventurous way that man has ever taken—a way beset with difficulties and demanding the fullest possible development of the powers of the race.

The current crisis of democracy, which is but an aspect of a general crisis in world society, may be traced primarily to two factors: the closing of the geographical frontiers of the earth and the rise of industrial civilization. Under the impact of forces so profound and pervasive in their influence any inherited social structure would be shaken to its foundations and men would be compelled inevitably to re-examine their traditional ideas and seek new ways of life.

With the discovery of the other half of the planet at the beginning of the modern period the peoples of Western Europe entered upon an epoch of expansion without parallel in history. Vast, fertile, and sparsely inhabited lands were opened to conquest, settlement, and exploitation. These lands doubled the area of the known world, provided territory for surplus populations, relieved the cramped conditions of the home countries, softened the acerbities of the struggle for existence, created opportunities for wealth accumulation on an unprecedented scale, enabled the oppressed to flee oppression, awakened hope in the damned of earth, shattered chains forged by custom and tradition, promoted communication and interchange of ideas, placed a high premium on individual initiative and daring, provided a material foundation for optimism, turned the attention of men irrevocably to temporal things, encouraged and even compelled novel experiments in social arrangements, and generally challenged the human mind to think, to hope, and to dare. This long period has already drawn to a close. The nations of mankind must now learn to live together in a world whose physical boundaries will never again be extended. Science can and will penetrate into the mysteries of mind and matter and place new sources of energy in the hands of men, but no unknown continents remain to be discovered and settled. Since America was one of the great, perhaps the greatest, of the frontiers of the earth, the repercussions of this change in human fortune and circumstance will be peculiarly profound in the United States.

The rise of industrial civilization was closely linked with the exploitation of the new lands and the attendant widening of the markets. And with the closing of the geographical frontiers it may be expected to take the place of those frontiers by opening new vistas for human development. Industrial civilization with its science and technology is inherently dynamic: it encourages the systematic advancement of knowledge, promotes discovery and invention by design, creates new materials unknown to nature, places practically unlimited power in human hands, multiplies fabulously the productivity of labor, gives man increasing power over life and death, causes war to take on a truly terrifying and hideous visage, extends the range of social integration, fosters the idea of rational control of the environment, propagates the principle of economic planning, and generally nurtures a naturalistic outlook upon the universe.

The coming of industrial civilization, moreover, is not to be understood as involving merely the introduction into the culture of certain new elements. This is due to the fact that a culture possesses a certain organic quality: it is not an aggregation of discrete items, each maintaining a separate existence; it is rather a system of relationships which, in response to impacts from without and strains from within, lives and changes its patterns. Thus science and technology, along with their varied fruits, have unsettled American and world culture from center to circumference, given rise to severe social and cultural dislocations, destroyed the authority of old sanctions, undermined traditional folkways and mores, put new meaning into inherited forms, and made necessary the creation of novel cultural patterns and configurations.

It is out of this situation that the crisis of American and world democracy has arisen. Man's "practical inventiveness" has run "ahead of his moral consciousness and social organization." When this has happened in the past, as it has at long intervals, according to Stanley Casson, "man has equally faced destruction." [7] For it must be kept in mind that profound changes in the culture, particularly in the modes of production and exchange, are not impersonal and mechanical in their incidence and implications. They involve changes in human relations and conflicts of interest among social groups and classes which set the stage for more or less severe struggles and thus place a strain on the democratic process. These changes have also affected the foundations of American democracy and altered the terms of the political equation. Already it is clear that the democracy of today is not and cannot be the democracy of the early years of the Republic.

It is no exaggeration to say that in all probability the present generation and the generation immediately to follow will be called upon to decide whether democracy is to survive and, if so, in what form. Indeed democracy has already disappeared in certain countries where it had established itself in some measure. While the major concern in these pages is with the situation in the United States, the fact must not be overlooked that the American people, sheltered though they are by the waters of two great oceans, cannot be indifferent to undemocratic tendencies elsewhere. Sooner or later such tendencies are likely to affect them. Little discernment is required to detect the beginnings of an attack upon democracy in the United States. The fact that this attack is commonly made in terms of the defense of "the American system" should confuse no one. In truth, blind loyalty to the traditional forms and symbols of democracy, without regard for its inner character and spirit, is doubtless the surest way to destroy it; and the way in which it will be destroyed, if its present and potential enemies should prove successful.

The American people should make no mistake about this. There is no spirit guiding the processes of social evolution toward a democratic goal or toward any worthy end or form of excellence. The past alone of any people is secure; the future can be only what they will to make it, working within those limits of the possible set by the forces of history. Humanity is raised to its highest levels only by long and sustained effort, discipline, and watchfulness. All too frequently in the past human societies have experienced catastrophe, cultural regression, and return to barbarism. Moreover, the fairly long tradition of democracy on the North American continent is by no means surety for its indefinite continuance. Future historians may record that American democracy was but an episode made possible by a peculiar set of conditions arising out of the mode of settlement of a new continent and the level of the technical arts in the eighteenth and nineteenth centuries.

If democracy is to survive in the United States, the American people, besides desiring it, will have to become familiar with its meaning and history, the conditions under which it arose, its changing fortunes and prospects, and the crisis which it faces today. They will have to acquaint themselves with this new industrial civilization within whose bounds it is compelled to live. They will have to study all rival systems of thought and society and discover the secret of their appeal, striving earnestly to understand why men, having experienced political freedom, turn to dictatorship and tyranny. They will have to search out the weaknesses, injustices, and deficiencies of the contemporary social order and seek to correct them. Above all, they will have to banish their complacency, recapture the spirit of an earlier day, fashion a truly challenging and realistic conception of democracy, and take the offensive in applying the conception to the reconstruction of American society. If the masses of the people lack the energy and the will to make this effort, that fact alone would presumably mean that the original democratic impulse, whatever its source, had spent itself and that the dream of a land of liberty and equality for the many was after all only a dream.

REFERENCES

1. A. G. Keller, "The Discoverer of the Forgotten Man," *The American Mercury* (November, 1932), 257.

2. J. B. Bury, *A History of Freedom of Thought* (Home University Library edition, New York, 1913), 247-248.

3. C. E. M. Joad, *Liberty To-day* (New York, 1935), 3.

4. Wilhelm Stuckhart, *Geschichte im Geschichtsunterricht* (Frankfurt, 1934), 84.

5. Benito Mussolini, "Fascismo" in *Enciclopedia Italiana* (Milan, 1932), XIV, 851.

6. H. N. Brailsford, *Property or Peace* (New York, 1934), 43.

7. Stanley Casson, *Progress and Catastrophe* (New York, 1937), 19.

CHAPTER *2:*

AMERICAN DEMOCRACY YESTERDAY

THE authenticity of American democracy cannot be successfully challenged. Whatever may have been its defects and limitations, and these have always been many and severe, it was and is one of the realities of history. In certain quarters, to be sure, it has become fashionable to deny that democracy ever played a significant role in American life and to contend that it was but a word which the few employed to deceive and govern the many. The record seems to show, however, that for generations the North American continent was the scene of a bold and humane experiment in the field of human relationships. Certainly such has been the conviction of the American people themselves and of ordinary men and women throughout the world.

The fact that during the single century from 1820 to 1920 approximately thirty-four million persons crossed the Atlantic, always with heartaches and often in the face of great hardship, is sufficient testimony to the substance of this conviction. The virtually unbounded economic opportunities of the country admittedly provided the fundamental motivation of this greatest migration of history, but those opportunities were the product of social and political institutions, of prevailing conceptions of society and human worth, no less than of geography. The meaning of America for the oppressed of Europe during the century following the establishment of the Republic was expressed in these lines of William Blake written about 1793:

> Why should I care for the men of Thames,
> Or the cheating waves of charter'd streams,
> Or shrink at the little blasts of fear
> That the hireling blows into my ear?

Tho' born on the cheating banks of Thames,
Tho' his waters bathed my infant limbs,
The Ohio shall wash his stains from me:
I was born a slave, but I go to be free.[1]

This same sentiment was expressed in vigorous language by an English farmer and master-bleacher, Thomas Hulme, who in the early eighteen-hundreds began to ponder over the future of his nine children. "I saw," he wrote, "that, of whatever I might be able to give to my children, as well as of what they might be able to earn, *more than one half* would be taken away to feed pensioned Lords and Ladies, Soldiers to shoot at us, Parsons to persecute us, and Fund-holders, who had lent their money to be applied to purposes of enslaving us."[2] In 1811 and 1812 in Lancashire, where he lived, "men were seized, dragged to prison, treated like convicts, many transported and put to death, without having committed any thing, which the law of the land deems a *crime.*"[3] In 1816 he set out for America on a trip of exploration and "was well pleased" with the country. He "saw an absence of human misery . . . a government taking away a very small portion of men's earnings . . . ease and happiness and a fearless utterance of thought every where prevail . . . no mobs, no riots, no spies, no transportings, no hangings."[4] He returned to England the same year and in 1817, having disposed of his property, he crossed the Atlantic with his entire family and made the United States his adopted country. In contrasting the New World with the Old he then wrote as follows: "There I should have been in constant anxiety about my family. Here I am in none at all. Here I am in fear of no *spies,* no *false witnesses,* no *blood-money men.* Here no fines, irons, or gallowses await me, let me *think* or *say* what I will about the government. Here I have to pay no people to be ready to shoot at me, or run me through the body, or chop me down. Here no vile Priest can rob me and mock me in the same breath."[5]

It must be remembered that at the time of the Constitutional Convention in 1787 oligarchy, autocracy, and despotism were in the saddle everywhere and the young republic, feeble in both wealth and population and torn by internal fears and jealousies, had set sail on relatively uncharted seas. Those who first directed the course of the ship of state, like all true revolutionaries, felt themselves charged with heavy responsibilities, not only to their own people, but also to mankind. In his first inaugural address, with the struggle for independence still fresh in his memory and in the memory of those present, Washington formulated this faith in words that still live. "The preservation of the sacred fire of liberty," he said, "and the destiny of the republican model of government, are justly considered as *deeply*, perhaps as *finally* staked, on the experiment intrusted to the hands of the American people." [6] In similar vein spoke Daniel Webster a generation later in his Bunker Hill Oration: "If, in our case, the representative system ultimately fail, popular governments must be pronounced impossible. No combination of circumstances more favorable to the experiment can ever be expected to occur. The last hopes of mankind, therefore, rest with us; and if it should be proclaimed, that our example had become an argument against the experiment, the knell of popular liberty would be sounded throughout the earth." [7] The same thought was expressed in one of the master-pieces of English prophetic literature by Abraham Lincoln during the dark hours of civil strife. And the great popular leaders of the contemporary epoch, notably Woodrow Wilson and the two Roosevelts, have addressed their appeal to the people in terms of this democratic faith.

To such an appeal the American people, particularly in times of distress, have always responded. On the one hand, they have believed themselves fortunate in living under free institutions; on the other, they have felt themselves responsible for upholding the democratic faith—for proving the falsity of the claims of aristocracy to an indefeasible right to rule and for demonstrating the ability of ordinary men and women to manage through their representatives the affairs of state and society. "Democracy everywhere," wrote Michael Chevalier, who was sent to America in 1834 by M. Thiers, Minister of the Interior of France, to inspect public works in the United States, "is intolerant towards foreign nations; the American democracy in particular, bred up in the belief that the nations of Europe groan ignobly under the yoke of absolute despots, looks upon them with a mixture of pity and contempt. When it throws a glance beyond the Atlantic, it affects the superior air of a freeman looking upon a herd of slaves. Its pride kindles at the idea of humbling the monarchical principle in the person of the 'tyrants who tread Europe under foot.' " [8]

This sense of destiny naturally engendered the vices of its virtues. Besides being intolerant of European political institutions, Americans developed a reputation for boastfulness during the first half of the nineteenth century. "The most striking circumstance in the American character, which had come under our notice," observed Captain Basil Hall, an English aristocrat traveling in the United States in 1827-28, "was the constant habit of praising themselves, their institutions, and their country, either in downright terms, or by some would-be indirect allusions, which were still more tormenting." [9] Sir Charles Lyell, the British geologist, relates an amusing but relevant incident which occurred on his second visit to the United States in 1845-46. Arriving at a hotel in Jackson, Mississippi, just as supper was to be served, he was ushered into the dining room where the landlord "first obtained silence by exclaiming, with the loud voice of a herald, 'Gentlemen, we are a great people,' and then called out the names of all the viands on his long table and side-board, beginning with 'Beef-steak, with or without onions, roast turkey, pork, hominy, fish, eggs, &c.' and ending with a list of various drinkables, the last of which was 'tea, foreign and domestic.' " [10] While this early intolerance and boastfulness of the American people was painful to European aristocrats, it marked the rise of the common man to power and revealed his militant faith in himself and his institutions.

The Conception of Equality

At the heart of American democracy is a great ethical conception that can be traced back to the beginnings of recorded history—the conception of the fundamental equality, brotherhood, and moral worth of all men. This conception has grown out of the deepest experiences of common people, has pervaded the life and work of the greatest prophets of the race, has expressed, motivated, and rendered significant innumerable struggles against tyranny and oppression, and in fond belief distinguishes civilization from barbarism and humankind from the beast. It is rooted in the life of free Athens, in the political experience of the Anglo-Saxon peoples, in all the great liberating and humanizing movements of the modern age—in the Renaissance, the Reformation, the Enlightenment, and the English and French revolutions; in the breakup of feudal institutions, the rise of the middle classes, the awakening of working men, the reconciliation of peoples, the emancipation of women, and the recognition of the personality of the child; in the overthrow of authoritarianism in church and state, the development of faith in the human mind, the advance of science, and the spread of a naturalistic outlook upon the world. It is proclaimed particularly in that gospel of the meek and the humble, of the slave, the serf, the laborer, and the common man, the doctrine that the earth is the rightful possession of the many and not the exclusive property of the few, which constitutes the central ethical tradition of Christianity. It is given its most universal expression in the second of the two great commandments of Jesus, and its most profound social application in these lines of the *Magnificat* which have been chanted by old and young alike in the Western World for fourteen hundred years:

He hath showed strength with his arm;
He hath scattered the proud in the imagination of their hearts.
He hath put down the mighty from their seats,
And exalted them of low degree.
He hath filled the hungry with good things;
And the rich he hath sent empty away.

This great conception, present, though generally unapplied, in that culture which the emigrants from the Old World brought to the New, found conditions attending the discovery, settlement, and conquest of the North American continent peculiarly favorable for its development and flowering. In imperishable form it was proclaimed in that sublime affirmation of popular rights—the Declaration of Independence. Although, in the case of various racial and class elements in the nation this charter of democracy has been grievously violated again and again, even those who have profaned it in deed have generally hesitated to denounce it in word. Forgotten or relegated to the copy-books of the schoolroom during periods of tranquillity, the American people return to it almost instinctively in times of stress for inspiration and guidance. Couched in general phrase, the Declaration stands today as fresh as when it was written—one of the most deeply cherished spiritual possessions of the American people.

It is of course true that the conception of equality has been attacked since the day it was first enunciated. The spokesmen of privilege have always contended that it is but a refuge for the weak and contrary to the laws of nature. In recent years persons versed in the measurement of human traits but unfamiliar with the history of morals and politics, being impressed by the great variability within the race, have contended in the name of objective science that the author of the Declaration of Independence was in serious error, that he was unfortunate in having lived before the day of the intelligence test, and that he should be called upon to revise or delete the opening sentences of the second paragraph of that historic document. These gentlemen, however, miss the point altogether.

Jefferson was by no means unaware of the physical and psychological differences among men—a fact that has doubtless been known since the Garden of Eden. Indeed he once wrote to John Adams of "a natural aristocracy among men" based on "virtue and talents." This aristocracy, he said, "I consider as the most precious gift of nature, for the instruction, the trusts, and government of society. . . . May we not even say, that that form of government is the best, which provides the most effectually for a pure selection of these natural aristoi into the offices of government?" [11]

The father of American democracy was but asserting that the experience of the race has shown the principle of equality in human relationships to be the only safe guide to the decent and civilized ordering of life—as necessary, paradoxically, for the full moral development of the strong as for the protection of the weak. He was giving practical expression to the great ethical imperative of Immanuel Kant: "So act as to treat humanity, whether in thine own person or in that of any other, as an end withal, never as a means only." And who, pondering world society today, can take serious issue with this doctrine. Let the principle of inequality prevail and the way is open for the return of tyranny and for the moral justification of the most grievous forms of exploitation and injustice—the lynching of Negroes, the shooting down of strikers, the driving of Jews back into the ghetto, the annihilation of Ethiopians with poison gas, the bombing of the civilian populations of Spain and China, the sanctification of cruel and inhuman practices, the deification of dictators. Lincoln, in a private letter, written in 1859, stated the case with admirable brevity and clarity: "The principles of Jefferson are the definitions and axioms of free society. And yet they are denied and evaded, with no small show of success. One dashingly calls them 'glittering generalities.' Another bluntly calls them 'self-evident lies.' And others insidiously argue that they apply to 'superior races.' These expressions, differing in form, are identical in object and effect—the supplanting the principles of free government, and restoring those of classification, caste, and legitimacy. . . . They are the vanguard, the miners and sappers, of returning despotism. We must repulse them, or they will subjugate us." [12] It would almost seem that Lincoln was viewing the present world situation.

American democracy, however, was not merely an ethical *conception*. If it had been only a construction of the mind, if it had never been translated into attitudes, ways of life, and social structure, it would scarcely be worth recording. The pages of history are literally strewn with glorious ideas, beautiful Utopian dreams, lovely pictures of paradise which left the lives of ordinary men and women unaffected. To the extent that democracy achieved special significance in America, it was expressed in the sentiments, the customs, the social arrangements, the modes of living of the people. And for those who are concerned about the future of free institutions in this country, who cherish the fundamental ideas and values of democracy, and who desire to fight the battles of popular rights in the difficult years ahead, the beginning of wisdom lies in the recognition of the fact that historically American democracy has assumed at least three forms—economic, social, and political. To identify it wholly with its political manifestation, important as that is, would be to play into the hands of the friends or tools of autocracy. Democracy is far more than a form of government. Indeed, in order to place its stamp upon government it must prevail beyond the bounds of politics. It is an attitude of mind to which the exploitation of man by man is abhorrent; it is a way of life in which human personality is judged of supreme, of measureless, worth; it is an order of social relationships dedicated to the promotion of the individual and collective interests of common folk; it is, in a word, a society in which ordinary men and women may grow to their full stature— a *society* "of the people, by the people, and for the people."

Economic Democracy

The most fundamental form of early American democracy was economic. This was clearly seen by a brilliant young Frenchman, Alexis de Tocqueville, who just over a hundred years ago came to the United States, traveled widely through the country, observed closely institutions and modes of life, brought to bear upon his observations deep philosophical insight, and returned to France to write a two-volume work on *Democracy in America*—the most penetrating study of American civilization ever made by a foreign scholar and one of the truly great political works of the nineteenth century. Tocqueville begins his analysis with a reference, not to politics, but to economics:

Amongst the novel objects that attracted my attention during my stay in the United States, nothing struck me more forcibly than the general equality of condition among the people. I readily discovered the prodigious influence which this primary fact exercises on the whole course of society; it gives a peculiar direction to public opinion, and a peculiar tenor to the laws; it imparts new maxims to the governing authorities, and peculiar habits to the governed.

I soon perceived that the influence of this fact extends far beyond the political character and the laws of the country, and that it has no less empire over civil society than over the government; it creates opinions, gives birth to new sentiments, founds novel customs, and modifies whatever it does not produce. The more I advanced in the study of American society, the more I perceived that this equality of condition is the fundamental fact from which all others seem to be derived, and the central point at which all my observations constantly terminated.[13]

Granted that Tocqueville may have viewed the young democracy through somewhat romantic spectacles, the essential soundness of his observation about "equality of condition" is supported by careful studies of the period. During the epoch of colonial settlement, to be sure, feudal arrangements were introduced into America, including a careful gradation of ranks and the holding of land by lease from an overlord. Only in Massachusetts, Connecticut, and Rhode Island was freehold ownership of land permitted. Thus the prevailing system of land tenure was originally feudal in character; but this system underwent rapid and radical change. "By the end of the seventeenth century," writes James Truslow Adams, "the strictly feudal tenures with the personal service exacted from tenant to lord had largely disappeared and the quitrent had come to be the measure and fulfillment of most of the tenant's obligations." [14] The quitrent, moreover, was often purely nominal and all but disappeared with the Revolution.

Feudalism simply could not survive in America. Under the impact of new and strange conditions of life—the act of crossing the Atlantic, the breaking of ties with the past, the distance from the cultural home-land, the selective character of the migration, the abundance of land and natural resources, the wide expanse of territory, the sparseness of population, the primitive means of transportation and communication, the reversion to a relatively simple economic and social pattern, the almost universal necessity of manual labor, the absence of both the material and spiritual manifestations of an old and settled community, and the comparatively free play of all those forces which in the western world were undermining the medieval system—under the impact of these conditions there developed an economy that, strictly speaking, was neither feudal nor capitalistic.

In the days of the founding fathers and until the rise of the present industrial order, America for the most part was a land of freehold farmers living a life of relative self-sufficiency and independence. In 1689, according to an estimate by Adams, of a total population of two hundred and six thousand in the twelve colonies, "nearly two hundred thousand persons must have been living either on isolated farms or in little communities of a few score souls, at most a few score families." [15] In the Constitutional Convention of 1787 Gouverneur Morris stated that "nine-tenths of the people are at present free-holders." There were, to be sure, slaves and slave-owners in the south, money-lenders in the north, a budding commercial class in the towns, land speculators everywhere, and a considerable body of persons, recruited from the indolent, the unfortunate, the grievously handicapped, and the recent immigrants, who were without productive property. Also among the freeholders there were fairly wide differences in circumstance, depending on inheritance, habits of industry, proximity to town and trading centers, and the accidents of fortune generally.

But after all necessary allowances have been made, the fact remains that in the time of Jefferson the American economy was marked by an extraordinary measure of equality. Tench Coxe, assistant secretary of the treasury under Alexander Hamilton, after an extended trip of observation through the country, wrote in 1794 that the poor taxes were "very small," the number of "menial servants" few, and the differences in circumstances relatively inconspicuous. "It is probable," he observed, "that all the jewels and diamonds worn by the citizens of the United States, their wives and daughters are less in value than those which sometimes form a part of the dress of an individual in several countries of Europe. . . . There are no *descriptions* of men in America and very few individuals, at the active times of life, who live without some pursuit of business, profession, occupation, or trade. *All the citizens are in active habits.*" [16] Even in the towns, if the testimony of foreign observers is to be credited, the extremes of poverty were far less apparent than in the Old World. "The United States," wrote Michael Chevalier from Charleston in 1835, "are certainly the land of promise for the labouring class. What a contrast between our Europe and America! After landing in New York, I thought every day was Sunday, for the whole population that throngs Broadway seemed to be arrayed in their Sunday's best. None of those countenances ghastly with the privations or the foul air of Paris; nothing like our wretched scavengers, our ragmen, and corresponding classes of the other sex." [17]

Since the freehold farmer provided the substance of American economic democracy, he merits further examination. The major fact regarding him was not that he was a farmer holding title to his land, but rather that he was much more than a farmer. With his sons he was also a hunter, a trapper, a fisherman, a butcher, a tanner, a cobbler, a carpenter, a mechanic, a mason, a "jack of all trades"; while his wife and daughters, besides "keeping house" in the sense of today, were adept in all the arts associated with the curing of foods and the preparation of clothing. His household was almost an entire economy in microcosm. As Horace Bushnell said, "the house was a factory on the farm, the farm a grower and producer for the house." [18] More than a generation ago, in 1885, Henry P. Hedges thus described the self-sufficiency of the farmer of Suffolk County, New York, a hundred years before:

From his feet to his head the farmer stood in vestment produced on his own farm. The leather of his shoes came from the hides of his own cattle. The linen and woolen that he wore were products that he raised. The farmer's wife or daughter braided and sewed the straw-hat on his head. His fur cap was made from the skin of a fox he shot. The feathers of wild fowl in the bed whereon he rested his weary frame by night, were the results acquired in his shooting. The pillow-cases, sheets and blankets, the comfortables, quilts and counterpanes, the towels and table cloth, were home made. His harness and lines he cut from hides grown on his farm. Everything about his ox yoke except staple and ring he made. His whip, his ox gad, his flail, axe, hoe and fork-handle, were his own work. How little he bought, and how much he contrived to supply his wants by home manufacture would astonish this generation.[19]

These farmers were self-sufficient, not from choice, but from necessity. They were self-sufficient because of the distances, the bad roads, the primitive modes of transportation, the absence of markets, the level of the technical arts. Percy Wells Bidwell in his study of the rural economy of New England at the beginning of the nineteenth century concludes that only from one-fifth to one-fourth of the population had access to the "market, such as it was." As to the rest of the people, they were "almost entirely isolated from commercial relations with the outside world."[20] In the middle states, the south, and the west the market played a larger or smaller role, depending upon circumstance; but with the exception of the southern plantation, the freehold farmer, with his self-contained household, was everywhere the dominant feature of the rural economy. And the American economy was essentially rural.

One of the fundamental consequences of this form of economy was a rough equality of condition. The lack of a market, given the abundance of land, the sparsity of population, the central position of the family, and the decay of feudal institutions, resulted, according to Bidwell, in an almost complete absence of tenancy and a large measure of

uniformity in the size of farms.[21] Where little or nothing
could be raised for sale, "the opportunities for business
profits, for the accumulation and investment of capital, all of
which are necessary steps in the development of inequalities
in wealth, were lacking." [22] Moreover, the scarcity of workers
meant that the labor available on the ordinary farm would
be the labor of the members of the family—parents, children,
and unattached relatives—and that the size of the farm could
not well go beyond a certain relatively modest acreage. Bidwell found that "the farms varied in size from 80-100 to 250-
300 acres, few having less than 100 acres and few more than
200." In these facts may be seen the most profound expression of American democracy and that equality of condition
which so impressed Tocqueville.

Social Democracy

This equality of condition, founded though it was on
unremitting toil, not a little privation, and an extreme simplicity of living, gave to the individual that independence
and dignity which have always characterized the American
farmer and distinguished him from the European peasant.
Out of this complex of forces arose the second form or expression of American democracy—an actual sense of equality
and a practice of equality in the ordinary social relationships.
On the frontier where the past was forgotten; on the freehold
farms where all men engaged in similar activities; in the
hard struggle with the raw forces of nature where false pretensions were quickly exposed; in the sustained fight for
independence where community of interest promoted a feeling of fraternity and the exigencies of the struggle called for
the propagation of democratic ideas, the feudal mentality
was all but obliterated and a passion for social equality
emerged which has been recorded in that very characteristic,
if paradoxical, American expression: "One man is just as

good as another, if not a little better." Thus did the commoner pay his respects to all who would claim superiority by reason of family, class, or rank.

Of particular significance in promoting this sense of social equality was the practical absence of occupational differentiation. Bidwell in his study of New England at the opening of the last century shows that, with the possible exception of the clergyman, the ownership and cultivation of land constituted the main source of livelihood for all, even for those who also practiced other callings. The representatives of the artisan, business, and professional classes were "standing on the borderline between agriculture and a specialized non-agricultural occupation. They were at times doctors, lawyers, innkeepers or storekeepers, fullers, carpenters, or tanners, but most of the time plain farmers. Thus we can see that the distinction between various occupations which we had set up for purposes of analysis tends to vanish. The broad outlines of a future division of employments were marked out, but the process of separation was as yet hardly begun." [23]

That Bidwell's exclusion of the clergyman from a preponderant dependence on the farm for livelihood during this period was only relative is suggested by the following plea for a salary raise made by Reverend Nathaniel Howe before his congregation in Hopkinton, Mass., in 1815: "Borne down with the fatigues of manual labor, pressed into the woods in the winter, to the plough in the spring, and into the meadow in the summer, to support my family comfortably and fulfil my promises, I felt the business of the ministry was greatly neglected;—that it was impossible for me to do what ought to be done in my profession, unless the people did more toward my support." [24] It is significant to note that this eloquent plea fell on deaf ears. The members of the Hopkinton congregation, doubtless farmers all, voted down unanimously every concrete proposal made by the minister for the improvement of his material condition.

Apparently they could see no reason why he should not be "pressed into the woods in the winter, to the plough in the spring, and into the meadow in the summer." Indeed they may have thought that the "fatigues of manual labor" were good for his immortal soul.

Isaac Weld, Junior, an Irishman who visited the United States toward the close of the eighteenth century, observed that "in the country parts of Pennsylvania" judges "are no more than plain farmers, who from their infancy have been accustomed to little else than following the plough." [25] And Edward A. Kendall, an Englishman traveling in America a few years later spoke thus of the legal profession in Vermont: "Of the judges, at present on the bench of the supreme court, only one was bred to the law. Of the others, one, at the present time, finds leisure, in the vacations, to drive a team between Rutland and Troy." [26] It is a truism of social psychology that men who live alike tend to become alike and to think alike. The freehold farmers and their professional servitors of 1800 engaged in much the same activities and lived largely according to the same pattern. For the sentiment of social equality to spread among them was natural and practically inevitable.

The most influential factor underlying the occupational uniformity and sense of equality was the relative ease with which a man of industry could become a landholder. This point is clearly developed by John Bradbury, British naturalist and traveler, who spent some years in the regions beyond the Alleghanies beginning in 1909. A simple laborer, without trade or profession, could in the course of "one year become so expert as to be entitled to what is usually paid to husbandmen, from twelve to fifteen dollars per month, and board." Then, having established himself in the community, "if his conduct is proper, he may associate with the sons of the neighbouring farmers, many of whom know that their ancestors became proprietors of land, from a beginning not more promising than his: even his employer was probably the helper to some one formerly." [27] Bradbury estimates, moreover, that "the savings of two or three years" will enable him to procure a farm of one or two hundred acres, "if he is prudent." [28]

Following the Revolution and the general tendency to obliterate the gradation of ranks widely propagated during the colonial period, the people apparently became militant, if not rude, in their assertion of social equality. At any rate various foreign visitors commented on the "want of common civility" on the part of the "lower classes of people in America." Weld observed that "the lower classes of people will return rude and impertinent answers to questions couched in the most civil terms, and will insult a person that bears the appearance of a gentleman, on purpose to shew how much they consider themselves upon an equality with him." [29] This same traveler reports a revealing incident taking place in a tavern in Pennsylvania where he passed the night when on the way to Philadelphia from Baltimore. Crammed together in a single room was a company of thirteen people, including "some eminent lawyers from Virginia and the southward," a "judge of the supreme court," and "two or three of the neighbouring farmers, boorish, ignorant, and obtrusive fellows." In the "acrimonious debate" which ensued the farmers seemed to be not at all over-awed by the learning, rhetoric, and logic of the distinguished representatives of bar and bench. Weld notes further that the former generally in America were "so very plain, both in their appearance and manners, that a stranger would not suspect that they were persons of the consequence which they really are in the country." [30]

A manifestation of the idea of social equality, often recorded by observers, was that of personal independence. "The generality of servants that are met with in Philadelphia," writes Weld, "are emigrant Europeans; they, however, for the most part, only remain in service until they can save a little money, when they constantly quit their masters, being led to do so by that desire for independence which is so natural to the mind of man, and which every person in America may enjoy that will be industrious." [31] The absence of servile manner and spirit on the part of persons engaged in personal service was remarked again and again by travelers. Weld experienced great difficulty in persuading attendants at taverns "to rub down" his horse, "or even to give him his food." Some attendants, he writes, "are so sullen and disobliging that you feel inclined to do every thing with your own hands rather than be indebted to them for their assistance: they always appear doubtful whether they should do any thing for you or not, and to be reasoning within themselves, whether it is not too great a departure from the rules of equality to take the horse of another man, and whether it would not be a pleasing sight to see a gentleman strip off his coat, and go to work for himself; nor will money make them alter their conduct; civility, as I before said, is not to be purchased at any expence in America." [32]

John Bradbury, deliberately replying to Weld, suggests that the European aristocrat, if he would travel pleasantly in America, should leave his sense of superiority in the Old World. He finds in the United States none of "that species of hauteur which one class of society in some countries show in their intercourse with the other," not even "amongst those clothed with judicial or military authority." If such an official "should be tempted to treat even the least wealthy of his neighbours or fellow-citizens with contumely, he would soon find that he could not do it with impunity." Bradbury then proceeds to answer the charges of Weld: "Travellers from Europe, in passing through the western country, or indeed any part of the United States, ought to be previously acquainted with this part of the American character, and more particularly if they have been in the habit of treating with contempt, or irritating with abuse, those whom accidental circumstances may have placed in a situation to administer to their wants. Let no one here indulge himself in abusing the waiter or hostler at an inn: that waiter or hostler is probably a citizen, and does not, nor can he, conceive that a situation in which he discharges a duty to society, not in itself dishonourable, should subject him to insult: but this feeling, so far as I have experienced, is entirely defensive. I have travelled near ten thousand miles in the United States, and never received the least incivility or affront." [33]

Half a generation later Captain Basil Hall observed that the "deep-rooted prejudice" against personal service "goes farther to make a residence on the western side of the the Atlantic inconvenient, than people can easily comprehend who have never been subjected to the absolute want of servants; or, what is often worse, to the necessity of submitting in patience to the ungracious, capricious, sluggish, disrespectful, and, at the very best, ill qualified nature of American attendance, which prevails from end to end of that country." [34] Hall was greatly exercised over the general absence of bells and all other means by which servants might be summoned by the patrons of public houses: "It is in vain that you thump the floor; or rap the plate with your knife. . . . It seems the servants themselves, or the helps, or hirelings, or whatever name they think it least degrading to go by, do not like being summoned by a ringing of bells." [35] The good captain was outraged one morning in Schenectady when he discovered that he had sat next to a man at tea who had twice served him "over night with a glass of iced-water at the bar." [36] Under these circumstances, it is not surprising that Sir Charles Lyell, speculating on the advisability of Englishmen bringing their servants with them on a visit to America, comes to the following conclusion: "If they venture on the experiment, they had better not take with them an English maid-servant, unless they are prepared for her being transformed into an equal." [37]

William Cobbett, the English journalist who lived in America from 1792 to 1800 and again from 1817 to 1819, summed the matter up in the observation that in America a man "will not wear a *livery,* any more than he will wear a halter round his neck" and that "neither men nor women will allow you to call them *servants."* [38] Of the "common laboring man," Cobbett said: "he crawls to nobody; he will call every man *Sir,* but he will call no man *master."* [39] He speaks also of the absence of hypocrisy in social relations in America: "The causes of *hypocrisy* are the fear of loss and the hope of gain. Men crawl to those, whom, in their hearts, they despise, because they fear the effects of their ill-will and hope to gain by their good-will. The circumstances of all ranks are so easy here, that there is no cause for hypocrisy. . . . The boasting of wealth and the endeavouring to disguise poverty, these two acts, so painful to contemplate, are almost total strangers in this country; for, no man can gain adulation or respect by wealth, and no man dreads the effects of poverty, because no man sees any dreadful effects arising from poverty." [40]

Perhaps nowhere is the old American sense of social equality expressed more succinctly than in a letter which Benjamin Franklin gave to the English press shortly after the Revolution in response to inquiries from persons interested in migrating to the United States. This letter, entitled *To Those Who Would Remove to America,* contains the following passage which could have been written by a citizen of no other country:

. . . it cannot be worth any man's while, who has a means of living at home, to expatriate himself, in hopes of obtaining a profitable civil office in America; and, as to military offices, they are at an end with the war, the armies being disbanded. Much less is it advisable for a person to go thither, who has no other quality to recommend him but his birth. In Europe it has indeed its value; but it is a commodity that cannot be carried to a worse market than that of America, where people do not inquire concerning a stranger, *What is he?* but, *What can he do?* If he has any useful art, he is welcome; and if he exercises it, and behaves well, he will be respected by all that know him; but a mere man of quality, who, on that account, wants to live upon the public, by some office or salary, will be despised and disregarded. The husbandman is in honor there, and even the mechanic, because their employments are useful. The people have a saying, that God Almighty is himself a mechanic, the greatest in the universe; and he is respected and admired more for the variety, ingenuity, and utility of his handiworks, than for the antiquity of his family. They are pleased with the observation of a negro, and frequently mention it, that *Boccarora* (meaning the white man) *make de black man workee, make de horse workee, make de ox workee, make ebery ting workee; only de hog. He, de hog, no workee; he eat, he drink, he walk about, he go to sleep when he please, he live like a gempleman.* According to these opinions of the Americans, one of them would think himself more obliged to a genealogist, who could prove for him that his ancestors and relations for ten generations had been ploughmen, smiths, carpenters, turners, weavers, tanners, or even shoemakers, and consequently that they were useful members of society; than if he could only prove that they were gentlemen, doing nothing of value, but living idly on the labor of others, mere *fruges consumere nati,* and otherwise *good for nothing,* till by their death their estates, like the carcass of the negro's gentleman-hog, come to be cut up.[41]

Almost identical advice may be found in the letters of Richard Flower, an Englishman of culture and refinement who in 1818 sold his estate in Hertford and removed to Illinois to participate in founding an English settlement. After stating that certain immigrants "to America find themselves as unhappy there as they were in their own country" he observes that "those who are averse to labour, fond of luxuries, and whose minds are rivetted to the artificial distinctions of society in Europe, have found to their cost, that America is not the country for them." Unless such persons "can learn wisdom," he continues, "and form resolution sufficient to alter some of their habits, and if not to despise, to regard with indifference most of those distinctions, they can never be reconciled to Republican manners and institutions. Respecting a few persons of this description at the Illinois, one of the principal settlers exclaimed:— 'What are such people come here for?' " [42] Apparently in this period of American history it was the conservative-minded individual who was advised "to go back to the country he came from."

Political Democracy

The third manifestation of the principle of equality appeared in the political sphere. Through the generations, from the days of the first settlements at Jamestown and Plymouth down to the present, the American people, building on Anglo-Saxon experience and traditions, have fought without ceasing for control over the institutions of government. But the interest here is in that seventy-five year period following the expulsion of the French power from North America under the provisions of the treaty of 1763 during which the foundations of political democracy were laid. This period witnessed the proclamation of the Declaration of Independence, the waging of the Revolutionary War, the formulation of the Articles of Confederation, the Shays and Whiskey rebellions, the adoption of the Federal Constitution, the amendment of the Bill of Rights, the rise of Jeffersonian and Jacksonian democracy, the general acceptance of the principle of universal white manhood suffrage, the overthrow of the doctrine of aristocratic rule, and an enormous amount of state and local political agitation, activity, and thought. Although at the close of Jackson's administration property qualifications were still required of voters in a few states, although more than one-half of the adult population suffered disfranchisement because of sex or color, and although the several branches of the federal government were only partially subject to direct popular control, the fact remains that this was the great creative epoch in the political history of the American people.

This struggle for human liberty was a glorious one—one of the most glorious and successful in history. But the story has been told so many times that it need not be repeated here. American political achievements have been extolled in every school history since the days of John McCulloch and celebrated in every Fourth of July oration since the founding of the nation. A major purpose of the present volume, as already stated, is to redress the balance between the political and the other supports of democracy in the United States. Attention will be directed therefore to those underlying conditions out of which political democracy arose.

The first point to be emphasized is that the American people, to an unusual degree, have been the heirs of the modern world. The discovery, settlement, and development of America coincided with the breakup of the medieval system, the rise of the middle class, the overthrow of the feudal economy, the growth of private capitalism, the spread of parliamentary institutions, the disestablishment of the church, and all of those great humanistic and liberating movements of the past five centuries—the Renaissance, the Reformation, the Enlightenment, the English and French revolutions, the advance of science, and the undermining of authoritarianism in the church, the state, and the ordinary relationships of life. Particularly was the rise of American political democracy associated with the intellectual and social ferment of the seventeenth and eighteenth centuries in England and France, with the thought of Harrington and Locke, of d'Alembert, Diderot, and Rousseau, with the ideas of natural law, the supremacy of reason, and the indefinite perfectability of man and his institutions. Moreover, because of their favored geographical and historical position, the American people were enabled to make a fresh start in the long human adventure. Coming largely from the oppressed classes of the Old World and having been the victims of the tyrannies of the past, their mentality was inordinately disposed to welcome and give rein to the creative forces of the time. Under the circumstances it is not surprising that the Enlightenment, though arising in France, found its most enthusiastic reception in America. The spirit of this great revolutionary age which cradled the young republic was immortalized in the oft-quoted lines of Wordsworth:

> Bliss was it in that dawn to be alive,
> But to be young was very Heaven! O times,
> In which the meagre, stale, forbidding ways
> Of custom, law, and statute, took at once
> The attraction of a country in romance!
> When Reason seemed the most to assert her rights
> When most intent on making of herself
> A prime enchantress—to assist the work,
> Which then was going forward in her name!
> Not favored spots alone, but the whole Earth,
> The beauty wore of promise—that which sets
> (As at some moments might not be unfelt
> Among the bowers of Paradise itself)
> The budding rose above the rose full blown.
> What temper at the prospect did not wake
> To happiness unthought of? [43]

The War of Independence, growing largely out of the conflict of economic interest between the colonies and the mother country, played a vital role in advancing the cause of political democracy on the North American continent. Among the most significant by-products of this struggle were the breaking down of the legal supports of class distinctions and the spreading among the masses of the people of the doctrines of equality. The representatives of the colonial aristocracy were inclined generally to remain loyal to the British crown and to look with disfavor and apprehension on the leveling tendencies implicit in the Revolution. The success of the colonists in the struggle consequently meant the weakening and the discrediting of the privileged orders. In the province of New York, where the Tory element was unusually strong, 35,000 persons out of a total population of 185,000 forfeited property valued at $3,600,-000 and "were scattered over the remaining parts of the empire." [44] Although the aristocracy recouped some of its losses in the years following the Revolution, it was never able to achieve complete recovery. Even the word "gentleman" fell somewhat into disrepute; and the fact that John Adams used the term occasionally was a matter of remark. [45]

The Revolution served as a great sounding board for the propagation of the egalitarian ideas developing on both sides of the Atlantic. In order to enlist and sustain the people in the struggle these ideas were widely disseminated. The Declaration of Independence, the pamphlets of Thomas Paine, and the writings of other revolutionary thinkers and propagandists of the time were read and discussed from Massachusetts to Georgia. This experience left an impression on the people of the United States that intervening generations have not been able to erase. Indeed the ideas popularized to win the war became a part of the American spiritual heritage and remain today to plague all persons of conservative and aristocratic temper. The dangers inhering in the situation were perceived and even foreseen by some of the more astute representatives of privilege as early as 1774. Thus Gouverneur Morris observed: "The mob begin to think and to reason. Poor reptiles! it is with them a vernal morning, they are struggling to cast off their winter's slough, they bask in the sunshine, and ere noon they will bite, depend upon it. The gentry begin to fear this." [46] And Fisher Ames, able and uncompromising spokesman of the New England aristocracy, pointed out in 1787: "The people have turned against their teachers the doctrines, which were inculcated in order to effect the late revolution." [47]

But underlying the Revolution and the propagation of democratic political ideas were the new conditions of life which for generations had been slowly undermining the mentality bred of feudal institutions. On the farms and along the advancing frontier the European serf, peasant, proletarian, or tradesman had been gradually losing that attitude of servility toward his "betters" which had seemed in harmony with the laws of nature in the Old World. The story of this transformation, of the emergence of a democracy of freehold farmers prepared to fight the battles of political democracy, was told by Frederick Jackson Turner more than a generation ago. For men, free, secure, and independent in the economic realm, to submit to political tyranny is unthinkable. The actual historic relationship between political and economic democracy was perhaps stated most clearly and unequivocally by J. Franklin Jameson, eminent historian and scholar, in the following passage from a lecture delivered at Princeton University in 1925:

The doctrine which underlies the present lecture is that political democracy came to the United States as a result of economic democracy, that this nation came to be marked by political institutions of a democratic type because it had, still earlier, come to be characterized in its economic life by democratic arrangements and practices. We do not look to see effects precede causes, and certainly political democracy came among us somewhat late, certainly long after the Revolution in most

states. If we take manhood suffrage as the most convenient symbol of political democracy, we have to say that it was 1840
before manhood suffrage came at all close to being the universal
rule of American political life. Long before this, however,
America stood committeed to economic democracy, which
meant, in a country so occupied with agriculture, to the system
of landholding which the classical economists called "peasant
proprietorship," the system of small holdings where landowner,
capitalist or farmer, and laborer are all one, the owner of the
land supplying the capital and working the fields with his own
labor and that of his family.[48]

Whether Dr. Jameson is correct in assuming, as he apparently does, that in the relationship between economics and
politics the former is always primary, is a question that will
be postponed for later consideration. Here it will suffice to
note, as historical fact, that economic democracy preceded
and provided a material support for popular government
in the United States. Being beholden to no man, the
freehold farmer could enjoy the luxury of relatively untram-
meled political judgment. The spirit of this economic democrat, as he exercised his rights of citizenship, is revealed in
a single sentence by James B. Ireland, describing an election
in Kentucky about the end of the first quarter of the nineteenth century. "Voters would step up to the Court
House," [49] he writes, "pull off their hat and request the
clerk to register their name and speak out independently
who they voted for." The political consequences flowing
from economic conditions were also brought out clearly by
Alexander Campbell, a representative from Western Virginia, speaking before the Virginia constitutional convention
in 1829:

But, Sir, it is not the increase of population in the west which
this gentleman ought to fear. It is the energy which the mountain breeze and western habits impart to these emigrants. They
are regenerated; politically, I mean, Sir. They soon become

working politicians; and the difference, Sir, between a *talking* and a *working* politician, is immense. The old Dominion has long been celebrated for producing great orators; the ablest metaphysicians in policy; men that can split hairs in all abstruse questions of political economy. But at home, or when they return from Congress, they have negroes to fan them asleep. But a Pennsylvania, a New-York, a Ohio, or a western Virginia Statesman, though far inferior in logic, metaphysics, and rhetoric, to an old Virginia Statesman, has this advantage, that when he returns home, he takes off his coat, and takes hold of the plough. This gives him bone and muscle, Sir, and preserves his Republican principles pure and uncontaminated.[50]

When Jefferson declared that "those who labor in the earth are the chosen people of God" he was at the same time glorifying the ordinary American citizen of the age and asserting the dependence of politics on economics. According to this view, a free government can remain free only as long as it rests on free men. And men cannot be made free by government. *They are made free or are enslaved by the conditions under which they live and gain their livelihood.* If those conditions encourage in them a spirit of independence, dignity, and integrity, then they will be free and capable of establishing and maintaining free government. The freehold farmer, given the economy and the laws of property of the time, was a *free man*. In the words of John Melish, a manufacturer of Glasgow who visited the United States several times between 1806 and 1811, "to view the American character fairly, we must go into the interior of the country, and there the first remark will probably be, that the inhabitants have a spirit of independence, and will brook no superiority. Every man is conscious of his own political importance, and will suffer none to treat him with disrespect." [51] This *free* man gave to America the institutions of political democracy.

In Conclusion

Despite its obvious imperfections and shortcomings, American democracy yesterday rested on solid economic foundations. Despite the survivals from feudal times, despite the shadow of Negro slavery in the South, despite the antici- pations of the new aristocracy of commercial, financial, and industrial capitalism, the people of the United States, hold- ing title to the means of livelihood and practiced in the arts of warfare, were relatively independent, equal, and free. With a confidence bred by the successful conquest of a wilderness and a sense of security nurtured by the broad waters of the Atlantic behind them and the rich lands of the boundless West before them, they gloried in their assertion of the worth and dignity of the common man. The entire social atmosphere made them fiercely jealous of their rights and scornful of the pretensions of birth and caste. "American society," wrote Chevalier in summary, "is essentially and radically a democracy, not in name merely but in deed. In the United States the democratic spirit is infused into all the national habits, and all the customs of society; it besets and startles at every step the foreigner, who, before landing in the country, had no suspicion to what a degree every nerve and fibre had been steeped in aristocracy by a European education." [52] With all of its cultural limitations, its crudities of life and manners, the land of the freehold farmer at the beginning of the nineteenth century was one of the most democratic ever to appear in the world.

REFERENCES

1. William Blake, *The Writings of William Blake* (Edited by Geoffrey Keynes, London, 1925), I, 224.

2. Thomas Hulme, "Introduction to the Journal," in R. G. Thwaites, *Early Western Travels 1748-1846* (Cleveland, 1904), X, 24.

3. *Ibid.*, 24.

4. *Ibid.*, 26.

5. *Ibid.*, 30.

6. George Washington, *The Writings* (Ford edition, New York, 1891), XI, 385.

7. Daniel Webster, *Works* (Tenth edition, Boston, 1857), I, 77.

8. Michael Chevalier, *Society, Manners and Politics in the United States* (Boston, 1839), 188-189.

9. Captain Basil Hall, *Travels in North America in the years 1827 and 1828* (Philadelphia, 1829), I, 61.

10. Sir Charles Lyell, *A Second Visit to The United States of North America* (New York, 1849), II, 160.

11. Thomas Jefferson, *The Writings* (Ford edition, New York, 1898), IX, 425.

12. Abraham Lincoln, *The Writings* (Lapsley edition, New York, 1923), V, 25.

13. Alexis de Tocqueville, *Democracy in America* (New York, 1898), I, 1.

14. James Truslow Adams, *Provincial Society 1690-1763* (New York, 1928), 12.

15. *Ibid.*, 2-3.

16. Tench Coxe, *A View of the United States of America* (Philadelphia, 1794), 441.

17. *Op. cit.*, 341-342.

18. Horace Bushnell, "The Age of Homespun" in *Work and Play* (New York, 1864), 392.

19. Henry P. Hedges, "Development of Agriculture in Suffolk County," in *Bi-Centennial History of Suffolk County* (Babylon, N. Y., 1885), 42.

20. Percy Wells Bidwell, *Rural Economy in New England at the Beginning of the Nineteenth Century* (New Haven, 1916), 318. See also Percy Wells Bidwell and John I. Falconer, *History of Agriculture in the Northern United States 1620-1860* (Washington, 1925), 131-144.

21. *Ibid.*, 371.

22. *Ibid.*, 371.

23. *Ibid.*, 266.

24. John Warner Barber, *Massachusetts Historical Collections* (Worcester, 1839), 395.

25. Isaac Weld, Jr., *Travels Through The States of North America and the Provinces of Lower Canada During the Years 1795, 1796, and 1797* (London, 1799), I, 130.

26. Edward A. Kendall, *Travels Through The Northern Parts of the United States in the Years 1807 and 1808* (New York, 1809), III, 266.

27. John Bradbury, "Travels in the Interior of America," in R. G. Thwaites, *Early Western Travels 1748-1846* (Cleveland, 1904), V, 302-303.

28. *Ibid.*, 286.

29. *Op. cit.*, I, 30.

30. *Ibid.*, 102.

31. *Ibid.*, 29.

32. *Ibid.*, 114-115.

33. *Op. cit.*, 291, 292.

34. *Op Cit.*, I, 157-158.

35. *Ibid.*, I, 77-78.

36. *Ibid.*, I, 67-68.

37. *Op. cit.*, II, 167.

38. William Cobbett, *A Year's Residence in the United States of America* (Third edition, London, 1828), I, 201.

39. *Ibid.*, 248.

40. *Ibid.*, 205.

41. Jared Sparks, *The Works of Benjamin Franklin* (Boston, 1836), II, 469-470.

42. Richard Flower, "Letters from the Illinois" in R. G. Thwaites, *Early Western Travels 1748-1846* (Cleveland, 1904), X, 116-117.

43. William Wordsworth, *The Poetical Works* (Oxford edition, 1911) "The Prelude," Book XI, line 108.

44. Alexander Clarence Flick, *Loyalism in New York During the American Revolution* (New York, 1901), 183.

45. William B. Weeden, *Economic and Social History of New England 1620-1789* (Boston, 1890), II, 858-859.

46. Jared Sparks, *The Life of Gouverneur Morris* (Boston, 1832), I, 25.

47. Fisher Ames, *Works* (Boston, 1809), 11.

48. J. Franklin Jameson, *The American Revolution Considered As A Social Movement* (Princeton, 1926), 41-42.

49. James B. Ireland was born in Kentucky in 1797 and lived through the nineteenth century in his native state, following the occupation of farming. In connection with the celebration of the one-hundredth anniversary of his birth in 1897 he set down his recollections under the title *Looking Backward Through 100 Years*. The manuscript was published in the *Hancock Clarion*, Harnsville, Hancock County, Kentucky, in 1898.

50. *Proceedings and Debates of the Virginia State Convention, of 1829-30* (Richmond, 1830), 119.

51. John Melish, *Travels in the United States of America* (Philadelphia, 1812), I, 44.

52. *Op. Cit.*, 187.

CHAPTER *3:*

AMERICAN DEMOCRACY TODAY

Aмerican democracy today bears little resemblance to that of yesterday. The closing of the frontier and the rise of industrial civilization have profoundly transformed the simple society of the times of Jefferson and Jackson; but whether there is more or less of democracy now than formerly depends upon definitions. Some say that it has all but disappeared, while others see a steady march of democracy from colonial days down to the present. Arthur Meier Schlesinger, taking into account the diverse manifestations of democracy and striving to strike a balance between the advances and retreats, concludes that it reached its highest point about 1870; or to put the matter conversely, as he does, "aristocracy in America appeared to have reached the nadir of its decline" shortly after the Civil War.[1] The most fruitful approach to the question would seem to be an examination of the present status of the several forms of democracy.

Economic Democracy

Perhaps the most striking change in the economic foundations of democracy, at least to superficial observation, is the radical transformation of the instruments and organization of production—the reduction of the role of human labor, the advance of the machine, and the harnessing of mechanical power. The per capita consumption of energy has increased approximately fortyfold in the course of a single century and the productivity of the economic mechanism has attained fabulous proportions. If the factor of social insecurity is disregarded and a general *average* of material well-being is considered, the economic advance of the American people since

the times of Jefferson seems incredible. The life of the freehold farmer who lived under a condition of rough equality
with his neighbors was one of hardship, privation, and incessant labor of a degree almost inconceivable to the present
generation. Henry P. Hedges thus describes the life of the
farmer of the period in Suffolk County, New York, now almost within the shadow of the Empire State Building: "All
day he labored in the fields. In the long autumn and winter
evenings he husked corn and shelled the ears over the edge
of his spade. No horse-rake; no corn sheller; no horse pitch-
fork; no horse-mower or reaper—the life of the farmer was
literally a battle against the forces of nature for little more
than the actual necessities of subsistence, and with the most
rude and unwieldly supply of weapons for the war."[2] The
lot of the woman was equally stern and exacting. The members of both sexes grew old beyond their years and carried
the scars of the harsh economic struggle to the grave. From a
technological standpoint the condition of scarcity is no
longer necessary.

But this transformation of the means and modes of production must not be permitted to obscure the issue of
economic democracy—an issue which can best be introduced
by noting the changes in the social position and relations
of the freehold farmer who fought the great battles for
popular rule. The dominant fact here is that he has declined
in proportionate numbers until now he constitutes but a
minority of the population. From a country of rural home-
steads and hamlets America has become largely a nation of
urban dwellers—the most powerful industrial state in the
world. A majority of the people now would fall into Jefferson's category of "the mobs of great cities" who "add just
so much to the support of pure government, as sores do to
the strength of the human body."[3]

The process of occupational differentiation which Bidwell
observed in embryo in the New England towns at the begin-

ning of the nineteenth century has continued through the years with an ever accelerating tempo. Today a totally new occupational configuration, of almost unimaginable complexity and characteristic of industrial society everywhere, meets the eye of the observer. So complicated is this new configuration that the Bureau of the Census finds it necessary to employ thousands of classifications to report the occupations of the American people. The freehold farmer constitutes but one element in this configuration. According to T. M. Sogge, in 1930 only 12.4 per cent of the 48,829,920 persons gainfully employed in the United States were classified as farmers. An additional 9.0 per cent were placed in the category of farm laborers, approximately one-half of whom were "members of the family working on the home farm." Of the remainder, 37.9 per cent were industrial wage-earners, 14.6 lower salaried employees, 8.7 proprietors and officials, 7.9 professional workers, 4.1 servants, and 5.4 unclassified. [4]

The farmer of the 1930 census, moreover, should not be confused with the freehold farmer to whom Gouverneur Morris referred in the Constitutional Convention. His attachment to his land is comparatively uncertain; and the support which his land gives him is relatively precarious. In more than forty per cent of the cases he is a tenant. In similar proportion the holding of the farm owner is mortgaged, with an average ratio of mortgage to farm value of approximately forty per cent. Of even greater significance perhaps is the changed relation of the farm to the total economy. In 1800 the rural household was relatively self-contained, deriving from the soil the needed raw materials and fabricating in the house the finished articles of consumption. Horace Bushnell, in a "secular sermon" delivered at the Centennial Celebration of Litchfield County, Connecticut, in 1851, thus described the economy of the early nineteenth century farmer:

Thus, if the clothing is to be manufactured in the house, then flax will be grown in the plowed land, and sheep will be raised in the pasture, and the measure of the flax ground, and the number of the flock, will correspond with the measure of the house market—the number of the sons and daughters to be clothed—so that the agriculture out of doors will map the family in doors. Then as there is no thought of obtaining the articles of clothing, or dress, by exchange; as there is little passing of money, and the habit of exchange is feebly developed; the family will be fed on home-grown products, buckwheat, maize, rye, or whatever the soil will yield. And as carriages are a luxury introduced only with exchanges, the lads will be going back and forth to the mill on horseback, astride the fresh grists, to keep the mouths in supply. The meat market will be equally domestic, a kind of quarter-master slaughter and supply, laid up in the cellar, at fit times in the year. The daughters that, in factory days, would go abroad to join the female conscription of the cotton mill, will be kept in the home factory, or in that of some other family, and so in the retreats of domestic life.[5]

In comparison, farming today is a highly specialized calling, a part of a far-flung and closely integrated economic fabric dominated by the market. While the farmer may be classified formally as an entrepreneur by traditional capitalist economists, in certain respects his position is quite as precarious as that of the factory laborer. In losing his self-sufficiency he has lost his independence; in losing his independence he has lost his freedom; and in losing his freedom he has in a measure become proletarianized. Though the politician may still titillate his vanity and, incidentally, secure his vote by addressing him in rounded tones as "the independent farmer," his independence was dealt a first mortal blow in 1790 when Samuel Slater installed his spinning machinery at Pawtucket, and a second in 1830 when the Baltimore and Ohio Railroad opened thirteen miles of line. Whether Jefferson would regard the farmers of today

as "the chosen people of God" would seem to be extremely
doubtful.

The age of homespun and wooden-ware, of simplicity and
self-sufficiency, of physical hardship and unremitting toil, in
which American democracy was nurtured and from which it
derived its character, is already so distant that its spirit
utterly defies recapture. In some of the documents of the
period, to be sure, a glimpse of that forgotten life may perhaps be obtained, but only a glimpse. Bushnell, in whose
lifetime the new order of machinery and power began to
emerge, did indeed place the past and the future in remarkable juxtaposition. "This transition from mother and
daughter power to water and steam-power," he said, "is a
great one, greater by far than many have as yet begun to
conceive—one that is to carry with it a complete revolution
of domestic life and social manners." He then proceeded to
the following reminiscence and prophecy:

If our sons and daughters should assemble, a hundred years
hence, to hold another celebration like this, they will scarcely
be able to imagine the Arcadian pictures now so fresh in the
memory of many of us, though to the younger part already
matters of hearsay more than of personal knowledge or remem-
brance. Every thing that was most distinctive of the old
homespun mode of life will then have passed away. The spin-
ning-wheels of wool and flax, that used to buzz so familiarly in
the childish ears of some of us, will be heard no more forever;
seen no more, in fact, save in the halls of the Antiquarian Societies, where the delicate daughters will be asking, what these
strange machines are, and how they were made to go? The huge,
hewn-timber looms, that used to occupy a room by themselves
in the farm-houses, will be gone, cut up for cord wood, and their
heavy thwack, beating up the woof, will be heard no more by
the passer by—not even the Antiquarian Halls will find room
to harbor a specimen. The long strips of linen, bleaching on the
grass, and tended by a sturdy maiden, sprinkling them, each
hour, from her water-can, under a broiling sun—thus to prepare

the Sunday linen for her brothers and her own wedding outfit, will have disappeared, save as they return to fill a picture in some novel or ballad of the old time. The tables will be spread with some cunning, water-power Silesia not yet invented, or perchance with some meaner fabric from the cotton mills. The heavy Sunday coats that grew on sheep individually remembered —more comfortably carried, in warm weather, on the arm—and the specially fine-striped blue and white pantaloons of linen just from the loom, will no longer be conspicuous in processions of footmen going to their homespun worship, but will have given place to processions of broadcloth gentlemen lolling in the upholstery of their coaches. . . . The churches, too, that used to be simple brown meeting-houses covered with rived clapboards of oak, will have come down, mostly, from the bleak hill-tops into the close villages and populous towns that crowd the water-falls and the railroads.[6]

Against the conquering march of the forces of industrialism the embattled farmers offered stout and valiant, if blind and ineffectual, resistance. Again and again, invoking the authority of holy scripture and everything they held sacred, they opposed the advance of mechanical invention and the market. In the name of the home and the virtue of their daughters they waged incessant war on factory and city. They fostered a pride in household industry, erected moral barriers against the spread of the pecuniary economy, and refused to buy factory-made goods. They fought highways, railroads, large enterprise, corporations, labor unions, Wall Street, "the money power." They organized political parties and sought to capture the federal government in order to halt the sweep of the new industrial order. But all of this resistance was fruitless. It died with William Jennings Bryan and Robert M. LaFollette.

The changing fortunes of economic democracy in America, however, are not to be understood merely in terms of the passing of the self-contained rural household, the rout of Jefferson's freehold farmers, and the emergence of a new and marvelously intricate and complex occupational configuration. Of even greater significance is the concentration of economic power which has marched hand in hand with the conquest of the continent and the growth of industrialism. Whether this tendency is to be regarded as an inevitable concomitant of the application of science and technology to the various branches of the economy or as the natural product of capitalistic modes of production and distribution is a question which will be considered in a later chapter.

The fact of concentration of economic power need not be dwelt upon unduly, nor documented. It imposes itself starkly on all who read the newspapers, attend the movies, listen to the radio, or even take the trouble to observe casually the world in which they live. Scholarship has done no more than refine and make more precise the observations and judgments of the ordinary citizen. Extreme contrasts of poverty and riches, misery and luxury, material degradation and ostentatious living have become so common that they excite neither comment nor thought. If Alexis de Tocqueville were to return today and write a comprehensive work on the life and institutions of the people of the United States, one wonders whether he would find his old title appropriate. Who would have the hardihood to take issue with him if he should change it to *Plutocracy in America?* Certainly he would not begin his account with a reference to the "general equality of condition among the people." It is more likely that he would quote the following from Franklin D. Roosevelt's second inaugural address:

In this nation I see tens of millions of its citizens—a substantial part of its whole population—who at this very moment are denied the greater part of what the very lowest standards of today call the necessities of life. I see millions of families trying to live on incomes so meager that the pall of family disaster hangs over them day by day. I see millions whose daily lives in city and on farm continue under conditions labeled indecent by a so-called polite society half a century ago. I see millions denied education, recreation and the opportunity to better their lot, and the lot of their children. I see millions lacking the means to buy the products of farm and factory and by their poverty denying work and productiveness to many other millions. I see one-third of a nation ill-housed, ill-clad, ill-nourished.[7]

Or Tocqueville might begin his work with a reference to the findings of any one of a large number of more or less competent studies of the distribution of income in the United States which have been made during the past generation. The following quotation, consisting of but three short sentences, taken from the best of these investigations, an inquiry by the Brookings Institution into the incomes of American families for the prosperous year of 1929, should serve his purpose well:

The 11,653,000 families with incomes of less than $1,500 received a total of about 10 billion dollars. At the other extreme, the 36,000 families having incomes in excess of $75,000 possessed an aggregate income of 9.8 billion dollars. Thus it appears that 0.1 per cent of the families at the top received practically as much as 42 per cent of the families at the bottom of the scale.[8]

To friends of democracy these facts are terrifying. Yet they fail to reveal the most disturbing features of the American economy. Meager incomes, crucial as they are from the standpoint of material welfare, social relationships, political power, and cultural opportunities, are not incompatible with the nurture of the democratic spirit. The eleven and one-half million families receiving incomes under fifteen hundred dollars in 1929 doubtless included in their standard of living many things that would have been regarded as impossible luxuries to the early nineteenth century farmer. Even fairly large differences in income need not necessarily destroy democracy. Undoubtedly there were large disparities in family income under the order of the self-contained rural house-

hold. It would seem that the most fundamental question
pertains to the relation of the individual or family to the
source of income—to productive property. Control of the
means of production, whether immediately by the power of
the sword or indirectly through the force of law and custom,
has always been the basis of popular liberty, as it has been
the bulwark of aristocracy.

During the nineteenth century, as the old household
economy decayed and disappeared, an aristocracy of industrial capitalism arose. Growing out of the merchant and
financial classes of colonial times, recruiting new members
from farming, laboring, and other elements, standing on the
rights of private property guaranteed in federal constitution
and judicial decisions, seizing the opportunities associated
with the exploitation of a fabulously rich continent and a
rapidly expanding population, promoting and utilizing to
the full technology and mechanical invention, employing
new devices of economic organization and financial manipulation such as the corporation, the stock market, and
monopoly, destroying with the assistance of northern and
western farmers the rival slave-holding aristocracy of the
South, taking into its service the ablest and most ambitious
talent of the legal profession, gaining substantial control of
the press, the school, and even the church, and bending to its
purposes the legislative, executive, and judicial branches of
government, this new aristocracy, composed in its origins of
daring, inventive, forceful, ambitious, and ruthless men,
created the present national economic structure and gained
practical control of the economic life of the nation.[9]

As a result of this peaceful revolution in the economy the
overwhelming majority of the American people find themselves today practically without title to *productive* property
and with but little control over their economic destiny.
While figures of precision are wanting and the estimates of .
competent authorities vary, it seems reasonably safe to

assume that the percentage of the gainfully employed whose livelihood is dependent wholly or mainly on the ownership of the means of production lies somewhere between ten and twenty. According to Sogge's analysis of the 1930 census, the two categories of the "gainfully employed" whose work bore an immediate relation to ownership of productive property, "farmers" and "proprietors and officials," embraced respectively but 12.4 and 8.7 per cent of the total. The character of the first group has already been described. The second embraces not only *bona fide* proprietors, but also managers and superintendents of both large and small enterprise, commercial travelers and real estate and insurance agents, and even auctioneers, hucksters, peddlers, and boarding-house keepers. "However one approaches the problem of income distribution," writes Ferdinand Lundberg after a careful and comprehensive study of the matter, "one is confronted with substantially the same conclusion: fewer than twenty per cent of the people possess nearly everything while eighty per cent own practically nothing except chattels. Wealth itself has become monopolized." [10] And the great numerical majority of this twenty per cent are in a sense but vestiges from the past—holders of small property, farmers, shopkeepers, and the "little fellows" of industry who for the most part have been fighting a losing battle with their larger and more powerful competitors. In the distribution of ownership of productive property the condition of the American people has been practically reversed in little more than a century. In the time of Jefferson probably at least eighty per cent of the people gained their livelihood through the ownership and personal operation of productive property.

Moreover, due to the rise of the corporation the concentration of economic power is far greater than the above percentages indicate. According to A. A. Berle and G. L. Means, on or about January 1, 1930, two hundred non-financial corporations controlled 49.2 per cent of the corporate wealth (other than banking), 38.0 per cent of the business wealth (other than banking), and 22.0 of the total wealth of the nation.[11] In commenting on this concentration of power these authors say: "If roughly half of corporate wealth is controlled by two hundred large corporations and half by smaller companies it is fair to assume that very much more than half of industry is dominated by these great units. This concentration is made even more significant when it is recalled that as a result of it, approximately 2,000 individuals out of a population of one hundred and twenty-five million are in a position to control and direct half of industry."[12] Lewis Corey has estimated that control over one-fourth of the corporate assets of the United States "is concentrated in 167 persons in the Morgan combination who hold more than 2,450 interlocking directorships in corporations."[13] Robert H. Jackson, counsel for the Bureau of Internal Revenue, concluded that in 1932 fifty-three per cent of the total corporate wealth of the country—$280,085,-000,000—was held by 618 corporations.[14] And Franklin D. Roosevelt, in his special message to Congress on April 29, 1938, basing his statement on statistics of the above-mentioned Bureau for 1935, said that "of all corporations reporting from every part of the nation, one-tenth of 1 per cent of them owned 52 per cent of the assets of all of them."[15] The economic domains ruled by the largest of these great organisms almost pass comprehension. The American Telephone and Telegraph Company, though title is widely distributed, say Berle and Means, "controls more wealth than is contained within the borders of twenty-one of the states in the country."[16] In meeting the argument that the great mass of the people share in the corporate wealth of the country through stock ownership, the President stated that in the "banner year" of 1929 "three-tenths of 1 per cent of our population received 78 per cent of the dividends reported by individuals."[17] Moreover, in order to complete the picture, the point should be made that, as corporations have increased in size, ownership and control have become separated and actual power has passed into fewer and fewer hands. Through various devices a small minority of stock, not infrequently as small as one per cent of the investment, will exercise control. Today, as regards concentration of economic power, the "great democracy of the West" is not to be distinguished from the larger industrial states of the Old World.

The tendency in the economy toward aristocracy was not of course wholly unforseen. From the days of the Constitutional Convention down through the succeeding decades of the nineteenth century not a few persons of knowledge and insight made observations and predictions recording and forecasting the disappearance of equality of condition and the concentration of economic power in the hands of some new privileged order. "The time is not distant," said Gouverneur Morris in the Constitutional Convention, "when this country will abound with mechanics and manufacturers, who will receive their bread from their employers." [18] And James Madison predicted on the same occasion that "in future times, a great majority of the people will not only be without landed, but any other sort of property." [19] Jefferson in a letter to George Logan in 1816 wrote: "I hope we shall . . . crush in it's birth the aristocracy of our monied corporations which dare already to challenge our government to a trial of strength and bid defiance to the laws of our country."[20] One of the many tragi-comic incidents of the present confused epoch was the effort by the American Liberty League, an organ of these corporations, to canonize the author of the Declaration of Independence and to make him their patron saint.

But the boldest, most penetrating, and most comprehensive analysis of the forces tending toward aristocracy, attempted during the first generation of the history of the Republic, was made by John Taylor of Caroline County,

Virginia—officer in the Revolutionary armies, member of the United States senate, and the most systematic thinker produced by the old agrarian democracy. Of him and his thought Jefferson wrote as follows in 1820: "Colonel Taylor and myself have rarely, if ever, differed in any political principle of importance. Every act of his life, and every word he ever wrote, satisfies me of this." [21]

In a powerful essay on *Aristocracy,* published in 1814 and worthy of republication today, Taylor analyzed the causes, the nature, and the methods of aristocracy in history, with particular reference to the United States of his time. He divided the long career of privileged orders in the Western World into three periods. The aristocracy of ancient times, "chiefly created and supported by superstition," he styled "the aristocracy of the oracle"; that of the Middle Ages, produced by conquest, "the aristocracy of the sword"; and that of the present age, derived from the manipulation of economic devices and institutions, "the aristocracy of paper and patronage." The change in the form of aristocracy, he pointed out, has led to confusion in the popular mind: "If aristocracy is the work of nature, by deserting her accustomed constancy, and slily changing the shape of her work, she has cunningly perplexed our defensive operations: to create the aristocracy of the first age, she used Jupiter; of the second, Mars; and of the third, Mercury. Jupiter is dethroned by knowledge; the usurpations of Mars are scattered by commerce and alienation; and it only remains to detect the impostures of Mercury." [22]

He charges his contemporaries with blindness to the real nature of aristocracy. Contending that an aristocracy exists whenever and wherever power resides "in the hands of a minority," * whether that power is derived from the superstitious, the military, or the fiscal methods "of enslaving

*This definition or conception of aristocracy is accepted in the present work.

nations," he observes that "the Americans devoted their ef-
fectual precautions to the obsolete modes of title and hierarchy, erected several barriers against the army mode, and
utterly disregarded the mode of paper and patronage." [23] He
aims his shafts particularly at John Adams for his concern
over the aristocracies of the past and his failure to face the
actual threat to free institutions in the aristocracy of the
present:

> Why has Mr. Adams written volumes to instruct us how to
> manage an order of nobles, sons of the Gods, of exclusive virtue,
> talents and wealth, and attended by the pomp and fraud of
> superstition; or one of feudal barons, holding great districts of
> unalienable country, warlike, high spirited, turbulent and dan-
> gerous; now that these orders are no more? Whilst he passes
> over in silence the aristocracy of paper and patronage, more
> numerous, more burdensome, unexposed to public jealousy by
> the badge of title, and not too honorable or high spirited to use
> and serve executive power, for the sake of pillaging the people.
> Are these odious vices to be concealed under apprehensions of
> ancient aristocracies, which, however natural, are supplanted by
> this modern one? [24]

Taylor argues that the modern form of aristocracy is peculiarly dangerous and difficult to control. "A nation exposed to a paroxysm of conquering rage," he writes, "has
infinitely the advantage of one, subjected to this aristocrat-
ical system. One is local and temporary; the other is spread
by law and is perpetual. One is an open robber, who warns
you to defend yourself; the other a sly thief, who empties
your pockets under a pretence of paying your debts. One is a
pestilence, which will end of itself; the other a climate
deadly to liberty." [25] He saw the new aristocracy already
firmly entrenched behind legal conceptions and working
through established and accepted institutional arrangements.

This powerful champion of democracy, however, focused

his attention primarily on the perils inherent in the operations of commercial and financial interests. It was too early to see the more serious threat resident in the new industrial economy which was still in embryo. But half a generation later Tocqueville, doubtless with the experience of western Europe in mind, penetrated beneath the surface of things to see the image of coming events and made a remarkable forecast. If he were to survey the present scene in America, he might point with some satisfaction to the following paragraph written in the "old horse and buggy days":

I am of opinion, upon the whole, that the manufacturing aristocracy which is growing up under our eyes is one of the harshest which ever existed in the world; but, at the same time, it is one of the most confined and least dangerous. Nevertheless, the friends of democracy should keep their eyes anxiously fixed in this direction; for if ever a permanent inequality of conditions and aristocracy again penetrate into the world, it may be predicted that this is the gate by which they will enter.[26]

As the Civil War cleared the way for the unimpeded advance of the new order, the decay of the economic foundations of American democracy became apparent to all who had eyes to see. In 1885, almost two generations after Tocqueville gave expression to his fears, Josiah Strong, "pioneer and prophet of social Christianity," thus announced the fulfillment of the prophecy of the French philosopher: "It is useless for us to protest that we are democratic, and to plead the leveling character of our institutions. There is among us an aristocracy of recognized power, and that aristocracy is one of wealth. No heraldry offends our republican prejudices. Our ensigns armorial are the trademark. Our laws and customs recognize no noble titles; but men can forego the husk of a title who possess the fat ears of power."[27] The remainder of the story has been told in the facts of the distribution of wealth and income.

Social Democracy

Although a new aristocracy has emerged in America, in superficial respects one of the most powerful in history, democracy in the ordinary social relationships is still fairly characteristic of the masses of the American people. In comparison with other nations they place relatively little store by ancestry, family, and social position: they still are inclined to judge an individual by his own powers and achievements. And yet, not being institutionalized, this form of democracy can scarcely be expected to long survive the disappearance of its economic foundations. Indeed, historically, it has been hardly more than a reflection in the sphere of social relationships of a widespread freehold agriculture in which the great majority of people followed the same occupations and "the young farm hand" advanced almost universally to land ownership.

To the close observer, moreover, the old sense of social equality manifests signs of decay. The feeling of caste is everywhere emergent; the search for ancestors and the dispensing of titles have become a profitable business; and exclusive clubs, country estates, and private hunting grounds dot the land. Wide differences in modes of life, in standards of expenditure, in cultural opportunities, in the actual exercise of power all combine to create differences in mentality and outlook. In the presence of the facts of property ownership and the human relations engendered by them, professions and even honest convictions of social democracy lose their reality and become but a cloak for hypocrisy. The growing advocacy of social doctrines of human inequality on "scientific" grounds by "scientists" is the expected fruit of gross economic inequality and constitutes the ethical foundation for the establishment in America of the "leader principle" of German fascism.

The spirit of personal independence also seems to be passing with the destruction of its economic base. Where today could be found "farmers, boorish, ignorant, and obtrusive fellows," who would refuse to be impressed or intimidated by the robes of the supreme court, the badges of esoteric learning, or the evidences of riches? Perhaps in the more remote parts of Maine or in a few other districts where the old frontier and agrarian life lingers on, but their number is small and rapidly dwindling away. In the absence of economic security and in the presence of those who control their means of livelihood, only fools, candidates for "suicide squads," and persons of deep moral conviction will indulge the luxury of independent thought and action. The American people today are ready, even eager, if the practice of the newspapers is a true guage of public sentiment, to listen with respect to the opinion of a man of great wealth on any subject whatsoever, regardless of his competence, from Greek art to sun spots.

With the passing of economic independence and security is going that sense of integrity which is essential to the successful operation of democratic institutions. While there are doubtless still many who would object to wearing the livery of another man, at least if it were done openly, their numbers also are steadily diminishing. Captain Basil Hall and Isaac Weld would encounter little difficulty in America today in finding servants ready and willing to rub down horses or even to jump at the sound of a bell. On the contrary, they would be besieged by persons eager not only to shine, but to lick their boots. Mr. J. P. Morgan stated in an interview not long ago that the level of a civilization is reflected in the number of its menial servants. But without pausing to expose the peculiar class conception of civilization implicit in this observation, it should be noted that with the concentration of economic power and the increase of insecurity has gone a decline in intellectual and moral integrity, a spread of the servile mentality, a growth in the number of "yes-men"—an appellation which, if used in the early American democracy, would have led to bloodshed. This process of personal degradation, moreover, is by no means confined to the lower ranks of society. Men of talent and education, graduates of ancient and honorable institutions of learning, desirous of enjoying the fleshpots of this world, make a business of selling themselves, their abilities, and their convictions to the highest bidder. Professor T. V. Smith has coined the term "plutogogue" as a very appropriate designation for these gentlemen. Even presidents of great universities will listen with unctuous attention to the educational ideas and proposals of a representative of the contemporary aristocracy, not because they possess merit, but because they are the pronouncements of economic power. For the same reasons every June the highest of academic honors are bestowed upon persons who, though in the higher financial brackets, make no pretensions to learning.

With the emergence of class divisions in American economy and society there emerge also, as surely as the night follows the day, the phenomena of class organization, class consciousness, and class conflict. Since the Civil War these manifestations of deep cleavage in the social order have appeared as dark clouds over the horizon, ever rising and growing more threatening in aspect. The organization of financial and industrial capital has been followed falteringly by the organization of labor and farming. From time to time the struggle between these clashing interests has burst forth into bitter and violent domestic war. Although class mentality is being forged on both sides by this struggle, its most aggressive, energetic, and effective manifestations have come from the upper strata. One of the most striking examples of this mentality, reminiscent of Mr. Tom Girdler of the Republic Steel Corporation in 1937, was displayed approximately a generation ago by Mr. George F. Baer, President of the Philadelphia and Reading Railway Company, at the

time of the great coal strike in 1902. It seems that a citizen
of Wilkes-Barre, by the name of W. F. Clark, had written
Mr. Baer, appealing to him as a Christian to grant the
strikers a slight concession, end the strike, and thus earn the
blessing of God and the gratitude of the nation. With the assurance and arrogance of a feudal lord holding his fief from
almighty God, Mr. Baer replied as follows:

I have your letter of the 16th instant.

I do not know who you are. I see that you are a religious man;
but you are evidently biased in favor of the right of the working
man to control a business in which he has no other interest than
to secure fair wages for the work he does.

I beg of you not to be discouraged. The rights and interests of
the laboring man will be protected and cared for—not by the
labor agitators, but by the Christian men to whom God in His
infinite wisdom has given the control of the property interests
of the country, and upon the successful Management of which
so much depends.

Do not be discouraged. Pray earnestly that right may triumph,
always remembering that the Lord God Omnipotent still reigns,
and that His reign is one of law and order, and not of violence
and crime.[28]

Evidence is accumulating that class relations in the United
States are beginning to congeal, that the high social mobility
so distinctive of American society in the past is disappearing,
that the land of opportunity for the poor is becoming a land
of security for the rich. This is not to say that, with the possible exception of the Soviet Union, American society today,
particularly for persons born into the middle ranks, remains
the most fluid in the world. But the handwriting on the wall
is already clearly discernible. The pre-emption of the continent, the closing of the frontier, the rounding out of the productive mechanism, the decline in the rate of population
growth, and the deepening contradictions of capitalist econ-

omy combine to limit the range and incidence of individual
opportunity.

In a recent study of business men F. W. Taussig and C. S.
Joslyn found a marked tendency for sons to follow in the
footsteps of their fathers.[29] And an investigation of two generations of millionaires by Professor Pitirim Sorokin reveals an
even stronger trend toward social stratification. "The percentage of the living millionaires," he writes, "whose fathers followed 'money-making' occupations is much higher than that
of the deceased group. This fact taken together with some
further data gives a basis to state that *the wealthy class of the
United States is becoming less and less open, more and more
closed, and is tending to be transformed into a caste-like
group*." [30] In conclusion Sorokin says that *"American society is being transformed—at least in its upper stratum—into
a society with rigid classes and well outlined class divisions."* [31] He even finds that "the percentage of hereditary
transmission of occupation among America's wealthiest
group is no less than in other European societies and is still
growing." [32] Robert H. Jackson, in testifying before the
Committee on Finance of the United States Senate in August, 1935, thus outlined the economic and legal foundations
of the tendency toward an hereditary aristocracy:

It is often asserted that large wealth is dissipated in three
generations, and it has become a proverb that it is "three generations from shirt sleeves to shirt sleeves." It was doubtless once
true that all a grandfather saved from the fruits of his labor
could be spent by a grandson. It is probably true today of very
moderate fortunes. It is not true of large invested fortunes under
present conditions. They not only perpetuate themselves, they
grow.

This is because they are now so large. A riotous living heir to
one of our larger fortunes would exhaust himself before he
could exhaust the income alone of the estate. Furthermore, such
estates are largely perpetuated in trusts, and every legal and

economic obstacle to their dissipation is employed. They are invested in the enterprises of the country where the income and management are not dependent upon the judgment or industry of the heir, or are invested in tax-free Government securities.[33]

An extraordinary corroboration of this analysis was made a matter of public record on August 4, 1937, when the trustees of the fifty million dollar estate left by William Rockefeller in 1922 made an accounting in the Surrogate's Court. Under the provisions of the will the principal is to be left intact for the great-grandchildren, the children and grandchildren being permitted only to share the interest. The remainder of the story is told in *The New York Times:*

While the principal is growing at the rate of a million a year, William's four children and fourteen grandchildren have been dividing among themselves an additional three-quarter million of annual interest.

The total net interest they have drawn since William's death in 1922 is $9,514,834, while the total increase in the untouched principal during the same period has been $13,947,361. The estate is now valued by Surrogate James A. Foley at $63,713,889 net, after payment of all debts, taxes and expenses.

At present there are twenty-eight young great-grandchildren in line for an eventual distribution of this, as their respective parents die. Only two of them are over 14 years of age and the other twenty-six average 4 or 5 years. The court recognized there were more yet to be born.

According to the family record of William Rockefeller's direct descendants, there will possibly be fifty such great-grandchildren in all. And at the rate of accumulation of the original $50,000,000 during the last fifteen years, they will divide about $75,000,000 some time after 1950.

Under the provisions of the will, which the court construed as a "continuing trusteeship," Mr. Rockefeller has supplied the country with fifty prospective millionaires in their own right.[34]

If the case of the Rockefellers stood alone, regardless of the social injustice involved in maintaining a family of social parasites through four generations, it would be a subject of curiosity rather than a cause for alarm. But it does not stand alone. It is but typical of the general tendency of the social order; it can be approached or duplicated wherever great fortunes have appeared. The fact is that the "aristocracy of paper and patronage" which John Taylor feared has reached maturity. Whereas in the first decades of the Republic's history it was largely an aristocracy of individuals, today it is an aristocracy of families. Through the laws of inheritance and property accumulation, operating in an economy of unforseen productivity, great dynasties are founded and perpetuated for five and six generations. The American people who fought a revolutionary war in part to throw off the shackles of monarchical and feudal tyranny find themselves today under the dominion of a new aristocracy of their own creation. That neither they nor the founders of these mighty families realized what was happening does not soften the threat to free institutions inherent in concentrated economic power. Jefferson, though fearing the tendency, completely underestimated the strength of the forces at work. Having fought entail and primogeniture in a country where land was the chief form of property, the productivity of the economy relatively low, and the birth-rate inordinately high, he believed that "the best corrective" of "overgrown wealth" would be "the law of equal inheritance to all in equal degree." [35] Clearly he reckoned without knowledge of the potentialities resident in the coordination of the resources of the law, the trust, the corporation, the institution of interest, and the energies of an industrial regime. Although income and estate taxes are already affecting the situation in favor of democracy, the consolidation and perpetuation of this moneyed caste are by no means halted.

This palpable American aristocracy, moreover, is more than a simple *aggregation* of families. While there are rivalries and even bitter conflicts among these dynasties of wealth, they are being welded through marriage into a fairly distinct and self-perpetuating caste with a mentality and a social outlook more or less distinct from those of the rest of the population. Ferdinand Lundberg, on the basis of a review of the available facts, finds that "the wealthiest Americans, with few exceptions, are already joined by a multiplicity of family ties, just as they are joined by interlocking directorates and mutual participations in economic undertakings." Wealth marries wealth so consistently that the exception is converted by the newspapers into a major sensation, if not a scandal, as in the case of the marriage of James A. Stillman, Jr., to a daughter of his mother's cook or of Ellin Mackay to a composer of popular music. "The continuation of intermarriage among millionaire families will, other factors remaining unchanged," predicts Lundberg, "in a generation or two give rise to a situation wherein all the big American proprietors will be blood relatives—first, second, or third cousins." [36] Already this trend is well advanced. When it is completed the cycle of democracy in America will have been closed and an era of feudalism founded on industrial capital instead of land will have opened.

But the account is not ended. Through ties of marriage and the more solid links of economic interest the American aristocracy is being bound to that of Europe. Franklin observed that in his time the "commodity" of birth and rank could not "be carried to a worse market than that of America." Today it cannot be carried to a better one. Indeed, unless he commits a serious social or political blunder, as did the Duke of Windsor in the autumn of 1937, the scion of European nobility can come to the United States with the assurance of receiving not only the fraternal greetings of the aristocracy but even the adulations of the multitude. How many decadent and bankrupt houses of the Old World have been regenerated and made solvent by matrimonial alliances with the puissant plutocracy of the New! According to Gustavus Myers, the number had reached half a thousand by 1909.[37] And Lundberg estimates that "by now the aggregate is easily six or eight times as great."[38] In the year of the Constitutional Convention Jefferson writing from France, where he could observe at first hand the fruits of aristocracy, admonished "our young Republic" to "prevent their citizens from becoming so established in wealth and power, as to be thought worthy of alliance by marriage with the nieces, sisters, &c., of Kings."[39] American social democracy has moved a long distance toward oblivion in one-hundred-and-thirty years.

Political Democracy

The century which has seen the rise of an economic aristocracy has also witnessed an almost uninterrupted advance of political democracy. By 1856 white manhood suffrage had become universal throughout the nation; in 1863 the Proclamation of Emancipation destroyed the legal foundations of Negro slavery; in 1870 the fifteenth amendment to the Federal Constitution formally bestowed full rights of citizenship upon male Negroes; in 1913 the seventeenth amendment abolished the indirect election of senators and gave the people direct control over the upper house of the Congress; in 1920 the nineteenth amendment crowned with success the long fight of women for equal political rights; and in 1937 President Roosevelt shattered the carefully nurtured aura of sanctity surrounding the Supreme Court and inaugurated a struggle to make the whole federal judiciary more responsive to popular interests and changing conditions. Today practically the entire edifice erected in the Convention of 1787 for the apparent purpose of keeping the control of the three branches of the federal government out of the hands of the populace lies in ruins. At the same time in the realm of state and local government the formal process of democratization has marched from one conquest to another. While much remains to be done before a full political democracy is achieved, a political democracy suited to the structure and character of industrial society, the advances have been fairly steady and substantial. In theory at least the American people are in a position to make their political institutions serve their purposes. An informed, determined, and united popular will cannot be thwarted long at the polls. *The question of the possibility of achieving such a will in a society dominated by an economic aristocracy is the central problem of the present volume.*

The actual successes of political democracy in protecting and advancing the interests of the people are far less impressive than the formal extension of popular control over the organs of government. To be sure, the responsibilities of government for the performance of needed and valuable services have been greatly increased. The conception of the police state, remote from the lives of men and women and dedicated primarily to the enforcement of the rules of the economic game, has been abandoned in practice, whatever the prevailing theory may be. Local, state, and federal authorities have taken an active interest in the promotion of health and education, in the administration of various public utilities, in the regulation of trade and commerce, in the improvement of minimum standards of working conditions, in the conduct of scientific inquiry and research, in the dissemination of useful knowledge, and in the performance of many other functions that cannot be enumerated here. Particularly should attention be directed to the establishment of that system of public schools, embracing primary, secondary, and higher institutions, which has gone far to destroy the class monopoly of knowledge. Recently, the federal government has assumed large obligations in the relief of unemployment and the mitigation of various hazards associated with the conduct of the economy. It has even accepted some responsibility for the operation of the economic system.

Also, through the income tax amendment adopted in 1913, it has established a principle of taxation possessing revolutionary implications for the economic order.

But after all is said on this score that can be said, the fact remains that political democracy has been extraordinarily ineffective in its efforts to halt the march of the aristocracy and to effect fundamental social reforms conceived in the general interest. Indeed ofttimes legislation designed to accomplish these ends has been either emasculated or actually turned to contrary purposes. As new millions have been added to the roster of voters the basic trend away from democracy in the organization and conduct of the economy has proceeded steadily on its course. The melancholy fact is that if political democracy had proved to be the effective instrument which the American people have traditionally thought it to be, their essential liberties would not now be in danger. A few illustrations will make the point clear.

A hundred years ago the American people possessed a public domain of almost unlimited natural riches—a vast domain beyond the Alleghanies of soil, timber, minerals, and water, not to mention the abundant animal life inhabiting stream, lake, timber, mountain, and prairie. John Quincy Adams, a man of great learning and sagacity who was deeply concerned about the future of the Republic, recognized the worth of this material heritage and saw in it boundless resources for the promotion of the general interest—the building of schools, the construction of highways and canals, and the advancement of the cultural level of the people. But he was helpless to stem the tide of plunder. "The thirst of a tiger for blood," he wrote to a friend in 1838, "is the fittest emblem of the rapacity with which the members of all the new states fly at the public lands. The constitutents upon whom they depend are all settlers, or tame and careless spectators of the pillage. They are themselves enormous speculators and land-jobbers. It were a vain attempt to resist them here." [40]

Soil, timber, minerals, water, and animal life, each in its turn, has served the ends of personal aggrandizement and the building of private fortunes. The result has been a wastage of irreplaceable resources that surpasses anything of its kind in history. Even the Homestead Act of 1862, deliberately designed to reserve the remaining public lands for bona fide settlers, failed utterly to achieve its purpose. By 1890, when "the closing of the frontier" was officially recognized in the report of the census, "only 372,659 homestead entries had been perfected, granting 48,225,736 acres to supposed settlers—an area less than that of the state of Nebraska and equal only to three and one half per cent of the total territory west of the Mississippi River. By that date more than four times as much land had been given to the railroad companies." [41] The resources which the democracy gave away, now in many cases badly depleted and mangled, can only be recovered at an exorbitant price.

The outstanding instance of the failure of political democracy was of course the resort to the sword in the decision of the slavery issue. In fact as the country drifted toward catastrophe, the Supreme Court of the United States in the Dred Scott case, while presuming merely to interpret and apply the fundamental law of the land, rendered far-reaching political judgments and practically forced the nation into civil strife. Scholars agree today that in their decision the majority of the court went beyond the boundaries of legal necessity to make the United States safe for slavery. A case that was capable of simple adjudication was employed to place the impress of a sectional social philosophy upon the nation. "The political character of the whole performance," says Professor Theodore Clarke Smith in his authoritative work on *Parties and Slavery,* "was stamped upon it in the phraseology of the opinions as well as in the logical incoherence and superfluousness of the arguments." [42] There is some evidence of collusion between the executive and the court in this case. The tragic consequences for American democracy of the ensuing struggle can scarcely be overestimated. The forces of the people were so thoroughly divided over the issue that even today, after the passage of more than two generations, the cleavage remains a major political reality. On the one hand, the slave-holding aristocracy succeeded in enlisting the loyalties of the great masses of white freehold farmers in the south in the defense of an institution in which they could have no genuine sympathy. On the other, the rising aristocracy of "paper and patronage" was able to enroll under its banners the northern and western farmers who had already established a tradition of struggle against the "money power." The ordinary men who fought in both armies were fighting, unaware of it though they were, not their own battles, but the battles of rival aristocracies. If they had maintained their solidarity through the middle decades of the century, or had regained it in the years immediately following the civil struggle, they might have checked the more serious abuses of capitalism and greatly reduced its power over government.

In 1857 the Supreme Court had come to the support of the southern aristocracy and its "peculiar institution"; after 1886, by a "tortured" interpretation of the Fourteenth Amendment, it became a powerful rampart of the rising northern aristocracy. That amendment, adopted in 1868, had been designed, at least in popular opinion and conviction, to protect the rights and liberties of the recently emancipated Negroes. And so it was interpreted by the court until 1886 when in the case of Santa Clara County v. Southern Pacific R. R. the term "person" used in the amendment was made to embrace corporations as well as Negroes. Thereafter the "due process clause" was generally employed to support property rights against human rights and to block popular efforts to curb the advance of the new aristocracy operating increasingly through corporate devices and agencies. "It is interesting to see," conclude Louis M. Hacker and Benjamin

B. Kendrick, "that so completely was the Fourteenth Amendment regarded as a bulwark against oppressive state legislation, particularly as it affected the rights of property, that between 1888 and 1914 the amendment was invoked in 790 cases brought before the Supreme Court." [43] To imagine a more complete distortion of the generally accepted meaning of a constitutional provision or a bolder thwarting of the popular will would be difficult. It is to be hoped that this long series of decisions by the court will not have the tragic sequel of the Dred Scott case.

Since the Civil War political movements aiming at the democratization of the economy have followed one another in an unending succession. Besides revolutionary parties inspired by European ideas and employing European methods, there have been the Knights of Labor, the Greenbackers, the Populists, the Progressives, the apostles of the New Freedom, and numerous minor voices of protest. But except for a few needed reforms embodied in such legislation as the Interstate Commerce Act of 1887, the Federal Reserve Act of 1913, and the Transportation Act of 1920, which carried no threat to the aristocracy, and the establishment of the principle of federal taxation of income and inheritance, whose full import is yet to be revealed, the forces of political democracy have shattered their lances in vain on the embattled hosts of the plutocracy. William Jennings Bryan charged in words of burning eloquence that the people were being crucified on a "cross of gold"; Theodore Roosevelt with his "big stick" stood at Armageddon and battled for the Lord; and Woodrow Wilson in the measured tones of the scholar declared that "until monopoly is abolished, until it is destroyed" the government cannot be free; but the concentration of economic power proceeded inexorably on its way. Beginning with the Sherman Anti-Trust Law of 1890 the Congress attempted by means of a number of enactments to prevent monopolistic practices in the economy, but always somewhere between the legislative chamber and the office of business enterprise the teeth of these enactments were thoroughly extracted. Whether at last under the leadership of Franklin D. Roosevelt and his successors the people will succeed in employing the institutions of political democracy for the protection and advancement of their interests is a question that will probably be answered during the coming decade. The record of the past two generations would seem to hold but little promise for the future.

In Conclusion

Despite the easily observable advances of the past century and the wide participation of the masses of the people in the processes of popular government, American democracy today is unquestionably far more apparent than real. However unpleasant the admission may be to friends of free institutions, the fact must be admitted that in the course of a century the people of the United States have lost control over the foundations of power in any society—the means by which they obtain their livelihood. When James W. Gerard in August, 1930, gave to the press the names of fifty-nine persons who, he said, are the real rulers of America, few took serious issue with his pronouncement. Ferdinand Lundberg pursuing this idea into the available records of the time has produced a heavily documented volume on *America's 60 Families* which, whatever may be its inadequacies, obviously contains far too much of truth to be cast lightly aside by the champions of democracy. These families, the great majority of which are practically unknown to the ordinary citizen, are shown not only to hold the major strategic positions in the economic order, but also to exert an extraordinary influence on government, the press, the church, the school, and international relations. While the pattern presented is doubtless more simple that the facts, while no clear line of demarcation can be drawn between the great financial lords of the nation and the princelings of region and locality, while the leading families are divided by rivalries and differences in interest, much as the kings and monarchs of Europe were divided a few centuries ago, the concentration of economic power constitutes the most profound reality in the contemporary social order in the United States. "Inequality of condition and aristocracy" have again penetrated into the world and they have entered through the very gate which Tocqueville foresaw a hundred years ago.

REFERENCES

1. Arthur Meier Schlesinger, *New Viewpoints in American History* (New York, 1928), 93.

2. Henry P. Hedges, "Development of Agriculture in Suffolk County," in *Bi-Centennial History of Suffolk County* (Babylon, N. Y., 1885), 43.

3. Thomas Jefferson, "Notes on the State of Virginia," in *Writings* (Ford edition, New York, 1899), III, 269.

4. Tillman M. Sogge, "Industrial Classes in the United States in 1930" in *Journal of American Statistical Association* (June, 1933), 199.

5. Horace Bushnell, *Work and Play* (New York, 1864), 378-379.

6. *Ibid.*, 376-378.

7. *The New York Times* (January 21, 1937).

8. Maurice Leven, Harold G. Moulton, and Clark Warburton, *America's Capacity to Consume* (Washington, 1934), 56.

9. This story is well told in Charles A. & Mary R. Beard, *The Rise of American Civilization* (New York, 1927), II; Louis M. Hacker and Benjamin B. Kendrick, *The United States Since 1865* (New York, 1932); Gustavus Myers, *History of the Great American Fortunes* (Modern Library edition, New York, 1936); and Ida M. Tarbell, *The Nationalizing of Business 1878-1898* (New York, 1936).

10. Ferdinand Lundberg, *America's 60 Families* (New York, 1937), 48.

11. Adolph A. Berle and Gardiner C. Means, *The Modern Corporation and Private Property* (New York, 1932), 32.

12. *Ibid.*, 33.

13. Lewis Corey, *The House of Morgan* (New York, 1930), 448.

14. Robert H. Jackson, "The Big Corporations Rule," *The New Republic* (September 4, 1935), 99-100.

15. *New York Herald Tribune* (April 30, 1938).

16. *Op. cit.*, 19.

17. *Op. cit.*

18. Henry D. Gilpin, *The Papers of James Madison* (Washington, 1840), III, 1252.

19. *Ibid.*, 1253.

20. *Op. cit.* (Ford edition, New York, 1899), X, 69.

21. *Ibid.*, 170.

22. John Taylor, *An Inquiry into the Principles and Policy of the Government of the United States* (Fredericksburg, 1814), 20-21.

23. *Ibid.*, 42.

24. *Ibid.*, 15-16.

25. *Ibid.*, 41.

26. Alexis de Tocqueville, *Democracy in America* (New York, 1898), II, 197.

27. Josiah Strong, *Our Country* (New York, 1885), 116.

28. Caro Lloyd, *Henry Demarest Lloyd, 1847-1903, A Biography* (New York, 1912), II, 190.

29. F. W. Taussig and C. S. Joslyn, *American Business Leaders* (New York, 1932).

30. *The Journal of Social Forces* (May, 1925), 635.

31. *Ibid.*, 636.

32. *Ibid.*, 635-636.

33. *Revenue Act of 1935, Hearings* before the *Committee on Finance, United States Senate, Seventy-Fourth Congress, First Session* on *H.R. 8974* (Washington, 1935), 177.

34. *The New York Times* (August 5, 1937).

35. Thomas Jefferson, *The Writings* (Washington edition, New York, 1854), VI, 575.

36. *Op. cit.*, 9.

37. *Op. cit.*, 378.

38. *Op. cit.*, 9.

39. Thomas Jefferson, *The Writings* (Washington edition, New York, 1853), II, 253.

40. Henry Adams, *The Degradation of the Democratic Dogma* (New York, 1920), 31.

41. F. A. Shannon, "The Homestead Act and the Labor Surplus," *American Historical Review*, (July, 1936) 637, 638.

42. Theodore Clarke Smith, *Parties and Slavery* (New York, 1906), 202.

43. Louis M. Hacker and Benjamin B. Kendrick, *The United States Since 1865* (New York, 1932), 199.

CHAPTER 4:

ARISTOCRACY OR DEMOCRACY

THE supreme social task facing the American people today is the rebuilding of the economic foundations of their democracy. If the analysis presented in the preceding pages is at all accurate, this conclusion seems to be irrefutable. Thus the current age bears a striking resemblance to that of the first half century of the history of the Republic: then as now the future of democracy was at stake. Yet the two ages are fundamentally different. Then a rough economic democracy sought political power and endeavored to place its stamp on the institutions of government; now a substantial political democracy is grappling with a financial, commercial, and industrial aristocracy and seeking to bring economic power under popular control. Whether the terms of the democratic equation can be reversed in this fashion, that is, whether the institutions and processes of popular government can be employed successfully in the reconstruction of the economy along democratic lines, is a question which will be considered in succeeding chapters. Here attention will be directed primarily to the location of the problem.

Underlying the above statement of the nature of the contemporary task are two somewhat related assumptions: first, that democracy is a desirable way of life and order of society; and second, that the American people can mold their economy along democratic lines by one means or another, if they purpose to do so. The former assumption is of course fundamental to this entire study; the latter will be subjected to critical examination.

The role of human choice and purpose in history will doubtless remain forever a subject of dispute and controversy. Persons with and without learning will continue, as in the past, to argue that men are but the pawns of fate; while others of equal erudition or ignorance will contend that they are free architects of their own fortunes. According to the former, democracy in the United States was the inevitable product of a peculiar set of conditions arising out of the discovery of the New World, the settlement of North America by Englishmen, the level of technology of the time, the simplicity of life on the frontier and the farm, the abundance of land and natural resources, and the rationalism of the eighteenth century. With the passing of these conditions democracy may be expected to disappear. By the same token the tendency toward aristocracy of the past three generations is seen to be but a reflection of the reestablishment of a social equilibrium upset by the discovery of new continents, or a necessary feature of complex social organization—in either case, fixed and irreversible. According to the apostles of freedom or voluntarism, on the other hand, American democracy was the deliberate and unfettered creation of the people who settled and developed the land—an expression of their thought, choice, and purpose. The trend toward aristocracy can be halted and reversed if the present inhabitants of the country so desire. They can make of their nation whatsoever they will.

The position assumed throughout this volume is represented in neither of these extremes. Acceptance of the first destroys the human will; assent to the second renders that will capricious and irresponsible. It is contended here that man in history is neither wholly bound nor wholly free, that his life, though always conditioned, is never fated. His past, his cultural heritage, his environing conditions at the same time set the limits within which he must make his choices and provide the materials with which he may build his future. While the historic process does not permit him to make an unconditioned choice, it does not bind him completely. Within the bounds of the possible human preference operates. Today the historic process would seem to have confronted the American people with the opportunity of choosing between democracy and aristocracy. But whether they have the resources, both material and spiritual, with which to build a democratic society in the age of industrialism cannot be foretold in advance. It is the function of scholarship and thought to define the problem, to reveal the resources available, to discover the limits fixed by the social process, and to devise the most promising ways and means of achieving the goal.

Crucial Character of the Economic Issue

Whatever may have been the origins of American democracy, it is in grave peril today. Though the superstructure may appear to be sound, the foundations are far more precarious than the ordinary citizen realizes. Sapping operations have been going on uninterruptedly for such a long period that the collapse of the entire building might possibly occur in the not distant future. But to say that the threat comes from the aristocratic tendency in the economy is not to assume an extreme economic interpretation of history. Although powerful arguments may be advanced to demonstrate the primacy of economic forces in the social process, such demonstration is not necessary to support the present thesis. The simple and obvious fact is that the *current* danger to free institutions can be traced in large part to developments in the economic quarter. As Aristotle observed more than two thousand years ago, "when the rich grow numerous or properties increase, the form of government changes into an oligarchy or a government of families." [1]

Since over a period of time any society tends to manifest a considerable degree of integration and unity, to become organized according to some specific set of values, the emergence of contradictory and irreconcilable forces must result sooner or later in the domination of the one or the other. As the one waxes, the other wanes; as the one advances, the other retreats. In a highly dynamic society like the present this is peculiarly true. The American nation cannot remain indefinitely half democratic and half aristocratic: the one principle or the other will eventually triumph. The logic of the contemporary struggle was outlined with remarkable clarity and consciseness by Daniel Webster in the following passage from his address before the Massachusetts Constitutional Convention in 1820:

The freest government, if it could exist, would not be long acceptable, if the tendency of the laws were to create a rapid accumulation of property in few hands, and to render the great mass of the population dependent and penniless. In such a case the popular power must break in upon the rights of property, or else the influence of property must limit and control the exercise of popular power. Universal suffrage, for example, could not long exist in a community where there was great inequality of property. The holders of estates would be obliged in such case, either in some way to restrain the right of suffrage, or else such right of suffrage would ere long divide the property.[2]

The issue as Webster saw it is now drawn in the United States. During the intervening century the course of events has proceeded according to his formula and brought American democracy to the deepest crisis of its history. The "tendency of the laws" has been "to create a rapid accumulation of property in few hands." While the vast majority of the people cannot be described as penniless, they are dependent —dependent on the holders of property and the uncertainties of a highly unstable economic system for the opportunity of earning their bread. The struggle to change "the laws," the great legal conceptions which support the inherited social structure, is advancing. Will the "holders of estates" restrain the right of suffrage in some fashion and thus render their holdings secure from popular attack? Or will the people, exercising the right of suffrage, "divide the property" (to use Webster's over-simplified phraseology) and usher in a new order under which the "tendency of the laws" will make impossible the "accumulation of property in few hands?" Such is the stern choice which history presents to the citizens of the United States in this generation. In the recent words of their President, they must know that "the liberty of a democracy is not safe if the people tolerate the growth of private power to a point where it becomes stronger than their democratic state itself." [3]

The contemporary human struggle throughout the world is rooted in economics. Everywhere political situations seem to be functions of economic situations. Whether in the sphere of international or in that of domestic relations, men are struggling bitterly for economic advantage. As abroad nations engage in an uninterrupted warfare, at one time through diplomacy and at another through armed forces, for markets, raw materials, concessions, spheres of influence, colonies, and outlets for surplus population; so at home economic classes are in perpetual conflict, now by negotiation and now by strike and lockout, over the distribution of this world's goods. Whereas in an earlier age ordinary men and women demanded the right to vote and freedom from the arbitrary exercise of political power, today they are demanding the right to employment, to leisure, to material security, and to participation in the fruits of technological advance. One of the truly terrifying phenomena of the present age is the apparent readiness with which men and women exchange political rights and privileges won through blood and tears for mere *promises* of economic guarantees. They are demanding what they call social justice, and will not take "no" for an answer. Just prior to the onset of the recent depression Nicholas Murray Butler called attention to this shift of attention from politics to economics:

For a generation and more past the centre of human interest has been moving from the point which it occupied for some four hundred years to a new point which it bids fair to occupy for a time equally long. Put bluntly, the shift in the position of the centre of gravity of human interest has been from politics to economics; from considerations that had to do with forms of government, with the establishment and protection of individual liberty, to considerations that have to do with the production, distribution and consumption of wealth.[4]

Form of a Democratic Economy

The precise form which the American economy should take in order to serve democratic ends most completely and satisfactorily in the emerging age of industrial civilization is a debatable question—a question about which genuine friends of democracy can and do disagree. To what particular port the ship of state should be directed is simply not known. Mankind has never traversed these seas before, and, though the past is not without its lessons, positive and detailed guidance from history cannot be expected. Also no experiment in social and economic reconstruction now under way in the world has proceeded far enough to be more than suggestive or admonitory to the American people. Moreover, the task of steering society on its course through the present tumultuous waters of domestic and international conflict is difficult and hazardous in the extreme. To say the least, the route to even a tolerable future, leaving aside entirely the question of an ideal state, is obscure and beset with great danger. Consequently, of all simple, wholesale, and final prescriptions for the ills of democracy intelligent citizens will be profoundly skeptical.

From this rather gloomy picture of the situation, however, the conclusion need not be drawn that the American people are engaged in a blind quest, that they are utterly without guidance as they face the future. Though they have no pillar of cloud by day and of fire by night to lead them unerringly to the promised land, yet they are not without some positive aids to assist them in finding their way out of the wilderness. Though the detailed specifications for a democratic economy in the age of technology are lacking and though the course to be travelled is shrouded in uncertainty, yet the general direction is known and certain relatively stable points of reference are at hand. The acceptance of the democratic conception of life and society itself provides a guiding principle of decisive worth and most far-reaching implications. In addition, the following five propositions would seem to be sound; first, an individualistic economy lies outside the realm of practical consideration; second, the social control of large aggregations of capital is essential; third, a fairly comprehensive solution of the problem will have to be achieved; fourth, the efficient operation of the economy is a necessary ideal; and fifth, the civil and political rights of the individual must be faithfully safeguarded. Each of these propositions will be elaborated.

Rejection of the Individualistic Economy

The rejection of the individualistic economy as a possible foundation for American democracy in the future is not due to any inherent conflict between the two traditions. In fact, as the merest novice in the history of American institutions knows, the debt which democracy owes to individual ownership of productive property is colossal. In its origins, as demonstrated in an earlier chapter, the former grew out of and was molded by the latter. And yet the close historical connection between them has left an ideological heritage which hampers the conservation and further realization of democratic principles. The great masses of the population today are equipped with ideas and loyalties which, because of a change in the whole structure of American society, stand athwart the road to a better future for themselves and their children. Because of this cultural legacy the representatives and defenders of aristocracy, by identifying democracy with economic individualism and manipulating certain outworn symbols of popular liberties and rights, are able to appear before the people as forthright and exclusive champions of democratic ideas and institutions. Perhaps the most poorly disguised move of this kind in recent years was the organization and campaign of the American Liberty League. The self-styled "Jeffersonian Democrats" and "the grass-root Republicans" are other unadorned examples of the same effort at popular deception.

Economic individualism is rejected as a possible support of democracy because *it has already ceased to exist.* It has been destroyed by the advance of technology, the spread of new agencies of transportation and communication, the nation-wide integration of the economy, the growth of large-scale enterprise, and the invention of new forms of economic organization. "But," some will say, "granted that it is no more, let it be revived." The answer to this proposal is that the technical foundations of economic individualism have been utterly demolished and that the American people could under no circumstances be persuaded to return to the old agrarian order. Practically the entire population has become dependent on the new modes of production which have come with industrialism. Any real attempt to return to the pre-industrial economy would of necessity mean greatly lowered standards of living, general social disorganization, widespread discontent, and probably attempts at violent revolution. And even as a few academicians ponder the desirability of introducing a far more complete form of economic individualism than ever existed under the sun, the actual march of events carries mankind farther and farther along the road to some form of socialized or collectivised economy.

Nobody today really desires a thoroughgoing individualistic economy, least of all those selfstyled "rugged individualists" who rise to power through their influence over government and their use of the new collective forms of economic organization. To go back to the age of the self-contained freehold farmer, to restore the wide distribution of small productive property, is technologically impracticable; to apply the principle of individualism in the present industrial economy would require, paradoxically, the establishment of a collectivism of the most complete and tyrannical type—the enforcement of competition, the abolition of corporations, trade unions, and cooperatives, the outlawing of every form of economic collaboration, the breaking up of all large-scale enterprise, the placing of a policeman on every corner and in every shop or place of business, and the organization of the most effective and pervasive system of espionage that the world has ever known. Economic individualism is simply contrary to the spirit of industrial civilization. Democracy therefore, if it is to survive, will have to seek other foundations. The solution of the problem lies not in the past but in the future. All appeals to the individualistic tradition in economy, however beautifully and eloquently phrased, if the preservation of free institutions is their object, must be classed as pure rhetoric.

The point should also be made that at no time have the American people as a whole practiced anything approaching the pure individualism of classical economic theory. The founding fathers, assembled in convention in Philadelphia in 1787, certainly were not individualists in that sense of the term. If they could be labeled at all, they were essentially mercantilists, devoted to the task of strengthening the power of government and seeking to hold in leash individualistic, sectional, and all divisive forces within the state. The freehold farmer, though ordinarily regarded as the perfect example of the species, was scarcely an individualist, at any

rate not that fiercely competitive enterpriser so dear to the
heart of the current propagandist for the alleged *status quo*.
In fact the term familism might be applied more appropriately to his mode of life. Also the record shows that he associated frequently and cheerfully with his neighbors in the
promotion of various undertakings which taxed the energies
of a single family. Individualism along the frontier and on
the farm, moreover, was always tempered by simple neighbor-
liness and a sense of community responsibility. Even the
business man, whether banker, merchant, or manufacturer,
perhaps the most vocal apologist of individualistic doctrines
in American history, has never been averse to combining
with his fellows or using the power of government if he
thought thereby to secure his own advantage. As a matter
of fact, through such action he has probably been the most
powerful single force in undermining whatever individualism may have characterized American economic life in the
past.

It would seem that the only genuine individualists bred on
the American continent were those daring and adventurous
trappers and hunters who lived lives of relatively complete
independence and isolation in the forests, on the prairies,
and along the streams of the furthest frontier, asking of civilized society only such things as rifle, lead, powder, axe, knife,
salt, and perhaps a little rum or whiskey. But these bold
spirits have long since gone to join their fathers in company
with the beaver, the buffalo, and the passenger pigeon. While
their exploits will doubtless continue to adorn the pages of
romance, the modern practitioners of their arts will lean
very heavily on Sears Roebuck and Montgomery Ward, while
deriving their livelihood from wages won by collective bar-
gaining or coupons clipped from the certificates of ownership
of corporate enterprise.

Social Control of Large Aggregations of Capital

The second guiding proposition is that large aggregations of capital must be subjected to some form of social control. If democracy in the economy cannot be preserved by a return to the ways of the great-grandparents and a wide dispersion of small productive property holdings through the population, then it follows that broadly speaking some form of collective oversight, management, and even ownership of the necessarily large holdings is the only recourse. Otherwise economic power drifts into the hands of a small class, the many become dependent on the few for their livelihood, the dual spirit of arrogance and servility arises, and genuine democracy fades away. As already noted, such has been the tendency of American society for several generations.

"We have never seen a venerated and wealthy hierarchy, an army stronger than the nation, an endowed, titled and privileged order of men, or an incorporated, enriched or united faction," wrote John Taylor, "without having at the same time seen the aristocracy of the first, the second, or the third age."[5] And in concluding his essay he brings his entire argument to focus on the rising aristocracy of modern times with these words: "An opinion that aristocracy can only exist in the form of a hereditary order, or a hierarchy, is equivalent to an opinion, that the science of geometry can only be illustrated by a square or a triangle."[6] It is an axiom of political science that concentrated economic power will either control or be controlled by government.

Precisely what form the social control of economic power and enterprise should take is a question that cannot be answered with assurance and finality. The part of government, the role of cooperative endeavor, the place of labor and professional organizations in a democratic economic order are all matters about which honest differences of opinion are possible and even inevitable. Nor is it at all clear how far the process of socialization should go—what industries and types of enterprise should be embraced. Also the problems arising out of relations between management and ownership, management and technical staff, and management and labor are by no means solved. There is no place in this relatively unexplored world to pit dogma against dogma or authority against authority. Clearly a prolonged period of invention and experimentation is to be expected during which the American people should strive to learn from the experience of other countries as well as their own. But the object of the present work is not to propose solutions to such problems, but rather to indicate the direction in which democratic society must move and to discover the limits within which the work of education may proceed.

This does not mean, however, that experience already gained suggests no immediate steps to be taken or lines of development to be followed. In fact some steps have been taken, and others are clearly on the way. In the case of certain services which are peculiarly identified with the general welfare, such as the mails, highways, education, water supply, and sewage disposal, public agencies long ago assumed large or major responsibility. Provision of medical care and the promotion of scientific research are similar services which are apparently headed in the same direction. It is also clear that the community must intervene in the conservation and development of the basic natural resources of land, water, timber, and minerals which are essential to the perdurance of society and which have been so grievously exploited by private enterprise. Almost equally clear is the mandate for the socialization in one form or another of all those economic functions which tend toward monopoly, such as communications, transportation, power, and banking. Beyond this, society should move as far as is necessary to introduce sufficient general planning and coordination of the total economy, including international commerce, to prevent the visitation of those twin destroyers of free institutions—war and depression. And in order that the power of the aristocracy may be checked, every encouragement should be given to the masses of the people to organize both as consumers and as producers, both in cooperatives and in labor unions, guilds, and granges. Finally, gift and inheritance taxes, becoming progressively heavier through the years and designed deliberately to halt and reverse the trend toward the growth of family wealth, should be levied on all fortunes exceeding the most modest proportions. Through such taxes the aristocratic threat would eventually be destroyed and society would be provided with funds for discharging its collective functions and for experimenting with various forms of social operation and control of economic enterprise.

Comprehensive Solution Necessary

While the precise nature of a desirable solution of the economic problem is not known today, a fairly comprehensive solution is necessary. Certainly if the trend toward aristocracy is to be halted, if the "business cycle" is to be abolished, if the chronic unemployment of millions and insecurity of all are to be prevented, if the productive forces of industrial economy are to be fully released, if a condition of general material plenty is to be established, the foundations of the system that has bred these evils will have to be reconstructed. At some point in the historic process a new economic and political configuration must emerge—a new configuration in which the orientation of the people will be directed away from the individualistic struggle for economic advantage and toward the promotion of the common good. That this would mean the complete abandonment of private enterprise is by no means implied. Doubtless in many fields this tradition could be maintained, but the focus of attention and the center of gravity would be shifted unmistakably to the socialized sector of the economy. How far this tendency should go is a question that should be answered not in terms of social dogma but in the light of experience and specialized knowledge.

The rapidity with which reconstruction should proceed, whether by gradual and relatively imperceptible stages or by sudden and sweeping changes, is a closely related question that is incapable of precise disposition. Although it is impossible to predict how much of suffering and insecurity the American people will endure, it seems not improbable that they would be prepared to follow a dictator if a depression equal to the last in depth and range should return. Because of their long democratic tradition and their exceptional economic reserves, they might conceivably undergo yet another without cracking under the strain, provided it did not follow too closely on the heels of its predecessor. But if depressions continue, if solutions to the urgent problems of food, clothing, and shelter are not achieved, the loyalty of the people of the United States to democratic procedures will sooner or later be shattered. They are not greatly unlike the other peoples of the world. If placed under similar conditions for a period, they may be expected to behave much as Russians, Italians, and Germans.

The point must be stressed that in a certain sense the essence of the matter is time. And time does not wait. The forces of history have precipitated a crisis which already has engulfed democratic tendencies in a large part of the world. The American people are by no means beyond the orbit of these disintegrating factors. Whether they in turn will be overwhelmed would seem to depend on their success in devising temporary measures for the relief of distress, on their capacity to achieve fundamental and far-reaching reforms, and on their ability to study, to learn, and to act, in a word, on their power to educate themselves in the fullest meaning of the term. H. G. Wells observed some years ago that the preservation of civilization is a race between education and catastrophe. If education is broadly considered, and not limited to the work of the school, the truth of his observation is far more apparent today than when he made it. The course of orderly social reconstruction cannot proceed more rapidly than the advancing experience, knowledge, and sentiments of the people. If change of some kind must proceed more rapidly, and in the contemporary interdependent world it may and often does, disaster, temporary or permanent, is the necessary consequence. The avoidance of dictatorship and the preservation of free institutions therefore would seem to depend on the rate at which the American people can and will be educated regarding the necessities and possibilities of their present situation. With the domestic and world order in rapid flux this clearly means that the processes of education, social invention, and orderly change must proceed without delay or interruption.

Ideal of Economic Efficiency

The successful conquest of economic power by the people requires the maintenance and advancement of standards of efficiency. While the major controlling purpose of economic enterprise will shift from profit-making for the few to guarding the more permanent material interests of the many, the ideal of adjusting means to ends through the most effective and least wasteful use of energies and materials will remain one of the great gifts of technology to mankind. If the popular struggle to gain control over the means of livelihood should result in the serious lowering of the productive efficiency of the economy, the entire experiment would end in disaster. Although such efficiency should not be converted into an absolute, only those who have never suffered poverty and physical privation will disparage the worth of material goods. During recent decades, as the enormous power of the new industrial mechanism has become manifest, the American people have caught a vision of a world of comparative security and abundance for all—a vision which is no longer Utopian but a practical possibility. This vision must not be permitted to perish. It cannot be emphasized too often that the present economic system, taken as a whole, is tragically inefficient, being incapable apparently of putting to effective use the great energies of technology.

The achievement of sustained productive efficiency under any conceivable organization of industrial society is fraught with great difficulty. To suppose that the unseating of the economic aristocracy will result automatically in the release of the necessary energies and talents is tantamount to belief in witchcraft. Particularly must the friends of popular freedom eschew any purely doctrinnaire approach to the problem and beware of the proposal to apply the concept of primitive democracy or the town meeting to the management of the economy—the immediate and indiscriminate participation of all workers in the launching and conduct of enterprise. The organization and administration of modern industrial economy is a most complicated and delicate undertaking, requiring the services of persons whose abilities are the product of special talent, systematic training, and years of experience. Men and women are not born into the world with the skills, knowledges, and powers necessary to adjust production to consumption and to coordinate all the resources of labor and technology. If efficiency is to be maintained, competence will have to be recognized, given authority, and charged with commensurate responsibility, the engineer will have to be accorded a status appropriate to his function in the economy. It is clear, moreover, that where so many factors have to be integrated, a high degree of discipline and *esprit de corps* must be achieved. A major educational task here is to prepare the individual to know the limitations of his own competence, to appraise the qualifications of others, to respect the judgment of the expert, and to evaluate the general operation of the economy. While the democratic principle of sharing in decisions should be carried as far as practicable, it should be tempered by a sober recognition of the just prerogatives of knowledge.

If economic efficiency is not to be attained by the dispersion of managerial responsibility through shop committees, it seems equally apparent that the solution of the problem does not lie in the direction of loading responsibility on the political state. The latter, standing outside the economy and deriving its authority from the general body of citizens, must rely upon the police power and on an extraneous system of rewards and punishments in the correction of abuses and the promotion of efficiency. Where it operates the economy directly, arrests and jail sentences, not to mention more severe measures, may be expected at critical times to take the place of business failure and bankruptcy. Here the architects of classical economic theory and the doctrines of *laissez faire* were fundamentally right. They saw clearly that the economy must be allowed to function with as few outside restraints and directives as possible and develop its own checks to waste and inefficiency. They made the mistake, however, of assuming the existence of a *natural* economic order whose laws and postulates were superior to or independent of history. As a matter of fact, the order which they knew and defended, like every other order that ever existed, rested on definite legal conceptions and arrangements established and supported by the political state. No strictly *natural* economic order has been known since man emerged from the brute and began to create cultures and build institutions.

Civil and Political Rights of the Individual

In the unseating of the aristocracy and the reconstruction of the economy the civil and political rights of the individual must be faithfully guarded—freedom to think, to read, to speak, to criticize, to petition, to protest, to organize with one's fellows, to participate in the processes of government, to live a personal life in accordance with one's lights and desires—freedom from unjust arrest, imprisonment, and discrimination—freedom from the capricious rule of state officials. This heritage of the American people, precious beyond the understanding of those who have never lived under dictators, must be recognized as an unassailable principle by all who would change the social order. This heritage is the very heart of the democratic conception of life. To scuttle it in the name of democracy would be to commit the grossest form of sacrilege.

The major virtue of the old agrarian economy was that it tended to guarantee to the ordinary individual a large measure of personal freedom. As already observed, that economy provided the freehold farmer with a solid material foundation for his social and political life. He was lord of his castle, and he had a castle. He could "stand erect on the middle of his farm," wrote John Melish, "and say, 'This ground is mine: from the highest canopy of heaven, down to the lowest depths, I can claim all that I can get possession of within these bounds; fowls of the air, fish of the sea, and all that pass through the same.' And, having a full share of consequence in the political scale, his equal rights are guaranteed to him. None dare encroach upon him; he can sit under his own vine, and under his own fig-tree, and none to make him afraid." [7] While this statement doubtless contains a degree of poetic exaggeration, it rests on substantial foundations.

A major vice of the present capitalistic and industrial economy is that, despite its enormous productive capacity, it fails to provide the masses of the people with the security necessary for a life of personal independence and dignity. They not only feel the rule of an aristocracy and occasionally the overt curtailment of civic and political rights, but they also experience the uncertainties and horrors associated with the grim specters of unemployment, sickness, and old age. Nevertheless, in building their future the American people must be ever watchful lest they exchange a lesser for a greater tyranny, the tyranny of a loosely organized, divided, and limited aristocracy for the tyranny of an all-powerful totalitarian state. The task of steering a course between these two forms of oppression is the central task of democracy.

That the world is entering an age of collectivism is everywhere apparent. Indeed the trend in this direction has been manifest for several generations, marching hand in hand with the rise of industrial society. The explanation of this trend is fairly obvious. The application of an advanced technology to one branch of the economy after another, has destroyed the economic independence of the individual and created a condition of interdependence. The time has now arrived when men must combine to obtain either material security or effective personal freedom. The danger resides in the fact that the former may be achieved at the expense of the latter. This is what has happened in those societies which have taken the road to totalitarianism, and in some cases certainly without actually attaining as yet the goal of material security. Whatever may be the professed objectives, the reality everywhere has been the reduction of the individual to the status of a mere subject of the political authority —a slave who finds the meaning of life in the subordination of his will to the command of party or dictator—a human sacrifice to the warring gods of class struggle and national egoism. If material insecurity and privation are thus exchanged for personal servitude and sychophancy, then will industrial civilization bring to mankind, not the realization of the age-long dream of an abundant life for all, but rather a frightful form of barbarism clothed in modern dress and armed with the weapons of the most advanced technology—a ruthless regimentation of the spirit and degradation of human personality, involving the immolation of the individual on the altar of some "popular despotism." Regardless of the name by which it is called, to the ordinary man or woman despotism remains despotism.

However, that collective forms of economy must inevitably assume such a harsh aspect is by no means self-evident. If this were so, then the future could hold out no hope to those who have been nurtured on the democratic and liberal tradition of the Western world and who continue to cherish the values embodied in these traditions. For the economic arrangements and political institutions associated historically with American democracy and liberalism can no longer perform their wonted functions. That many apologists for the contemporary aristocracy are assiduously propagating the doctrine that collective action in the economy on the part of the people or their representatives necessarily breeds despotism is to be expected. While their arguments must be met, the fact that they are pursuing this course merely demonstrates that the modern battle ground of social ideas and systems has been located. In whose interests are the resources of technology to be employed? This is the basic issue.

Friends of democracy, above all others, must oppose both the totalitarian state and every manifestation of spiritual regimentation, under whatever auspices they may present themselves. At the same time, they cannot endorse the aristocratic trend of the economy, since that trend, if permitted to proceed uninterrupted on its course, would sooner or later bring society to the same goal. It is their responsibility to fashion a collective economy in terms of the democratic ideal—a collective economy that is regarded and employed wholly as an instrument to serve both the material and spiritual interests of individual men and women. The course of history may prove this to be impossible; but in that case democracy will be destroyed only after it has endeavored to save itself. It will go down fighting for its ideals in a world that has lost the power of humane aspiration. For contemporary democracy in America to surrender without a struggle would be to acknowledge itself unworthy of those bold and free spirits who officiated at its birth and have ever been ready at critical times to give their lives that it might live.

The experience of the past two decades, not to mention the experience recorded in the many preceding centuries of human history, suggests that men who love freedom will hesitate to place too much power in the hands of the political state. In its historic form this institution has ever been the symbol of arbitrary authority and coercive might. Even when subject to the will of the people it may be guilty of tyranny. Whatever the source of its power, it will always be administered by men who possess the vices as well as the virtues to which the race is heir. Jefferson, peerless apostle of freedom, who once swore "on the altar of God eternal hostility against every form of tyranny over the mind of man," had good grounds for fearing the concentration of too much power in the hands of government. From the standpoint of the preservation of civic and political liberties therefore the emerging collectivism must avoid in so far as possible the aggrandizement of the state. The readiness with which political authorities enact legislation designed to restrict freedom in education suggests a tendency toward tyranny. All of which would seem to mean that the political state, indispensable as it is, must not be regarded as the sole agency of democratic purposes and that a perpetual alertness for signs of tyranny on the part of government must be encouraged in the electorate. The people should know that they alone are the dependable guardians of their own liberties.

Functional Organization of the Economy

The general tenor of the argument may lead many to the conclusion that all roads to collective forms of economy are closed. If the political state is not to be the administrative agent, it might seem that there is no alternative to the prevailing system. Yet a moment's thought is sufficient to demonstrate that state ownership, control, and operation are by no means the only mode of achieving an appropriate measure of social direction. Indeed, the present economic order, with its corporations, trade associations, banking syndicates, farmers' organizations, labor unions, and consumers' cooperatives is a far cry from the extremely individualistic conceptions of traditional economic theory. The fundamental criticism of these existing arrangements and practices is not that they are dominated by the ideas of Adam Smith, which they are not, but rather that they serve preponderantly the interests of a special class.

While the political state will doubtless always administer certain services directly and while in the period immediately ahead it will be called upon to assume large obligations in the conduct and coordination of economic activities, the best outlook for individual freedom and economic efficiency in the long run would seem to lie in the direction of the recognition of the great divisions of the economy and the placing of the responsibilities of operation on their respective laboring, technical, and managerial personnel. The integration of the economy could presumably be achieved through some kind of parliament, commission, or even economic state composed of representatives from the several branches or divisions. That at some point the political state would have to intervene for the establishment of the necessary legal conceptions and institutional arrangements is clear. But that it would not have to be loaded permanently with the obligations associated with the detailed operation of the economy is equally clear. The civil liberties of the masses of the people can be preserved and developed, not by making the democratic political state responsible for the entire conduct of the economy, but rather by breaking the hold of property ownership and introducing the democratic principle into the economic system.

REFERENCES

1. Benjamin Jowett, *Aristotle's Politics* (Oxford edition, London, 1926), 193.

2. *Journal of Debates and Proceedings in the Convention of Delegates Chosen to Revise the Constitution of Massachusetts* (Boston, 1853), 311-312.

3. *New York Herald Tribune* (April 30, 1938).

4. Nicholas Murray Butler, *Looking Forward* (New York, 1932), 77.

5. John Taylor, *An Inquiry into the Principles and Policy of the Government of the United States* (Fredericksburg, 1814), 73.

6. *Ibid.*, 74.

7. John Melish, *Travels in the United States of America* (Philadelphia, 1812), II, 357-358.

CHAPTER *5:*

BULLETS OR BALLOTS

THE struggle between an economic aristocracy, deeply entrenched and powerful, and a political democracy, numerous and supported by tradition, is on. The most fundamental issue to be decided by the American people is that of the method to be employed in this struggle. Inasmuch as the few do battle with the many and victory is presumably determined by the counting of heads, the ultimate triumph of the popular cause would seem to be assured. Yet, in the world as it is, even the most optimistic friends of democracy, provided they are informed and thoughtful, cannot be certain of the outcome. The aristocracy, by transforming its overwhelming economic power into political power, directly through the purchase of votes and officials and indirectly through the control of the mighty agencies for the molding of opinion, can greatly increase its weight at the polls. The masses of the people, moreover, are confused and divided, ignorant of the nature of the issue, not knowing at all clearly in what direction their true interests lie; and it is obviously a part of the strategy of the privileged orders to keep them so. Moreover, that the ordinary citizen either understands or prizes greatly the virtues and institutions of democracy is by no means certain. Already he has been molded far more than he realizes by the propaganda of the aristocracy and the life of subordination and regimentation demanded by the economic order.

The central concern of this chapter, however, is not with the probable strength of the people at the polls, but with a more fundamental consideration. It cannot be assumed without analysis and discussion that the democratic method of deciding the deep issues at stake will prevail. The conflicts of interest and purpose to be resolved may prove to be so bitter and irreconcilable that men will refuse to accept the verdict of the ballot box and turn to the machine gun. In such an event economic power would again increase many times the crude numerical strength of the aristocracy and give it great advantage in the contest. In both politics and war the party with the longer purse is rarely worsted. Thus in the present age the democratic process itself, as well as the democratic order of society, is in danger. The American people should understand this situation thoroughly, realize that the grim choice of bullets or ballots may be forced upon them at any time, know the sequence of events which is likely to lead to organized violence, and be fully aware of the price that civil strife invariably exacts. That in their calmer moments and under conditions of maximum enlightenment they would choose the way of the ballot box is practically certain; but there come times in any society when men go mad and lapse into savagery.

Possibilities of the Democratic Process

Of what the democratic process is capable under a given set of circumstances, no one can speak with certainty. In a society of free and equal men, that is, in a society where men have an independent means of livelihood and are consequently masters of their own souls, it could probably sustain whatever weight might be placed upon it. But this is due to the fact that in such a society those fundamental issues over which men fight are not raised. "With property divided, as we have it," said Daniel Webster in 1820, "no other government than that of a republic could be maintained, even were we foolish enough to desire it." [1] The situation in America, if the analysis of the preceding chapters contains any merit, falls far short of the ideal conditions for the functioning of the democratic process. The question here is whether it can be employed successfuly in setting men free or in destroying the power of an actual aristocracy.

To such questions no categorical answers can be given. The portrait of no society, whether the most oppressive or the most just, can be painted truly in blacks and whites. Certainly America does not lend itself to any such simple representation. Men are never wholly enslaved nor wholly free. Neither does aristocracy always wear the same countenance, possess the same strength, employ the same methods, or worship the same gods. Joints may be found and probed in the finest of armor; even the mighty Achilles carried a vulnerable heel. The democratic process itself has its virtues and vices, is a creature of time and circumstance, and varies from age to age and from society to society. Weak today, it may be strong tomorrow, responding to those waves of passion and sanity that sweep over the vast industrial populations composing the nations of the contemporary world. The customs, the traditions, the loyalties, the enthusiasms, the aversions, the prejudices, the intelligence, the general cultural level of a people are all of prime significance.

The invention and spread of a new instrument of propaganda and enlightenment such as the radio may shift the balance of power in the struggle to command popular loyalties. The emergence of genius in the ranks of democratic leadership at a time of crisis may prove decisive in the effort to make free institutions operate effectively, even as the rise of a gifted demagogue or plutagogue may turn the scales in the other direction. The factors of geography, the productivity of the economy, and the fortunes of the international struggle, under certain conditions, may affect most profoundly the course of American democracy. Also the outbreak of revolutions and the appearance of new social patterns and philosophies in foreign countries may either encourage or discourage the abandonment of the democratic process in the United States. Possibly a full realization of the uncertainties and hazards in the situation, on the part of the masses of the people, might turn the tide in favor of the ballot. Doubtless the period of time to elapse before the fateful decision must be made, during which the processes of education can be carried on, is of the very essence of the problem.

Argument for Bullets

Against the probability that the democratic process can be used effectively in democratizing the economy distinguished names and powerful arguments can be marshaled. The founding fathers generally seemed to doubt that it could be done, assuming almost without debate that the perpetuation of free political institutions would depend on continued wide distribution of productive property. Gouverneur Morris, contending in the Constitutional Convention that some property qualification should be attached to the right of suffrage, maintained that if votes are given to "people who have no property," they "will sell them to the rich, who will be able to buy them." [2] Madison agreed and, foreseeing the eventual rise of vast propertyless elements in the population, argued that in all probability "they will become the tools of opulence & ambition." [3] Jefferson saw free institutions undermined and destroyed by the "mobs of great cities." Webster assumed in a statement quoted in an earlier chapter that, if property were ever concentrated in few hands, the "holders of estates," in order to forestall an effective attack on property, might in some way "restrain the right of suffrage." That the restraint would be exercised through the ballot, while possible, is not likely. Webster went on to declare that "it was the popular magistrates . . . that laid the neck of Rome at the foot of her conqueror." It should of course be borne in mind that the urban populations of pre-industrial times, with which these men were acquainted, were unlike those of today. Consequently, to what extent their arguments are applicable to the present situation is open to some question. From the standpoint of the future of popular rule in the United States, however, these views of the architects of the Republic are disconcerting.

Equally disconcerting are various inquiries into the origin and development of American democracy. Dr. Jameson in his study of the period of the revolution, to which reference has already been made, after pointing out that as historical fact economic antedated political democracy, proceeds to say, at least implicitly, that this is the necessary sequence. Stating that "we do not look to see effects precede causes," he definitely implies that in the historic relationship economic forces were primary. That the new aristocracy of property which has appeared during the past several generations will encompass the destruction of democratic political institutions and extend their sway over the organs of government would seem to be a just inference. It appears that the "flag follows the dollar" in domestic no less than in foreign policy. At any rate Jameson's analysis holds out relatively little promise to those who would employ the ballot in the reconstruction of the economy.

Lord Balfour, English conservative statesman and philosopher, who could scarcely be charged with advocating violent revolution, was of the opinion that the institutions of political democracy in Anglo-Saxon countries had not yet proved themselves. He certainly believed that the English people at any rate had never fully demonstrated their ability to achieve the more profound changes in social structure by means of the ballot. To be sure, since the establishment of the parliamentary system, they had not been called upon to pass through a truly revolutionary epoch. But Balfour's doubts were more than the refusal of a careful and cautious mind to judge the success of an experiment before it had been completed. They arose out of a deep insight into the nature of social forces and the springs of British politics. Not long before his death, in a critical and penetrating introduction to a new edition of Walter Bagehot's *The English Constitution,* he gave clear expression to his misgivings. To emphasize the delicate balance necessary for the successful functioning of British political machinery he asked what would happen if the chasm dividing the two great political parties should "be so profound that a change of Administration would in fact be a revolution disguised under a constitutional procedure." Here is his answer:

It may perhaps be replied that if a majority of the House of Commons want a revolution they ought to have one; and no doubt if the House of Commons on this point fully represented the settled convictions of the community the reply suffices. But if not? Is there any means of ensuring that in these extreme cases the House of Commons *would* represent the settled will of the community? Is there any ground for expecting that our Cabinet system, admirably fitted to adjust political action to the ordinary oscillations of public opinion, could deal with these violent situations? Could it long survive the shocks of revolutionary and counter-revolutionary violence? I know not. The experiment has never been tried. Our alternating Cabinets, though belonging to different Parties, have never differed about the foundations of society. And it is evident that our whole political machinery pre-supposes a people so fundamentally at one that they can safely afford to bicker; and so sure of their own moderation that they are not dangerously disturbed by the never-ending din of political conflict. May it always be so.[4]

The most powerful and uncompromising challenge to those who would employ the institutions of political democracy to transform the economic foundations of society has come from the revolutionary socialists. Marx and Engels, and their disciples, employing the hard realism of a materialistic philosophy, deriving their insights and conclusions primarily from a monumental study of the history of Eu-

rope, perceiving the merciless exploitation of peoples by
nineteenth century capitalism, and rejecting as illusory all
sentimental appeals to members of privileged orders, have
contended that until all productive property is socialized
and a classless society is established the succession of social
systems will always be attended by revolutionary violence.
"The history of all hitherto existing society," they proclaimed to the workingmen of all countries in 1848, "is the
history of class struggles. Freeman and slave, patrician and
plebeian, lord and serf, guildmaster and journeyman, in a
word, oppressor and oppressed, stood in constant opposition
to one another, carried on an uninterrupted, now hidden,
now open fight, a fight that each time ended, either in a
revolutionary reconstitution of society at large, or in the
common ruin of the contending classes." [5]

In each social system, according to the argument, whether
slave, feudal, or capitalistic, and regardless of political forms,
the class owning and controlling the tools of production
holds the reins of actual power. Openly or covertly, directly
or indirectly, this master class rules the state; or more accurately, it is the state. In a capitalistic society, said Marx,
government is but "a committee for the administration of
the consolidated affairs of the bourgeois class as a whole."
This class names monarchs and elects presidents, forms parliaments and cabinets, appoints judges and justices, controls
the police and all armed forces, molds the family according
to the desired pattern, and dominates the entire cultural
apparatus of school, church, university, press, and theater.
The general exercise of civil liberties is permitted, if at all,
only in that interval after the new class, having thoroughly
routed its enemies, has consolidated its rule and before a
rival class, sufficiently strong to attempt the seizure of power,
has appeared. To expect an aristocracy to surrender its
essential privileges at the ballot box, to expect political democracy to be the instrument of social regeneration, is to

expect miracles. Whatever may be the professions of the master class during periods of domestic peace and harmony, it will never submit to the loss of those prerogatives which are the source of its being and power until it has had recourse to that final arbiter of all human disputes—the sword. Such, in the view of these prophets of revolution, is the verdict of history.

The soundness of this body of doctrine is no longer an academic question. It possesses a following in the world today that can be rivaled only by the great religions. Having served to inspire and guide the course of the most profound and comprehensive revolution in history, it constitutes the official philosophy of the largest and potentially most powerful country in the world. It is espoused by organized parties operating within or outside the law in some fifty-eight nations, all bound together in a powerful international federation, and enrolling millions of devout members who believe firmly it is certain to conquer the earth. To an extraordinary degree it has influenced and permeated the thought of mankind, from the dock hand in Shanghai, Seattle, or Hamburg to the scholar at Harvard, Oxford, or Paris. And to many thoughtful people the course of events in Europe from the Russian revolution to the rebellion in Spain practically demonstrates the essential truth of the Marxian interpretation of history, analysis of social forces, outline of revolutionary method, and forecast of the future. While as yet none of the older political democracies has turned to violence and dictatorship, either to defend the old or establish a new order, it is also true that none has witnessed fundamental changes in its class structure.

The foregoing arguments for bullets, or at least for the inevitability of bullets, are formidable. This must be admitted at once, and more particularly by all who may hope and work for the success of the ballot in effecting fundamental social change. Certainly the employment of the institutions of political democracy in reconstructing the economic foundations of American society will be no child's play. The history of the United States gives grounds for grave anxiety over the outcome. When the democratic process was subjected to its only really severe test in the middle of the last century, it broke down completely and the nation was plunged into one of the bitterest and bloodiest civil struggles of history. Also it has been suspended in large measure during every major war in which the nation has engaged; and in times of domestic crisis it has often been subject to more or less severe limitation. Certain underprivileged racial and economic groups, notably Negroes and immigrant laborers, have been practically denied membership in the democratic community. Finally, it may be argued, if American democracy was not able to save itself two generations ago, before the advance of industrialism had undermined its original agrarian foundations, while the new economic aristocracy was yet in comparative infancy, and when the democratic spirit of the people was still militant and self-confident, there can be little hope for a successful issue of the struggle today. The logical grounds for expecting civil strife or the eventual peaceful obliteration of all remaining supports of American democracy are many and powerful.

Argument for Ballots

The arguments for ballots are far less tangible and demonstrable than those for bullets, resting largely on an appeal to the future instead of the past. It must be admitted that throughout history armed might has been the common mode of altering the relations of classes, as well as changing the territorial boundaries of peoples and nations. And yet political democracy has had its successes, not the least of which has been its establishment as one of the great and living traditions of western culture. With shifting fortunes it has maintained itself in the United States for almost a century and a half and worked itself into the fabric of American life and character. The victories under Jefferson and Jackson were of the first rank—magnificent victories of the people which in other times and places could only have been bought with blood and iron. While, as already noted, the Civil War registered a tragic failure of free institutions, this struggle has been more aptly called a war between states that had never fully acquiesced in the surrender of sovereignty to a federal authority.

Generation after generation of men and women have been taught from the cradle that the American way of social change and settlement of differences, even the most profound, is the way of peaceful discussion and the ballot. Jefferson's declaration that "the suffrage of the people" is "the rational and peaceable instrument of reform" is a deep-seated conviction of the masses of the people. This doctrine was given explicit expression in the third or 1807 edition of the first history of the United States ever written for the schools. "And it is the glory of our republican government," concludes this textbook in reporting the election of 1800, "that the people have the supreme controul; and that when they apprehend their rulers err, they can effect a change of measures at the periods of election, without tumult, or the hazard of revolution." [6] Thus, George H. Mead, distinguished social psychologist and philosopher, was merely putting an old popular belief into the words of the scholar when he stated that the moral superiority of democracy over other systems of society is "its institutionalization of revolution." [7] Whether the American political system will prove capable of bearing the strain suggested in this statement, will only be known after it has been put to the test. But such has been the conception of the democratic process held by the people of the United States.

The fact of the matter is that America is neither Europe

nor Asia. It possesses a unique history that may be extremely
significant for the future of the democratic method. The
Marxian theory was founded primarily on the experience of
the Old World. That the course of events would follow the
same pattern in all countries Marx himself did not believe.
Speaking before the Amsterdam branch of the First International in September, 1872, after declaring that the worker
"must conquer political supremacy" and "must overthrow
the old political system," he said: "Of course I must not be
supposed to imply that the means to this end will be everywhere the same. We know that special regard must be paid
to the institutions, customs, and traditions of various lands;
and we do not deny that there are certain countries, such as
the United States and England, in which the workers may
hope to secure their ends by peaceful means. If I mistake
not, Holland belongs to the same category." [8] Marx may be
proved wrong in this instance, as he has been proved wrong
in others; but it would be tragic if those who have been
nurtured in the democratic tradition for generations should
exhibit less faith in the efficacy of that tradition than the
reputedly grim and inflexible founder of revolutionary
socialism. American democracy possesses resources for surviving the general world crisis that cannot be found in any
other country. It may also be burdened with certain special
difficulties and weaknesses. The purpose at this point in the
argument, however, is not to review the assets and liabilities
in the situation, a task to be undertaken in later chapters,
but rather to challenge the view that the institutions of
political democracy are uniformly moribund and useless
throughout the world. They may actually be found to be as
helpless to stem the tide of dictatorship in the United States
as they were in Italy and Germany, but the case remains to
be argued in the arena of social forces. There is certainly no
sufficient justification for the spread of a spirit of defeatism
through the ranks of American democracy today. On the

contrary, the situation calls for a girding of the loins for battle in defense of free institutions.

And what do those have to offer who would abandon democratic procedure? The answer is written in indelible letters on the pages of European history and on the map of the contemporary world—civil war and dictatorship—rivers of blood, desolation, military justice, secret police, arbitrary arrests, persecutions, individual and mass terror, intellectual slavery, and the creation of a heritage of hatred and bitterness to corrupt the relations of men for generations. The answer is also written on the pages of American history of the eighteen-sixties. James B. Ireland, the Kentucky farmer who was born in 1797 and lived through the nineteenth century, relates with simplicity, honesty, and power the meaning of civil strife to ordinary men and women: "All was peace, good will, and prosperity; and then alas! came the war—the cruel bloody war, the third war of my recollection, and the worst of all—fratricidal war, in which brother was against brother, son opposed father, neighbor was suspicious and fearful of neighbor, and the best of friends became deadly enemies; people were afraid to talk, afraid to give an opinion or express a sentiment. Men were afraid to stay at home and afraid to leave home, and no one felt safe or secure in his rights or liberties. For four long years there was anxiety, trouble, and sorrow, and the war ended."[9] Such an alternative to the democratic process, made yet more terrifying and debasing by modern engines of death and torture, violates the spirit and essence of civilized life.

To what end, moreover, violent revolution may lead is utterly unpredictable. It can no more be controlled than an earthquake or a tornado; it may destroy its own parents and trample upon its own children; it may be betrayed by its own leaders. Napoleon betrayed the French revolution; Mussolini betrayed Italian socialism; Hitler betrayed the German working man; and who has betrayed whom in Russia remains to be determined. Although the sword has been employed with success by vast popular majorities in overthrowing dictatorship, it has not yet proved itself to possess the slightest merit as a substitute for the operation of free institutions. Even where it is successful, its path is generally strewn with disillusionment and shattered idols, the road back to peace and reason is beset with difficulties, and the positive tasks of social invention and reconstruction always remain.

The masses of the American people should know that their political liberties, imperfect though they may be, are precious beyond price and that, if they once surrender this heritage, they may lose it for ever. In the critical years ahead the citizens of the United States may forsake all sanity and draw the sword of class strife; but let no friend of democracy either advocate or welcome this course. If revolutionary violence should come, regardless of the banners it carried, it might well write the final chapter to the American experiment in government and social relations launched in 1776. It is the uncompromising position of the present volume therefore that the method of peaceful change must be neither scorned nor abandoned, that it offers the only reasonable hope for a tolerable future. Instead of flirting with the machine gun and extolling the virtues of bloodshed, those who really believe in advancing the cause of popular liberty should be devoting their energies to the marshalling of the available cultural resources and the formulation of a program designed to make the institutions and procedures of political democracy function effectively in the popular conquest of economic power. The fate of American democracy is largely in the hands of its friends.

REFERENCES

1. *Journal of Debates and Proceedings in the Convention of Delegates Chosen to Revise the Constitution of Massachusetts* (Boston, 1853), 311-312.

2. Max Farrand, *The Records of the Federal Convention of 1787* (New Haven, 1911), II, 202.

3. *Ibid.*, 204.

4. Earl of Balfour, "Introduction" to Walter Bagehot, *The English Constitution* (The World's Classics edition, Oxford, 1928), xxiii-xxiv.

5. Karl Marx and Friedrich Engels, *Manifesto of the Communist Party* (Edited and Annotated by Friedrich Engels) (New York), 9.

6. John McCulloch, *A Concise History of the United States from the Discovery of America, till 1807* (Third edition, Philadelphia, 1807), 205-206.

7. Charles W. Morris, *Pragmatism and the Crisis of Democracy* (Public Policy Pamphlet No. 12, Chicago, 1934), 20.

8. G. M. Stekloff, *History of the First International* (London and New York, 1928), 240-1.

9. *Looking Backward Through 100 Years.* See page 42.

CHAPTER 6:

SOME LESSONS FROM THE PAST

As the American people wage the battles of democracy in the twentieth century, they would do well to look into their own past for any lessons which history may have to teach. Of particular urgency is an examination of the methods employed by privileged orders from age to age to thwart the advance of popular rule. While nearly every period is worth studying, one of the most fruitful for present purposes is that around 1800 which saw the dethronement of the dogma of aristocracy in politics and, in the words of Jefferson, witnessed "as real a revolution in the principles of our government as that of 1776 was in its form."[1]

This period is peculiarly worthy of examination because it was so like the present in certain respects. Then, as observed in an earlier chapter, a rough economic democracy, composed for the most part of freehold farmers, fought for political rights; today a rough political democracy, the achievement of a century of struggle, is fighting for economic rights. Then the fight was one of extreme severity and bitterness, as that of today promises to be. Even in the international field the resemblance between the two periods is striking. Then the French Revolution awakened the masses of mankind throughout the world, even as today the Russian Revolution sends its reverberations from continent to continent and nation to nation. Moreover, then as today, the aristocracy was badly frightened and prophesied the end of civilization, if the advance of the populace could not be halted. It will be interesting and instructive to observe the methods employed in the effort of the aristocracy to beat back the march of the people. This effort assumed two forms: first, a powerful campaign of propaganda was directed against the ideas and leadership of political democracy; and second, overt steps and measures were taken to hamstring the democratic process and frustrate the verdict of the polls. Thirteen years after the Constitutional Convention the nation narrowly escaped shipwreck on the rocks of party conflict and counter-revolution.

The Campaign of Propaganda

The present has been called the age of propaganda, and not without reason. The invention of powerful instruments of communication, such as the locomotive and automobile, the rotary press and moving picture, the telegraph, telephone, and radio, has enormously increased the range and authority of propagandist operations. Yet the pattern of the effort on the part of the privileged order to mold the thought of the public according to its own desires shows surprisingly little novelty and remains amazingly uniform from generation to generation. Every popular movement, from the formation of the democratic societies in the seventeen-nineties to the rise of the Committee for Industrial Organization today, has been damned as subversive and un-American; every legislative enactment designed to protect or advance the interests of the people, from the establishment of free schools to the adoption of the income tax amendment or the passage of the Wagner Act, has been denounced as dangerous to government and society; every leader of American democracy, from Thomas Jefferson to Franklin D. Roosevelt, has been charged with treasonable intent and mental instability. A few examples from the period of the Republic's infancy will serve to illustrate these generalizations.

In the early struggle for political democracy a favorite method of attack was to proclaim as an axiom the utter incompetence of the people to govern themselves, to point to certain alleged historical occurrences to support the axiom, and then to predict certain and dire ruin as a consequence of the equal enfranchisement of all classes of men. It is well known that Alexander Hamilton, the leader of the aristocracy and an avowed admirer of the English monarchical system, had no faith in the people. "The people is a great beast!" he exclaimed in the heat of passion. "All communities," he observed in a more sober moment, "divide themselves into the few and the many. The first are the rich and the well born, the other the mass of the people. The voice of the people has been said to be the voice of God; and however generally this maxim has been quoted and believed, it is not true in fact. The people are turbulent and changing; they seldom judge or determine right. Give therefore to the first class a distinct, permanent share in the government." [2] In these short sentences may be found the essence of the political doctrine of the great Federalist leader. Since the experience and learning of farmers and mechanics were commonly insufficient to sustain a contrary argument and since the weight of authority, supported by habits of submission deeply ingrained by custom, was on the side of privilege, such assertions must have seemed reasonable and wise to many ordinary men serving in the ranks of the democracy. The fact that the defenders of the *status quo* generally believed their propaganda made it the more effective.

One of the most complete and devastating denunciations of government by the people as inherently dangerous to law and order and subversive of the general welfare may be found in a Fourth of July oration given in 1805 by Isaac C. Bates, distinguished son of Massachusetts and graduate of Yale College, who served in both houses of the federal congress, fought Jeffersonian and Jacksonian democracy, and remained a staunch defender of Federalist and Whig doctrine to his death in 1845. In this oration which was delivered before the Federalists of Northampton and vicinity and which was thought so "elegant and spirited" by the Committee on Arrangements as to merit publication, he spoke thus concerning popular rule:

On subjects so complicated, as *general policy*, the least informed are the most liable to err. Hence it is the highest absurdity, for rulers to be governed, by the ever veering weathercock of popular opinion. It may shew the direction of the wind, but it will never point the mariner to the pole. Yet the contrary is a doctrine, which flatters our vanity, and we will believe it, though the paths thereof lead down to ruin. Vox populi vox Dei, is an apothegm, that has gone, hand in hand, with destruction; has made more mothers, widows, and children orphans, within a century, than the armies of oppression; has committed crimes one day, for which it has covered the face in sackcloth the next; has veiled the earth in darkness, and crucified the Son of God. Yet this is the wandering star, which rules, and guides the destinies of our nation.[3]

In combatting the struggle for political democracy the spokesmen of the conservative classes then employed the French Revolution, much as the Russian Revolution is used today, to excite emotion, obscure issues, and balk the popular effort to reconstruct the social order. In bitter and sweeping phrase the entire Jeffersonian movement was damned as an importation from France and was loaded with all the excesses of the mobs of Paris and the conquests of Napoleon. Near the close of his oration Bates points to the desolation of Europe as the certain consequence of "this leveling system" of popular rule:

The prospects, which the leading Democrats hold up, possess a charm which the magic of Umbro can hardly dissipate. But, God forbid, that they should charm us into maniacs; or, allure us into slavery by the lustre of their manacles. Beware of the Golden chain! It has the strength of iron. France seized the glittering pendant. "It bit like a serpent and stung like an adder." Gabriel himself could not have convinced that nation but that she was in the full pursuit of liberty and glory. Yet after she had committed crimes, at which those of Gomorrah brighten into day; after she had rolled her mad and sanguinary waves over Europe, and in successive undulations swept away every republic on the continent; the illusion vanished; and she settled down into a despotism more absolute, and more profound than the dominion of the grave. This leveling system as certainly leads to tyranny as sin to perdition.[4]

In conclusion this Federalist orator makes one of those "grass-will-grow-in-the-streets" prophecies which are so much in vogue today. Indeed, in words that almost bring tears to the eyes now he proclaimed the death of liberty and of all the values and institutions which the American people had cherished. After lamenting in man that "strange fatality" which nurtures a blind optimism and after asserting that "the testimony of all history without a single exception or contradiction" proves that the road on which the party of Jefferson had launched the nation would lead inevitably to anarchy and tyranny, he transported himself into the distant future and delivered a funeral oration over the ancient remains of the Republic:

But the judgment will come; and if we refuse to listen to the warning voice that whispers from the ruins of our predecessors, the period is on the wing, rapid as the flight of time, and certain as the shaft of fate, when it will be forever too late; when our liberty will be gone and with it all that can cheer, can animate, or console. Some future traveller may sit, like the son of Hilkiah on the ruins, and apostrophise the desolation that surrounds him. Here once was the seat of a great empire. Under the smiles of Heaven and of freedom she was virtuous and happy. But parties arose, freedom fled and now she is left desolate. "How doth the city mourn that was full of people. All her friends have dealt treacherously with her." The sound of the lute is no more heard in her cottage; innocence no more sports upon her mountains; but the streams murmur to the silence of the forest; and the blasts of the evening sigh through the wide and melancholy waste.[5]

Clearly this gentleman was an artist of no mean powers. One finishes these lines even now with a sinking sensation in the region of the abdomen and the conviction that Bates was right, even though the historical record of one hundred and thirty years would seem to demonstrate the contrary. Who among his successors in public life today can stand beside him? Certainly not Walter Lippmann or Alfred E. Smith, nor the distinguished lawyers of the American Liberty League. Even among the presidents of America's greatest universities not one comes to mind who could reach the eminence of this staunch New England Federalist in the art of halting thought and playing upon the loyalties of his audience. The best of contemporary apologists for aristocracy occasionally break over into lucid and meaningful discourse. How have the mighty fallen! But lest some reader, under the spell of this literary magician of the early nineteenth century, may wish to return to the rule of the "rich and well born" before it is too late, his views on the Louisiana Purchase will be quoted:

On the purchase of Louisiana, *two* facts are *obvious; the one, that we had lands before, of an excellent quality, more than we can ever cultivate;* the other, *that a nation compact is more powerful and happy, than when thinly scattered over half the globe.* Louisiana therefore, can be of very little importance, except to secure a passage through the Mississippi. But that passage it never can secure, while Spain, or any other nation holds the Floridas. . . .
REPUBLICS are never remarkable for energy.—When therefore, their territory becomes immense, they are like a *gigantic body,* with a *little spirit*; an huge hydropsie, with limbs soft, bloated, all bursting out with tumefaction, in whom the blood scarcely circulates from one extremity to the other, too unwieldy to be moved, without vigour, without activity, without use. Yet, my countrymen, for this state of things, we give 900,000 dollars per annum.[6]

Another powerful device employed through the centuries to discredit new ideas and movements has been to attach to them the label of atheism or infidelity. This device was employed generally during the period under review, as it is employed today, to bring the extension of democratic principles and leaders into disrepute. During the heat of the presidential campaign in 1800 it was predicted that, if Jefferson were elected, "all the meeting-houses and bibles in the country would be burnt." In September of that year the Reverend John Mitchell Mason, a New York clergyman and friend of Alexander Hamilton, published a pamphlet entitled "The Voice of Warning to Christians, on the Ensuing Election of a President of the United States." The dedicatory announcement runs as follows: "To Christians, who prize a good conscience, a consistent character, and the honour of their Redeemer, above all personal and political attachments; the following pamphlet is dedicated: with the single request, that, laying aside passion, they will give it such a calm, serious, and considerate perusal, as they owe to an argument relative to the best interests of themselves, their families, their country, and the Church of God."[7] The Reverend Mason, disregarding all contrary evidence, assembles fact and rumor concerning Jefferson's religious beliefs with this result: "CHRISTIANS! Lay these things together: compare them; examine them separately, and collectively: ponder; pause; lay your hands upon your hearts; lift up your hearts to heaven, and pronounce on Mr. Jefferson's Christianity. You cannot stifle your emotions; nor forbear uttering your indignant sentance—INFIDEL! !"[8]

In his conclusion, apparently aware of the growing power of democratic sentiment and fearing that his appeal might be unsuccessful in turning back the tide of "infidelity," this gentleman of the cloth made his own peace with his Creator and called on God to intervene in the election:

If you are resolved to persevere in elevating an infidel to the chair of your President, I pray God not to "choose your delusions"—but cannot dissemble that "my flesh trembleth for fear of his judgments." It is my consolation that my feeble voice has been lifted up for his name. I have addressed you as one who believes, and I beseech you to act as those who believe, "That we must *all* appear before the judgment seat of Christ." Whatever be the result, you shall not plead that you were not warned. If, notwithstanding, you call to govern you an enemy to my Lord and your Lord; in the face of earth and heaven, and in the audience of your own consciences, I record my protest, and wash my hands of your guilt.

ARISE, O LORD, AND LET NOT MAN PREVAIL![9]

One passage in the pamphlet is remarkable for its frank advocacy of one of the oldest methods of social control—the paying of lip-service to doctrines which are not believed but which are thought to be "good for the masses." In answer to the argument, apparently advanced at the time, that no likely candidate for the presidency was a "true believer," that Jefferson was as much a Christian as any of his rivals, and therefore that the citizen with religious scruples could with conscience free vote for the author of the Declaration of Independence, Mr. Mason came out flatly for hypocrisy:

But there is no prospect, you say, of obtaining a real Christian, and we had *better choose an infidel than a hypocrite.* By no means. Supposing that a man professes Christianity, and evinces in his general deportment a regard for its doctrines, its worship, and its laws; though he be rotten at heart, he is infinitely preferable to a known infidel. His hypocrisy is before God. It may ruin his own soul; but, while it is without detection, can do no hurt to men. We have a hold of him which it is impossible to get of an infidel. His reputation, his habits, his interests, depending upon the belief of his Christianity, are sureties for his behaviour to which we vainly look for a counterbalance in an infidel; and they are, next to religion itself, the strongest sureties of man to man. His very hypocrisy is an homage to the gospel. The whole weight of his example is on the side of Christianity, while that of an open infidel lies wholly against it. It is well known that the attendance of your Washington, and of President Adams upon public worship, gave the ordinances of the gospel a respectability in the eyes of many which otherwise they would not have had: brought a train of thoughtless people within the reach of the means of salvation: and thus strengthened the opposition of Christians to the progress of infidelity. You can never forget the honorable testimony which Mr. Adams bore, in one of his proclamations, to a number of the most precious truths of Revelation; nor how he was abused and ridiculed for it, by not a few of those very persons who now strive to persuade you that Mr. Jefferson is a Christian. In short, your President, if an open infidel, will be a center of contagion to the whole continent: If a professed Christian, he will honor the institutions of God; and though his hypocrisy, should he prove a hypocrite, may be a fire to consume his own vitals, it cannot become a wide-spreading conflagration.[10]

In this verbal attack on the democracy of the time the prize should doubtless go to a citizen of the rock-ribbed state of Connecticut, home at that time of political and clerical fundamentalism—Theodore Dwight, a member of the so-called "ruling family" of the state and brother of Timothy Dwight, famous president of Yale College—a pillar of the Church, a lawyer of repute, a citizen of highest probity, a man of talent and learning and of unquestioned respectability—in a word, a gentleman and a scholar who assumed with solemnity the responsibilities traditionally associated with his station in society. And perhaps among his utterances the premium should be awarded an oration delivered at New Haven on July 7, 1801, before the Society of the Cincinnati, an organization open to officers of the Revolutionary armies and designed to form the beginnings of an hereditary social caste. An earlier oration, however, "spoken at" Hartford on July 4, 1798, merits examination.

The Hartford oration was devoted entirely to tarring democratic ideas and leaders with the brush of the French Revolution. At the outset Mr. Dwight advances the proposition "THAT THE UNITED STATES ARE IN DANGER OF BEING ROBBED OF THEIR INDEPENDENCE, BY THE FRAUD AND VIOLENCE OF THE FRENCH REPUBLIC." [11] The instruments of this conspiracy in America were the person and party of Jefferson. The latter, while on his mission to Paris, having "imbibed no small portion of the unfettered notions of the French respecting philosophy, government, and religion," was "solicitous that his country should follow France, in her tremendous career" and plunge "again into the Revolutionary furnace." Being compelled, because of "the sober habits of Americans," to employ the method of indirection, Jefferson sought to achieve his treasonable purposes by steadily pursuing as Secretary of State a course of friendship toward the French Republic. His writings, and particularly his famous letter to Mazzei, are examined for the purpose of demonstrating that he had indeed imbibed the worst of the Jacobinical doctrines. Finally, in order that his hearers might harbor no misunderstandings regarding the nature of the goal toward which Jefferson would lead the country, Dwight painted a picture of the course of the French Revolution which remains to this day a classic of its kind:

In surveying the events which have happened in France, since the establishment of Republicanism, the mind recoils from scenes, sickening to the heart of man. There we find simple murder set so low in the scale of crimes, as almost to become a virtue. The ingenuity of a people, celebrated beyond all others, for its quickness, and versatility, has been exhausted in discovering new species of wickedness, more heinous than those heretofore known, and in adding aggravations to those which had already been practised. The common modes of destroying lives, among a people, which seemed bent on becoming a nation of murderers, soon became dull, and unpleasant; they therefore substituted the Guillotine, as a more expeditious, and to their hearts, a more enlivening engine of death. But, as the fashion became more general, this also was found too slow in its operations, for the zeal of Jacobinism; and new methods were invented, more cruel to the victims, and, of course, more exhilarating to their executioners. By the invention of "republican marriages," and "republican baptisms," hundreds, and thousands, of innocent men, women, and children, have been chained together, and plunged into a watery grave. Instances, too disgusting to hear, too horrid to relate, without number, have happened, in which fathers and their sons, mothers and their infants, husbands and wives, brothers and sisters, have been blown from the mouths of cannon, torn to pieces in the streets, or sacrificed to the infernal fury of cannibal fishwomen. Victims, whose hearts sunk at the prospect of the apparatus of death, have been forced to kiss the bleeding heads of their fellow victims, as a preparative to the awful change. Delegates from the National Convention, charged with the work of general extermination, lest they should lose some part of their bloody pleasure, have ordered the bodies of those butchered by their direction, to be brought, and piled in heaps before their doors, that they might regale themselves with "the trophies of their patriotism." And, as an encouragement to this work of slaughter, it is said, that the Convention, ordered the Corpses of the national victims to be flayed, in order to procure leather for the use of the army.[12]

But it was in his oration in New Haven on July 7, 1801, that Theodore Dwight painted the full length portrait of democracy and, released completely from the hampering bonds of fact, permitted his imagination to range freely over past, present, and future. Perhaps he was spurred to extraordinary endeavor by the thought of Jefferson in the White House and the sympathetic mien of the Chevaliers de Cincinnati before him. But whatever the source of his inspiration he soared to heights of genteel and scholarly vituperation which have rarely been reached on this continent and

which might well serve as an all-American record against
which contemporary efforts should be judged. Isaac Bates
could reach great altitudes, but he was unable to equal his
rival from Connecticut in sustained performance. He could
not, like Dwight, rise immediately from the take-off to the
empyrean and remain in this thin atmosphere without
thought of oxygen until the very end of his flight.

As the student peruses this masterpiece of political persuasion, he finds nothing omitted. Dwight was familiar with
the entire range of his instrument, knowing the black as well
as the white keys, and using them all. He knew about the
machinations of the "outlaws of Europe," the "foreign rene-
gades," the "fugitives from the gallows," the "blockheads and
knaves," and "our own abandoned citizens"; he knew how
these elements were plotting in their "drunken revelings"
and on the "profligate pages" of their newspapers to undermine religion and morals, to violate the shrine of liberty, to
turn class against class, to desecrate home and family, and in
general to destroy civilization. It is indeed surprising how
little the defenders of "law and order" have learned in a
century and a half. If one should take Dwight's oration and
introduce the verbal substitutions necessary to lift it out of
the age in which it was delivered, it would serve admirably
today as a campaign utterance in defense of privilege. In fact
the present author actually performed the experiment before
an audience of twenty-thousand persons assembled in Madison Square Garden, New York City, several years ago, to protest the enactment of "gag legislation." After reading the
quotation he asked those in attendance to guess the author.
From every quarter of the vast auditorium was shouted the
name of one man—William Randolph Hearst. It is true of
course that the high literary standard of the original was
lowered somewhat in order to make the disguise complete.
A few excerpts will show that the pattern of the attack upon
democracy remains unchanged through the generations.

In the early part of his discourse Dwight pronounced the democratic movement essentially unAmerican and identified it with French Jacobinism and the activities of the criminal element in society:

Yes, my fellow-citizens, the outlaws of Europe, the fugitives from the pillory, and the gallows, have undertaken to assist our own abandoned citizens, in the pleasing work of destroying Connecticut. Scarcely an Aurora appears, without an attempt to accomplish this desirable end. Every Republican Watch-Tower bears on its profligate pages, an effort towards the downfal of Connecticut. In the drunken revellings of the fourth of March, over the infuriated cup of Democratic intoxication, has been hiccupped out the ruin of this devoted state.[13]

After developing the theme that "the great object of Jacobinism, both in its political, and moral revolutions, is to destroy every trace of civilization in the world, and to force mankind back to a savage state," he asserts that this disruptive force begins its work of destruction by undermining "all moral and religious principle." Then, the heart having been "thoroughly divested of all its refinement, and humanity, and of all fear of accountableness," government is attacked, "every passion and every vice" are enlisted, "the poor are excited to hostilities against the rich," the "means of science" are destroyed, and the "authenticity of Religion denied, and ridiculed." All of which will finally "force men backward to that barbarous state, in which they were grovelling, when the light of christianity beamed upon the world."[14]

The reader might suppose that at this point the orator had exhausted his subject, but in that event he would not know the powers of Mr. Dwight. As yet nothing has been said about "the home" and "female virtue"; the peroration lies ahead. The speaker advances from one extravagance to another, and, having exhausted the historical record, he draws aside the veil of time, peers into the coming years, and describes the future state of society in Connecticut, the nation, and the world, if democracy should finally triumph:

We have now reached the consummation of Democratic blessedness. We have a country governed by blockheads, and knaves; the ties of marriage, with all its felicities, are severed, and destroyed; our wives, and our daughters are thrown into the stews; our children are cast into the world from the breast, and forgotten; filial piety is extinguished; and our surnames, the only mark of distinction among families, are abolished. Can the imagination paint any thing more dreadful on this side [of] hell? [15]

But further reading of the oration shows that Mr. Dwight has underestimated his powers. He surpasses himself. He does paint something "more dreadful this side [of] hell":

Some parts of the subject are, indeed, fit only for horrid contemplation. But let me point out to you, the progress of a being through this dreadful society. The offspring of—he knows not whom; instead of feeding on the nectar of his mother's bosom, cast out a vagabond among cosmopolites, with hearts harder than adamant, and colder than the frosts of Greenland, to pick a miserable support in a world where Charity lets not a crumb fall from her table; trained up without a filial, or a fraternal sentiment; loving, and beloved by, no human being; ignorant of himself, and ignorant of his God; in sickness friendless; in death deserted. What can such a state of Society breed but vice; what can it end in but misery? [16]

A Democratic Rebuttal

In the face of this flood of propaganda the friends of democracy were not helpless. They had their clubs and societies in most of the centers of population and they were probably far better armed with newspapers than they are to-day. Also they developed leaders, local as well as national, who were able to carry the battle to the enemy. Of these, few of whom below the highest rank are remembered in the school histories, Abraham Bishop of Connecticut is peculiarly worthy of acquaintance. Graduate of Yale, lawyer, teacher, lecturer, pamphleteer, and politician, he espoused the cause of Jefferson and for a half-dozen years around the opening of the century waged a relentless struggle against the very citadel of Federalism. Possessing "a command of simple, forcible English, a distinct satirical bent, and some sense of humor," he became a "dreaded and hated opponent of that conservative, religious, legal, and propertied alliance which completely dominated Connecticut prior to 1818."

In his preface to the published version of an oration delivered in Wallingford on March 11, 1801, "before the Republicans of the State of Connecticut, at their general thanksgiving, for the election of Thomas Jefferson to the presidency," Bishop gave the complete answer to the charge of lack of patriotism which is so frequently hurled at those who would criticize or change the existing order of things. Having often been the victim of this charge, he met it squarely by admitting that he had been "obliged to speak freely" of his native state. "And why not," he asks, and then proceeds to take the offensive:

If a likeness is to be taken, ought not the features to be drawn truly and without flattery? If we have serpents in our country, shall we call them doves? Shall our weeds be called flowers and our barberry bushes be nursed and cultivated, lest the world should know that there is something in New England which will blast our grain? Shall the canker worm and hessian fly be held sacred, because they are found in Connecticut? [17]

The leaders of democracy, then as now, were accused of fomenting unrest and revolution. Exploiting the natural desire of ordinary men for security, even at the price of enduring injustice, the aristocracy sought to frighten them from attempting reforms in their own interest. Bishop responded by placing the ultimate responsibility for resort to violence at the door of his opponents and by proposing to demonstrate the "truth of this proposition, *that the self stiled friends of order have, in all nations, been the cause of all the convulsions and distress, which have agitated the world.*" [18] He then goes on to make an observation which lies at the heart of the science and practice of politics, but which has often been neglected by political scientists. He observes that interest and social position, as well as learning and talent, give insight into how the world is run. Thus, he says, a recognition of the role of the "friends of order" in society did not come from those "mighty men" who have "filled the thrones of this world and led its armies," but rather *"from weak men, from fools,* in which class the writer of these pages has the honor to hold a high rank by the unanimous suffrage of *the friends of order.*" [19]

This man understood well the methods of political propaganda. He charged the aristocracy with resort to the device of the "red herring" to divert the popular attention from the real issues of the struggle. "The federal 'friends of order'," he observed, "never *reason* about the merits of republicanism. They abuse, they attack private character, talk of power and national honor, and gratitude; of jacobinism, atheism and philosophism. But among all their preachers, orators, poets or other writers, you will find no one serious attempt to address to the body of the people a dispassionate defence of federal measures, or any reasons why a republican government was not *attempted* to be supported." [20] Presumably Mr. Rob Roy McGregor, Assistant-Director of the Illinois Committee on Public Utility Information, an organ of the Insull interests, had read Bishop's oration. When asked by his chief, as revealed in the investigation by the Federal Trade Commission of the propaganda of the public utilities, what arguments he would use if running for United States senator against a man friendly to public ownership, he replied with the following formula: "My idea would not be to try logic or reason, but to try to pin the Bolshevik idea on my opponent." [21]

In another oration delivered in New Haven in September, 1800, on the subject of *The Extent and Power of Political Delusion,* Bishop exposes with clarity and realism the methods employed in tearing down and building up public characters. Here is his answer to Theodore Dwight:

A great art on these public occasions has been to paint up a certain character in every deformity of vice, then to rob the infernal wardrobe to dress him, then to present this a democrat, disorganizer, jacobin and satanist. Their creed is to be as monstrous as their appearance, they are made to believe things incredible, to practice things horrid, and to meditate mischiefs infinite. There say they, ladies and gentlemen, is a republican, and this is republicanism. Then to shew the power of contrast, you have presented, a charming, amiable, divine character, dressed in celestial robes, believing, practicing and contriving all which is good and deserving. This say they, is a federalist, and this is federalism. They then proceed to muster up all the infernal actions of all the bad men in the world, and set them up as the admiration of these infernals. They make them look complacently at blasphemy, smile at murder, and fall into a broad laugh at atheism. They then assign to them as companions all the wretches, who have in every age disgraced humanity, and on the other side, all the good actions throughout the world—all men famous for piety, goodness and science are presented as the objects of love and esteem for their celestials. They claim all holy men of every age as federalists. Then to crown the work, they send these infernal jacobins to the infernal world and translate the federalists to a state of glory.[22]

And those who are familiar with the partisan exaggerations of newspapers, with the universal practice of editorializing through the news, will see in this statement that the world of politics has changed but little since 1800:

Another electioneering delusion is, *"that the Aurora, and other republican papers are full of lies, and the conclusion is to be that the federal papers are full of truths."* Here let me ask how many times did the federal papers drown, shoot, or massacre Buonaparte, while in Egypt? How often was Suwarrow victorious when he was flying before the French? How often was Moreau's army defeated by the humane conquerer of Ismael? How often was Holland taken by the Duke of York? How often has rebellion been completely quelled in Ireland? How many illuminats have been found in this country? How often has Mr. Ross been governor of Pennsylvania? How completely did Mr. Monroe fail of his election to the chair in Virginia? What great federal concussions have been wrought in North-Carolina? What plots in in the South? And finally, when nearly all the federal papers in the last year published the success of the federal ticket in New-York, and added that democracy would never again raise its head there: I ask how true was it? The federal papers tell you that all New-England is federal; and even the same Boston papers, which announce 20,000 votes in favor of the democratic ticket, proclaims the integral federalism of that state; but unfortunately, the federalists came in such throngs, and so darkened their air, that 20,000 of them got benighted and voted for Gerry. Delusion, these are thy weak tricks! [23]

The Use of State Power

In combating the rise of political democracy the friends of aristocracy did not confine themselves to the organization and spread of propaganda. Being in power in Washington and in many local governments they employed state power to fight their battles. The Sedition Act of 1798, as every school boy should know, but does not, was passed to destroy the Republican forces and halt the march of democracy. It throttled the Republican press, crippled the democratic societies, practically prohibited the free discussion of political issues and personalities, suspended the bill of rights of both federal and state constitutions, and inaugurated a reign of terror. At least ten editors of Republican papers, among them Matthew Lyon and Anthony Haswell of Vermont, Thomas Adams of Massachusetts, Charles Holt of Connecticut, Thomas Cooper of Pennsylvania, and James Thomas Callendar of Virginia, were charged with sedition, tried, and sentenced. [24] Particularly was the law directed against the four most influential Jeffersonian journals of the time, *The Aurora* of Philadelphia, *The Examiner* of Richmond, *The Argus* of New York, and *The Independent Chronicle* of Boston. Under the influence of the general hysteria of the time, vigilantes tore down Republican liberty poles and beat their defenders. Artisans professing Jeffersonian principles were threatened with discharge. At a dinner in Boston in June, 1800, Hamilton was reported to have told his friends that within four years "he would either lose his head or be the leader of a triumphant army." Whether this story had any foundation or not, it serves to reveal the intensity and bitterness of the struggle. The colleges, centers of conservatism, played their expected role by bestowing honorary degrees on Federalist statesmen, while passing by Thomas Jefferson, President of the American Philosophical Society and the most learned man in public life.

As the election of 1800 approached and the possibility of the elevation of Jefferson to the presidency assumed the aspect of probability, the aristocracy became more and more alarmed. The inner council of the Federalist party were prepared apparently to employ practically any method, however desperate, if only it offered good chances of success—the overruling of the expressed will of the electorate. Following Federalist losses in New York City, Hamilton on the seventh of May, 1800, wrote a letter to John Jay, governor of the state, predicting a Jeffersonian majority in the next legislature and beseeching Jay, while time permitted, to call a special session of the existing legislature and to ask it to revise the method of choosing the presidential electors whereby a Federalist victory could be assured in state and nation. In support of his proposal he argued that "in times like these in which we live, it will not do to be over-scrupulous"; that *"it is easy to sacrifice the substantial interests of society by a strict adherence to ordinary rules";* that "the scruples of delicacy and propriety, as relative to a common course of things, ought to yield to the extraordinary nature of the crisis"; that such scruples "ought not to hinder the taking of a *legal* and *constitutional* step to prevent an atheist in religion, and fanatic in politics, from getting possession of the helm of state"; and that the measures proposed would be "justified by unequivocal reasons of PUBLIC SAFETY." [25] Fortunately for the experiment in free government Jay ignored the suggestion and penned the following note on the back of Hamilton's letter: "Proposing a measure for party purposes, which it would not become me to adopt."

A yet more far-reaching attempt to control the election of 1800 was embodied in a bill introduced into the United States Senate on January 23rd by Senator Ross of Pennsylvania. Entitled "A bill prescribing the mode of deciding disputed elections of President and Vice President of the United States," this measure was apparently designed to change the method of election prescribed in the Constitution and to shift power from the state legislatures, where the Republicans were strong, to the federal congress, where the Federalists were in control. It provided for the creation of a "Grand Committee" composed of thirteen members—the Chief Justice of the Supreme Court and six persons chosen by ballot from each house—and having "power to examine and finally to decide, all disputes relating to the election of President and Vice President of the United States." [26] The Committee was to "sit with closed doors"; and its majority report would "be a final and conclusive determination of the admissibility or inadmissibility, of the votes given by the electors for president and vice president." [27]

When the contents of this bill were made public in *The Aurora,* a storm broke. William Duane, editor of the paper, was prosecuted under the Sedition Law on the charge that the issue of *The Aurora* for February 19, 1800, "contained assertions and pretended information respecting the Senate, and Committee of the Senate of the United States, and their proceedings, which were false, defamatory, scandalous, and malicious, tending to defame the Senate of the United States; and that the said publication was a high breach of the privileges of the House." [28] One of the little ironies of the case is that the warrant was signed by Thomas Jefferson, as President of the Senate—the warrant for the apprehension of the editor of the most powerful Jeffersonian paper of the time. The bill passed the Senate, but was killed in the House largely by the efforts of John Marshall who abandoned his party in the interests of constitutional government.

Finally, when the election returns showed a Republican triumph, a powerful movement was launched in the Federalist party to prevent the choice of Jefferson, the unquestioned candidate of the people for the presidency, by throwing their weight on the side of Aaron Burr, Jefferson's running mate. To the credit of Hamilton it can be said that he opposed this move, though not on constitutional grounds but rather because he feared Burr more than Jefferson. In the end, however, while some Federalists talked of secession, the will of the people was victorious, the country escaped a revolution from the right, and a tradition of reliance on the ballot was established which constitutes one of the most precious elements in the American political heritage.

The Observations of a Contemporary

Perhaps the most penetrating American observer who lived through this critical period and who put his thoughts in writing was John Taylor. Although he did take part in the struggle on the side of the democratic forces, he played a relatively minor role in the action of the time. This fact lends to his observations a measure of detachment and authority which should be useful and significant today. He realized fully that the aristocracy, though defeated, had not been vanquished; that the dynamics of the economic and legal system were working on the side of privilege; that the battle for free institutions in the United States had only begun. In view of these considerations his analysis of the methods by which the aristocracy of modern times, the "aristocracy of paper and patronage," enforces its rule may serve as a fitting conclusion of this look into the past.

The apologists for aristocracy, according to Taylor, begin their argument for the defense by employing a device used to support every privileged order in history. They say it is "natural and inevitable":

"It is the will of Jupiter," exclaimed some artful combination of men. "The will of Jupiter is inevitable," responded the same combination to itself; and ignorance submitted to a fate, manufactured by human fraud . . . whenever it is impossible to prove a principle, which is necessary to support a system, a reference to an inevitable power, calling it God or nature, is preferable to reasoning; because every such principle is more likely to be exploded, than established by reasoning . . . Hence have been derived, the sanctity of oracles, the divinity of kings, and the holiness of priests; and now that these bubbles have become the scoff of common sense, experiment is to decide, whether there remains in America a stock of superstition, upon which can be ingrafted, "an aristocracy from nature." [29]

This aristocracy will rule by concealing itself. And here Taylor makes an observation of extraordinary penetration: any age can detect the frauds of an aristocracy that has passed away, while submitting unwittingly to the depredations of an existing privileged order. The causes of earlier aristocracies "are distinctly seen," he says, "because they do not exist.

They have no counsel in court. They are, therefore, better understood than when they flourished." But the cause of the contemporary aristocracy "is not seen, because it does exist; and the more oppressive it shall become, the greater will be the difficulty of discovering its existence." The aristocracies of "superstition" and of "motto and blazon" are "exposed naked to our view," while that of "paper and patronage," "disguised in the garb of republicanism, and uttering patriotick words, joins the mob in kicking them about, by way of diverting the publick attention from itself." [30] The former, "being substantially dead, their bodies may be cut up, the articulation of their bones exposed, and the convolution of their fibres unravelled; but whenever the intricate structure of the system of paper and patronage is attempted to be dissected, we moderns surrender our intellects to yells uttered by the living monster, similar to those with which its predecessors astonished, deluded, and oppressed the world for three thousand years." [31]

One mode of concealment, as suggested above, is to "utter patriotick words," to profess democracy, to attack all other aristocracies, to drape oneself in the flag. "Fine words are used to decoy, and ugly words to affright," says Taylor.[32] Closely related is that age-long device of using symbols to which are attached sentiments of love or hate, anger or fear: "The aristocracy of superstition defended itself by exclaiming, the Gods! the temples! the sacred oracles! divine vengeance! and Elysian fields!—and that of paper and patronage exclaims, national faith! sacred charters! disorganization! and security of property!" [33]

Through the exercise of economic power this modern aristocracy takes control of government and dominates the whole of society. "A legislature . . . will be governed by that interest, and legislate in its favour . . . to the injury of the other interest, that is, the great mass of the nation." [34]

Thus does the aristocracy entrench itself behind what Taylor calls the law charter:

This modern system of law charters, is founded in the same design, with the ancient system of a social compact. Under the sanction of social compact, governments have formerly tyrannised over nations. Under the sanction of law charters, governments now buy a faction, rob nations of enormous wealth, and soar beyond responsibility. The inviolability of a social compact was the old dogma; the inviolability of law charters is the new; for effecting the same end. The last is however an engine in the hands of avarice and ambition, of power far superior to the first. It is able to corrupt and pillage a nation without limit. The first was an opinion unable to purchase partisans; the last offers every thing to its disciples, which can gratify pernicious passions, and meets arguments with bribes. Thus a nation, which won self-government by exploding the doctrine of the antiquated compact dogma, may lose it again in the modern law charter dogma; and thus a nation, which thought it morally wrong to suffer slavery from troops hired by clothes, pay and rations, may be persuaded that it is morally right to suffer slavery from troops hired by dividends, interest upon stock, and protecting duty bounties.[35]

In defending a given law charter, counsel for those enjoying the privileges which it guarantees appeals to "publick faith." And "publick faith," in the words of Taylor, "is made with great solemnity to mount the rostrum, and to pronounce the following lecture:

Law enacted for the benefit of a nation is repealable; but law enacted for the benefit of individuals, though oppressive to a nation, is a charter, and irrepealable. The existing generation is under the tutelage of all past generations, and must rely upon the responsibility of the grave for the preservation of its liberty. Posterity, being bound by the contracts of its ancestry, in every case which diminishes its rights, man is daily growing less free by a doctrine which never increases them. A government intrusted with the administration of publick affairs for the good of a nation, has a right to deed away that nation for the good of itself or its partisans, by law charters for monopolies or sinecures; and posterity is bound by these deeds. But although an existing generation can never reassume the liberty or property held by its ancestor, it may recompence itself by abridging or abolishing the rights of its descendant.[36]

"By this artifice," Taylor concludes, "whenever men cut off their shackles with the sword, they are riveted on again by the pen."[37] And gradually the whole of society will become enslaved by the aristocracy of paper and patronage—"that political hydra of modern invention, whose arms embrace a whole nation, whose ears hear every sound, whose eyes see all objects, and whose hands can reach every purse and every throat."[38] Under its exactions the burden on the backs of the people will become more and more difficult to bear. But, according to Taylor, "as grievances gradually excite national discontent, they [the aristocracy] will fix the yoke more securely, by making it gradually heavier. And they will finally avow and maintain their corruption, by establishing an irresistible standing army, not to defend the nation, but to defend a system for plundering the nation."[39]

The Record of American Democracy in the Past

Under the leadership of Jefferson the American people carried through a political revolution. The pattern of the struggle bears a striking resemblance to that of the present. As the people moved to the conquest of political power the aristocracy was far more badly frightened than it is today. Its spokesman charged democracy with every sin on the calendar, from the nationalization of women to the overthrow of religion; they predicted the destruction of civilization and the end of the world; they employed substantially the same arguments that their spiritual descendants are using today. Failing to halt the popular advance by such

means the "representatives of the few" brought the engines
of state power into their service, suspended civil rights,
and even toyed with the idea of arbitrarily repudiating the
election returns. The final triumph of the cause of political
democracy by peaceful means constitutes one of the glories
of the Republic—an achievement which may serve as a
precedent to be followed in the contemporary struggle for
economic democracy. At the same time the American people
must ever be watchful lest the aristocracy forsake, corrupt,
and destroy the democratic process when the verdict of the
polls begins to go against its interests. So it labored once,
and so it may again.

The triumph of democracy, however, was less complete
than it seemed. The period which witnessed these great
victories in the sphere of politics also saw the laying of the
foundations in law and custom of the "aristocracy of paper
and patronage." Although the people ostensibly won the
elections year after year, they steadily lost their economic
independence. This "tendency of the laws" was clearly perceived by John Taylor. As the student ponders today his
bold, realistic, and unsentimental analysis of the interplay
of ideas and interests in American society of the time, he
sees unfolding before him much of the history of the intervening century—the decline of agriculture, the rise of commerce and industry, the pillaging of the common domain,
the steady conversion of public into private property, the
increasing concentration of economic power, the subordination of human to property rights, and the extension of the
sway of business over all departments of economy, government, and culture. Whether the American people can now
strike off with the ballot shackles "riveted on with the pen"
during these hundred years is a question which will doubtless be answered in the proximate future. Their behavior
and achievements around 1800 give some grounds for hope.
And if they would study that period and the methods em-

ployed by the aristocracy in an effort to maintain its privileges, they might gain moral and intellectual support for the contemporary struggle.

REFERENCES

1. Thomas Jefferson, *The Writings* (Ford edition, New York, 1899), X, 140.

2. Jonathan Elliot, *The Debates in the Several State Conventions, on the Adoption of the Federal Constitution* (Second edition, Washington, 1836), I, 466.

3. Isaac C. Bates, *An Oration* (Northampton, 1805), 8-9.

4. *Ibid.*, 29.

5. *Ibid.*, 30.

6. *Ibid.*, 25.

7. John Mitchell Mason, *The Voice of Warning to Christians, on the Ensuing Election of a President of The United States* (New York, 1800), 4.

8. *Ibid.*, 25.

9. *Ibid.*, 40.

10. *Ibid.*, 29-30.

11. Theodore Dwight, *An Oration* (Hartford, 1798), 4.

12. *Ibid.*, 24-25.

13. Theodore Dwight, *An Oration* (Hartford, 1801), 15-16. The *Aurora* and *Republican Watch-Tower* were Jeffersonian papers.

14. *Ibid.*, 20.

15. *Ibid.*, 29.

16. *Ibid.*, 29.

17. Abraham Bishop, *Oration* (New Haven, 1801), iv-v.

18. *Ibid.*, v.

19. *Ibid.*, vi.

20. *Ibid.*, 28.

21. Ernest Gruening, *The Public Pays* (New York, 1931), 147.

22. Abraham Bishop, *An Oration* (Newark, 1800), 43.

23. *Ibid.*, 52.

24. Frank Anderson, "The Enforcement of the Alien and Sedition Laws," in *Annual Report of the American Historical Association* (1912), 120-121.

25. Alexander Hamilton, *The Works* (Lodge edition, New York, 1904), X, 372-373.

26. *The Aurora*, February 19, 1800.

27. *Ibid.*

28. *Annals of the Congress of the United States* "Sixth Congress Comprising the Period from December 2, 1799 to March 3, 1801, inclusive" (Washington, 1851), 123.

29. John Taylor, *An Inquiry into the Principles and Policy of the Government of the United States* (Fredericksburg, 1814), 11-12.

30. *Ibid.*, 73-74.

31. *Ibid.*, 31.

32. *Ibid.*, 558.

33. *Ibid.*, 31.

34. *Ibid.*, 39.

35. *Ibid.*, 64.

36. *Ibid.*, 61.

37. *Ibid.*, 62.

38. *Ibid.*, 23.

39. *Ibid.*, 40.

CHAPTER 7:

SOME LESSONS FROM THE PRESENT

Since the outbreak of the Great War the world has been the scene of an unending succession of dislocations, convulsions, and revolutions—economic, political, and cultural. The outwardly stable relationships, arrangements, and institutions of the opening years of the century have cracked and crumbled: daring flight into the future on the wings of revolutionary doctrine has been attempted in Russia; violent reaction against both the substance and the spirit of modernism has established itself in Italy, Germany, and a number of the smaller countries of Europe; and a struggle of life and death among rival social programs and philosophies, each straining to capture the soul of mankind, has engulfed a large part of the earth. Some of these movements invoke the name of democracy; others curse it as the source of all the maladies and ills of the age. To those in America who would preserve free institutions, this experience of the Old World should be of value. It is proposed here to examine briefly the rise of communism in Russia, the emergence of fascism in Italy and Germany, and the outbreak of the rebellion in Spain. The object of such examination of course is not a comprehensive study of these events, but rather the illumination of the question of the prospects of democracy in the United States. In all four cases the fate of democracy is profoundly involved. Perhaps from the agony of European peoples, grappling with the forces released by the advance of industrial society, American citizens may gain some insight into the problem of preserving their own liberties.

Russia

When the Russian revolution broke upon the world in 1917 it was not unexpected. In fact many thoughtful observers were surprised that the imperial regime—corrupt, inefficient, brutal—was able to endure the strain of more than two and a half years of war, marked by an indescribable slaughter of unequipped Russian soldiers and an almost uninterrupted succession of defeats for Russian arms. For at least two centuries and a half, beginning with the blind peasant revolt led by Stenka Razin in 1667, the blackest autocracy of the western world, modeled after the despotism imposed upon the Slav by the Tartar, was threatened with revolution in practically every generation. So apparent were the rottenness of the old order and the bitterness of the people that an ordinary American traveler on his honeymoon in 1902 could write as follows to his father:

This morning as I walked upon the Nevsky Prospekt, the Broadway of the Imperial capital, and watched the movement of mankind along the way, and beheld the extraordinary contrasts between those who walked and those who rode; as I saw the burly policeman arrest the shabby foot-farer for nearly being run down, while he let the haughty grandee drive freely on; as I beheld poverty and wealth in such flagrant contrast, and realized that a standing army is kept ever armed and girt to protect and uphold the privilege and security of the rich; as I beheld the surly, sour, sombre faces of those who wore no gaudy covering of broadcloth and gold lace, my fancy harked back to the time, somewhat more than a century ago, when the King and Nobles of France drove through the Rues of Paris in all their glittering splendor, trampling down in their pride of power the pedestrian who failed to escape from their sudden approach. How secure they felt in their arrogant enjoyment of prerogative and rank! How contemptuously they disdained the humble claims of the gutter-proletarian, of the peasant on the land! Louis XIV had cried *"L'etat c'est moi."* Was that not enough! And yet, I had stood in the Place de la Concorde, almost on the very spot where, inspired by the hatred of the Sansculottes, Mademoiselle La Guillotine had bit off the dull head of Louis XVI, and cut through the fair throat of Marie Antoinette.

It may be possible for Russia and her governing men, her Bureaucratic Autocracy, yet a little while to postpone the fateful hour. By means of foreign wars it may be possible to play the old game of diverting the public mind from its own bitter ills; by promises of fair and liberal dealing it may be possible to calm the public mind—cajole it until the promises are duly broken, as is invariably the case. Whatever fair-speaking and fat-feeding officialdom may to the contrary assert, the impression I gain amidst all this splendor and pomp and glare of supreme, concentered power of the few is that, beneath this opulent exterior, deep down in the hearts and even below the conscious working of their minds, there to-day abides among the masses of the Russian people—who after all hold in their hands the final power—a profound and monstrous discontent: a discontent so deep-rooted and so intense that when the inevitable hour strikes, as strike it must, the world will then behold in Russia a saturnalia of blood and tears, a squaring of ten centuries' accounts, more fraught with human anguish and human joy than ever dreamed a Marat and a Robespierre, more direful and more glad than yet mankind have known.[1]

The revolution passed rapidly from right to left and lodged finally in the hands of a revolutionary party professing the doctrines of Marxian socialism, as modified and adapted to Russian conditions by its own leadership. In its fundamental social ideas this party was linked with and carried on the movement of popular protest which dates from the breakup of the medieval system. In militant spirit it proclaimed the liberation of the masses, the reconciliation of races and peoples, the economic, political, and intellectual emancipation of women, the secularization of all cultural activities and interests, the ascendance of science and scientific method, the rejection of authoritarianism in every field, and the acceptance of a naturalistic world outlook. Marx himself, in developing the basic philosophy of revolutionary socialism, was profoundly influenced by three characteristic manifestations of the modern spirit—German philosophy, English industrial development, and the French revolution. The new Soviet constitution, adopted in December, 1936, provides for the social control of all important forms of productive property, lays the legal foundations of a socialistic society, and thus gives one answer to the current world-wide question of the control of economic power. Also, while affirming in word most of the rights guaranteed in the liberal constitutions of the eighteenth and nineteenth centuries, it adds certain rights over which the social struggle is being waged in the age of industrial civilization: the right to work, the right to rest, the right to material security, the right to free education, the equality of the sexes, and the equality of races. In the Soviet Union the new constitution is heralded as the "most democratic in the world." In *theory* the revolution identifies itself fully and without reservation with the democratic movement in history.

In actuality the Communist Party repudiated political democracy completely and established, almost from the beginning, a rigid dictatorship. Seizing political and military power, it achieved a monopoly of legality, gained control of the institutions of government, abolished civil liberties, converted the courts into revolutionary organs, conducted an unremitting struggle against all enemies, molded the entire cultural apparatus to its purposes, and shaped in detail both domestic and foreign policy. Though, according to the Marxian doctrine, the dictatorship was organized and sustained in the name of the industrial proletariat, supported by the poorer peasantry, it was in fact a dictatorship by a highly disciplined party whose membership was guarded with extreme care. Moreover, as appears to be inevitable under such circumstances, a struggle for power developed among the leaders and actual authority came to reside in the hands of a very small body of men.

To what extent these men have expressed the will of the masses of the people, even of the proletariat, is not known and never will be known. Under the dictatorship the public mind has been deliberately shaped by school, press, and other organs of opinion or, where the method of propaganda and persuasion has failed, by systematic and ruthless use of the police power. This has meant the suppression of all criticism of a fundamental character, although criticism of methods and means, criticism within the framework of the ideas and purposes established by the "party line," has not only been permitted but at times encouraged. The dictatorship has also destroyed without mercy every movement that might be thought to harbor even the seeds of organized opposition. What is known in America and the political democracies of the West as freedom of thought and expression for the individual has been thoroughly outlawed during these years. Real dissent, however mild its forms, has been forced into subterranean channels.

The achievements of the revolutionary forces in lifting an extremely backward country into the age of technology, and of altering the psychology of the people, have been unprecedented. An enormous program of construction has been carried through in an astonishingly brief period of time. The tempo of this construction has been particularly rapid during the past ten years—the years that have been marked by a tightening of the dictatorship. The economy in both its rural and urban divisions has been socialized; a coordinated program of production and distribution in the community interest has been instituted; a modern industrial plant has been built; an agriculture of a quasi-feudal type has been mechanized; a powerful system of military defense has been organized; unemployment has been abolished; illiteracy has been reduced to less than ten per cent; educa-

tional opportunities have been extended to the people on a
tremendous scale; and numerous social services have been
established. These are but the outstanding achievements
of the revolution, and the list might be considerably length-
ened. Although the country is still marked by a low standard of living and other evidences of cultural backwardness,
the solid accomplishments of the dictatorship cannot be
disputed.

At the same time, the struggle within the party, involving
both policies and personalities, has introduced a sharp note
of uncertainty with respect to the future. Numbers of old
party leaders, men and women whose names had come to be
identified with the revolution both at home and abroad,
have been arrested, declared guilty of sabotage and conspiracy, and sentenced to exile, imprisonment, and death. Being
in profound disagreement with the methods and program
of the controlling faction and being unable under the conditions of the dictatorship to conduct open opposition, these
persons apparently resorted to underground activities reminiscent of the activities of revolutionists under the autocracy
of the tsar. While the complete story of these events, which
have shocked the sensibilities of the world and practically
destroyed the radical movement, will probably not be known
for years, it seems safe to assume that they were the natural
fruit of dictatorial rule in a period which required radical
changes in revolutionary policy. Whether the bitterness and
hatred inevitably generated by such procedure will permit
the gradual and peaceful dissolution of the minority control
and the final establishment of a democratic regime founded
on popular control of economic as well as political power,
the avowed goal of the revolution, is a question which only
history itself can answer.

As pointed out in an earlier chapter, there are those in
America, and elsewhere, who believe that fate has decreed
that every social system must enter and leave the world

through the door of revolutionary violence and dictatorship. Some further believe, and they have been very vocal, that Russia has prescribed the method by which the more profound changes in social structure will take place in the modern world, if economic power is ever to be made subservient to the popular will and interest. While only the rashest of men would today presume to pass final judgment on what is perhaps the greatest social convulsion of history, there are excellent grounds for believing that this convulsion has provided no universal pattern for the political struggle, that America at any rate will follow a very different course, and that all who look to Russia as an example to be copied will be subject sooner or later to severe disillusionment.

The Russian revolution, in spite of the indebtedness of its leaders to the doctrines of Marx and Engels, was a *Russian* revolution, and is becoming more patently Russian with every passing year. The very disappointment which many persons have come to feel toward the course of things in the land of the Soviets, persons whose loyalties have been international in character, is clear evidence of this. For generations the old regime with its face set steadfastly toward the past and bent on defending the feudal principle of autocracy in state and church, effectually barred the way to reform and the incursion of modern ideas. Violent revolution seemed the only road to the future. In the course of its long career the imperial despotism had piled up a huge debt of injustice and misery that could only be paid in blood and tears. Having lived by the sword, it was destined to perish by the sword. Only if the ruling elements of America choose to incur a similar debt, which, unfortunately, some among them seem desirous of doing, will they be required to pay in the same coin. The great law of history that "those whom the gods would destroy they first make mad" is fully demonstrated in the Russian revolution.

The pattern of that revolution has also been profoundly

influenced by a number of other factors. Not only was there little basis for political democracy in the immediate experience of the people. There was little basis for it in the culture. At the time of the revolution, according to the best estimates, well over sixty per cent of the prospective citizens were illiterate—grossly and abysmally so. And, as Lenin once truly remarked, "an illiterate person is outside of politics." One hundred and forty millions of people, with such a rate of illiteracy, were scattered in a few cities and two hundred thousand villages over that vast land reaching from the Baltic to the Pacific and from below the Caucasus to the Arctic —a land so boundless that even an American has difficulty in grasping its immensity—a land as large as the United States, Canada, Alaska, and Mexico combined. Also this great population was divided into more than one hundred and fifty different races and nationalities, among whom there existed bitter animosities and jealousies bred of centuries of oppression and struggle. Clearly, only a strong central government, dominated by some coherent and determined minority, would have been able to hold together such a far-flung empire inhabited by such diverse, backward, and politically untutored peoples. Any genuine attempt to establish democratic rule would have thrown the country into warring sections and led eventually to the founding of separate nations.

If these peoples were unprepared for political democracy, how much less prepared were they for any modern form of economic democracy. Socialism assumes an advanced technology and a closely integrated economy. Except for the emergence here and there of large scale capitalism, chiefly under the control and direction of foreign interests, Russia was a land of handicrafts. The machine was only beginning to make its appearance. The peasantry, comprising eighty-five per cent of the population, was dependent on tools and processes almost indescribably backward from an

American standpoint. The flail and wooden plow were still in use in many parts, while the tractor was practically unknown. Except for a few great highways constructed for military purposes the roads were but tracks across the plains or through the forests. Of railroads in 1913 the empire could boast but thirty-seven-thousand miles, of telephone subscribers but two-hundred-eighty-thousand. For the United States at the same time, a country of only about one-third the size, the corresponding figures were approximately two-hundred-fifty-thousand and eight million seven-hundred-thousand. Consequently, if the revolutionary forces were resolved to build both political and economic democracy, they were constrained to hold power by whatever means until the necessary underlying conditions could first be established. Whether for the people of the Soviet Union the end will justify the means cannot be known today. But it is clear that any effort to extend democracy in the United States to the economic realm cannot follow the Russian pattern. Indeed, whether the revolutionary forces released in the land of the tsars in 1917 will ultimately promote democratic values is one of the deep uncertainties of the epoch. And, in view of the basic differences between the two countries, it is self-evident that any attempt to impose upon America a precedent established in Moscow is doomed from the start to futility and disaster. This should be thoroughly understood by all who are engaged in the struggle for the extension of the principles of democracy in the United States.

This is not to say that the Russian revolution is without general significance. Whatever may be its course in the future, whether it succeeds or fails in terms of its original professed purposes, it has served to shatter complacency and to awaken the nations to the economic ills under which the masses of mankind still live and suffer. Regardless of its excesses and perversions, the common accompaniment of violent revolution, it has proclaimed to all races and peoples the vision of a society sensitive to the needs and confident of the potentialities of the ordinary man. Like the American and French Revolutions of an earlier age, it has so dramatized and vitalized certain great social ideas that they cannot be disregarded. Its methods may be the product of Russian tyranny and cultural backwardness; certain of its purposes are the common possession of mankind. The American people, identified in their history with the championship of the ideal of justice and opportunity for all, are already responding to these ideas. But in their efforts to bring economic power under control, it is to be hoped and expected that they will make full use of their own glorious heritage and the peculiarly favorable circumstances which they enjoy.

Italy

Italian Fascism repudiates emphatically and completely both the letter and the spirit of democracy. It scorns and ridicules the whole body of social and political thought underlying free institutions. Though lacking a clear-cut philosophy of its own and developing its doctrines after the event, it conceives itself as a reaction against the entire liberating movement of the past three or four hundred years— a reaction against the Reformation, the Enlightenment, and the English, American, and French revolutions—a reaction against rationalism, equality, individual freedom, civil liberty, majority rule, parliamentary government, and international peace. "The plain truth," said Mussolini in March, 1923, "is that men are perhaps tired of liberty." For the "intrepid, restless, and hard" youth of today, "there are other words of much greater power . . . order, hierarchy, discipline." The ideal of personal freedom for which men fought valiantly in the eighteenth and nineteenth centuries has lost its vitality and its power of arousing deep loyalties.

"Let it be known therefore once and for all," Il Duce announces, "that Fascism knows no ideals and worships no fetishes; it has already passed over and if necessary will turn once more and quietly pass over the more or less decayed corpse of the Goddess Liberty." [2] Fascism resurrects from the past the principle of authoritarianism and makes it the guiding star of the new Italy.

In a statement, admirable for its clarity and frankness, a leading spokesman of Fascism once declared that "fascism has the character of an anti-revolution." This idea he expounds as follows:

The March on Rome is to the French Revolution what the Council of Trent was to the Protestant Reformation. Living is reaction. In fascism, Italy has again found itself by reacting. It has found its very self, not as formerly in scattered regional tradition, but in the unity of its new consciousness.

In the name of Romanity Italy casts off its false prophets, breaks down the profaned altars of golden and silver idols built during the century of perdition. We are at last tired of hearing the text of the Nordic lie. Better for us the pagan orgies than to take lessons in morality from Emerson or Ruskin. . . . Man of the Revolution, abstract man, deified man, a grotesque parody of his Creator, has not succeeded in giving us law. Human will is by nature discordant and can never give birth to a moral order. Order can not rise from disorder nor peace from the conflict of individual wills, truth from discussion, law from free-will, the state from contract, authority from liberty. Peace is possible only there where all bow before the authority of a transcendent power.

In the face of European civilization, moth-eaten by individualism, imperial Italy solemnly asserts the necessity of a law imposed by God on human minds. The tide of history has turned. From Luther to Lenin, the cycle of the great heresy is closed. The society of the future will not be based on the "Declaration of the Rights of Man" but on the Syllabus.[3]

On its positive side Italian Fascism affirms the fundamental inequality of individuals and peoples, interprets history essentially as a struggle of nations, identifies national vigor with conquest and the spread of empire, and exalts to supreme rank the virtues of the soldier. Also it regards the organization of society into classes as natural and inevitable, apotheosizes the state as a transcendent entity standing over and embracing all generations of Italians, looks upon the state as engaged in a sacred mission to be "realized in the course of the historical process," presents *Il Duce* as the divinely anointed personification of the state, and preaches to the individual the doctrine that he finds his true self only as he subordinates himself to and loses himself in the will of the state. "Fascism," writes Mussolini in a sober and authoritative article in the *Enciclopedia Italiana,* "conceives of the State as an absolute, in comparison with which all individuals are relative, only to be conceived of in their relation to the State . . . the Fascist State is itself conscious and has itself a will and a personality." [4] And the mission of the state, living today in the person of the Italian dictator, is "the expansion of the nation"—war and conquest. Under the cloak of idealistic and mystical phrases man is converted into a soldier, woman into a bearer of soldiers, the school into a soldier factory, society at large into a military encampment, government into a charismatic dictatorship, and civilization into barbarism armed with modern technology.

The operational meaning of this doctrine of empire is already written large on the map of the world in Ethiopia and Spain. It is disclosed with utter candor in a volume written by Marshall Emilio de Bono and published in 1937 by the National Fascist Institute of Culture in Rome. It is called *Preparation and the First Operation* and is numbered Volume I in a proposed series to be issued under the general title of *The Conquest of Empire.* In this book the man who with Mussolini deliberately planned from 1933 the rape of

Ethiopia and who commanded the Italian forces during the early months of the campaign tells the "inside story," and not without pardonable pride, of the first imperial adventure under Il Duce. He tells how early in 1935 he went to Eritrea for the purpose of destroying the political unity of Ethiopia and sowing the seeds of dissension among the native princes. "In case the Negus has no intention of attacking us," wrote Mussolini to his lieutenant in February, "then we must take the initiative. For this purpose I want to send you two hundred thousand men within the year."[5] Doubtless when the rebellion in Spain has been successfully consummated a second volume will be added to the series.

The circumstances under which a political democracy was transformed into a dictatorship, a peaceful country into an international brigand, should be of the greatest interest and concern to the American people. Although it is a far cry, in terms of history, geography, social organization, and national temperament, from Italy to the United States, yet the experience of the Italian people in abandoning democratic political practices should contain some lessons of fairly general application. Whereas the dictatorship of the Communist Party in Russia followed the dictatorship of the tsar, the dictatorship of Mussolini in Italy followed a regime generally committed to the extension of free institutions. This fact makes the Italian experience far more significant to Americans who desire to preserve their own democracy.

The pattern of events out of which Italian Fascism emerged is fairly clear. Immediately following the war Italy entered a period of disillusionment, economic distress, and moral breakdown. At the beginning of the struggle in August, 1914, Rome refused to honor her engagements under the Triple Alliance, remained neutral for approximately nine months, and finally threw in her lot with the Allied Powers. On the battlefield the Italian armies won little glory and suffered several disastrous defeats. Though

the war was unpopular from the beginning with great masses
of the people, victory was celebrated as a vindication of the
policy pursued and for a time popular rejoicing was general.
Then came "the great humiliation of Versailles" under
which Italy, having won the war, "lost the peace." In wide
circles the idea was propagated and believed that the war
had been a great blunder. Among idealistic elements the
publication of the text of the secret understandings and
treaties of the Allies created a feeling of deep disillusionment and led to the conviction that the war had not been a
crusade for democracy, self-determination, internationalism,
and world peace, but rather a grim struggle among the
nations for existence, dominion, and empire. So bitter was
the feeling that in certain quarters of the industrial cities
the military uniform became an emblem of disgrace: returning soldiers were occasionally stoned, insulted, and spat
upon.

Economic crisis and distress followed the war in Italy as in
other countries. The conclusion of hostilities found the nation staggering under an enormous debt and facing general
economic paralysis. In the course of the months the currency
depreciated; prices rose; real wages declined; savings disappeared; factories shut down; unemployment spread; labor
grew restless; the economic struggle sharpened; strike followed strike; the middle classes suffered impoverishment;
and the whole population lost its sense of security. A spirit
of pessimism and defeatism gripped the nation. It was freely
said that Italy was a beaten country, that Italians were "the
poor products of a poor soil," that the glories of the Italian
peninsula were a thing of the past.

The situation bred a revolutionary temper among the people. The earliest manifestation of this temper followed for
the most part the established lines of popular protest in
Europe—those of Marxian and Christian socialism, supplemented and modified by syndicalist, anarchist, and cooper-

ative ideas and methods. During the generation immediately preceding the war, these doctrines had been widely propagated among the Italian working classes and had profoundly influenced the labor movement, in both its economic and its political phases. During the war the spread of revolutionary ideas continued at an ever accelerating pace; following the Russian revolution the drift toward Bolshevism became pronounced. The cause of the war and the general distress was located in the capitalistic system of production and exchange. By 1920, when the peak was reached, trade-unionism enrolled in its several branches approximately five million members. Supported by elements from the middle and intellectual classes, organized industrial workers demanded the immediate socialization of the more important forms of productive property and the inauguration of an era of socialism. In support of this program the more extreme elements resorted increasingly to direct action and violence; they seized factories, intimidated city administrations, and often took law into their own hands; they preached the complete, the totalitarian revolution, the overthrow of the institutions of property, family, church, and state.

A reaction soon set in. Self-styled patriotic clubs, avowedly organized to oppose Bolshevism, sprang up in various places under diverse leadership and rapidly spread through the country. Supported financially by wealthy landholders and industrialists and composed for the most part of returning soldiers and members of the lower middle class, the motive of the actual participants was doubtless a mixture of fear, patriotic sentiment, and love of excitement. As societies of army veterans joined the movement, military organization and discipline were introduced. In order to create loyalty and solidarity, rites and ceremonies were devised, shirts and insignia adopted, meetings and parades organized. Wearing the uniform of the order, bearing the national colors, and armed with clubs, guns, and castor oil, the members of a particular organization would go forth professedly to do battle with the representatives of revolutionary socialism and their sympathizers. Actually they attacked the entire labor and liberal movement without discrimination. They put down strikes and smashed labor unions and cooperative societies alike, placing in a single category Christian-Democrats, Socialists, Communists, Syndicalists, and Anarchists, beating and killing leaders and destroying property. Battles were fought in the streets, demonstrations were converted into invitations to violence, raids were systematically organized, and strikes were made the occasion for bloodshed. This civil war, for such it was, though undeclared and unrecognized, grew ever more bitter and determined. The extremists on both sides thirsted for the revolutionary struggle. The forces of labor, however, were so badly divided by personal rivalries and ideological differences that they were utterly incapable of joint action against the common enemy.

In the presence of this conflict, government abdicated. Unable to formulate any positive policy adequate to the situation, it adopted for a time the negative policy of *laissez faire,* of throwing its weight on one side or the other as circumstances suggested, of following the line of least resistance. But gradually, as the nature of the struggle revealed itself, government, under the domination of the propertied classes, inclined increasingly toward the reactionary party. According to Professor Gaetano Salvemini, "the Fascists were provided with arms, ammunition, and means of transportation by the military authorities, and could almost always count upon the passive and frequently even the active connivance of the police." [6] In the years 1919-20 government resigned its executive and police functions, in 1922 its legislative functions. In a word, constituted authority lost its power to command; government its power to govern. When action was required, parliament was paralyzed by party divisions and degenerated into a debating society in which the debate was conducted with bitter acrimony but to no purpose. Whatever of political democracy Italy ever possessed had lost its vitality and its title to respect. It was incapable of making the decisions that the times required. Consequently, the March on Rome on October 28, 1922, merely recorded a shift in power that had already occurred. One of the ironies in the situation is the fact that no representative of parliamentary government took Mussolini seriously. Although he had made no effort to conceal his intentions, the friends of democracy were so blinded by the inherited symbols of power which they held in their hands that they did not realize how their own ineptitude and pusillanimity had emptied those symbols of all content.

The appeal of Mussolini, a man of boundless ambition, who eventually succeeded in capturing the undisputed leadership of the counter-revolutionary forces, was diverse. As an active and militant figure in the ranks of socialism down to the World War, he had come to know intimately the popular mind; by natural gift and training he was a masterful propagandist and showman. When in 1918 and 1919 the socialists placed responsibility for the distress of the nation on the system of capitalism, he placed it on the institutions of parliamentary government and the unjust distribution of the resources of the earth among the nations. He organized his Fascisti, as the Standard Dictionary defines the term, "to oppose Bolshevism in Italy," to combat internationalism in every form, to arouse the Italian nation to gird itself for a struggle in the world arena. He charged the government with the failures of the war, of the peace, and of the domestic economy—with the betrayal of Italy. He made political democracy the scapegoat for all the misery and humiliation which the nation had suffered and was suffering. Although two years before he came to power the orthodox Marxian movement had begun to recede, he employed with great effect the bogey of Bolshevism to frighten the middle and conservative classes and rally them around his standard.

The real enemies of the Italian workers, Mussolini declared, were not the Italian bourgeoisie, but foreign nations —plutocratic nations under whose iron heel Italy had been exploited and robbed and forced into a position of economic servitude. The only freedom worth fighting for was freedom, not for the individual, but for the nation. He proclaimed the "supremacy of moral over material forces," appealed to tradition against the spirit of reason, revived the fire but not the ideas of the Risorgimento, contracted to bring back the glories of ancient Rome, promised to make every Italian proud to be a citizen of Italy, and swore to establish order at home and to inspire respect and fear abroad. Where in all the world could a political leader make such an appeal more effectively than in the Eternal City, center of western civilization for two thousand years, home of the Christian Church and capital of Christendom, symbol of both spiritual and temporal power? And the youth of Italy responded and have followed him steadfastly to this day, even into Ethiopia and Spain. To the mighty men of Italian society, to industrialists, bankers, merchants, and large landholders, he promised law and order, an end to strikes, protection of property rights, an opportunity to make profits, and generally the preservation of the system of private capitalism. Although the ultimate course of Fascism defies prediction, and although a regime of "law and order" has been indubitably established, there is every reason for believing that Italian business men have been profoundly disillusioned and would give much to restore that freedom of enterprise which the Fascist state has destroyed. The fact remains, however, that by destroying political democracy Il Duce did succeed in halting the extension of popular power into the sphere of economics. For this service these same business men are doubtless grateful. Italian democracy was a

casualty of the first great economic depression following the
World War.

Germany

In its essential pattern German National Socialism follows
very closely Italian Fascism. In fact Hitler regarded Mussolini as the prophet of a new political dispensation on earth
and modeled his method and program after the design fashioned by the dictator below the Alps. Democracy in all of its
forms is repudiated more completely and uncompromisingly
by the Third Reich than by the new Italy. Correlatively, National Socialism through its affirmation of the leader principle and its proclamation of the divinity of Hitler's person
and mission surpasses Fascism in its devotion to the doctrine
of authoritarianism. It permits no phase of the life of the
German people to escape its grasp; it places its stamp not
only on economy and government, but also on every department of the culture. With the thoroughness characteristic of
the German temperament, it carries to a logical conclusion
the conception of totalitarianism. Also, and perhaps most
fundamental of all, National Socialism, like Italian Fascism,
while loudly attacking capitalism as a system, destroys labor
unions, establishes a form of monopoly capitalism, and places
the power of the state behind the interests of property. By
elevating the business man to the position of leader of those
beneath him in the economic hierarchy, it drapes him with
the mantle of Hitler and gives to his decisions and com-
mands something of the finality and sanctity attending the
words and acts of Der Fuehrer himself. As in all autocratic
regimes, power descends from the top, while obedience and
discipline are the lot of the many.

In certain superficial respects the two dictatorships differ.
Whereas Mussolini once declared that Fascism was not a
commodity for export, being a peculiar manifestation of the
Italian spirit, Hitler and his associates from the beginning
have promoted an international movement and endeavored

to organize a worldwide front against "Communism," a label generally applied to any manifestation of liberalism or democracy. Also, while Mussolini called upon the Italian people to avenge the "humiliation of Versailles," his language was temperate in comparison with that of Hitler. "How could each one of these points (of the Treaty)," the latter shouted in *Mein Kampf*, "be burnt into the brain and feeling of the people for so long a time that in the end in 60,-000,000 heads, in men and women, the common feeling of shame and common hate would flare up into a single fiery sea of flames out of whose glow there would then arise a will hard as steel and a cry would be raised: We want arms again!" [7]

In Italian Fascism there is nothing comparable to Hitler's cruel, bitter, and sustained persecution of the Jews—the most barbarous attack upon any people recorded in the history of modern times.* Closely related to this item in his program is the new "racial science" which is made to pervade and color every aspect of life in the Third Reich. The nationalism of Mussolini, which is only an exaggeration of a general tendency of the past several centuries, is sharpened and perverted into the racialism of Hitler, a practical application of the teachings of Gobineau, Houston Stewart Chamberlain, Madison Grant, and Lothrop Stoddard—a doctrine which proclaims the measureless superiority of the Nordic over all other races and identifies the appearance of this people with the final realization of the purposes of creation—a doctrine which has been thoroughly discredited by the findings of contemporary anthropology. Wilhelm Stuckhart in his manual for history teachers thus summarizes this peculiar and terrifying aberration of the Nazi mind:

When taking account of German history, the pupil must begin to realise that the Third Empire, based on the immortal values of the Nordic race and rooted in the depths of the Ger-

* Since these words were written the views of anti-Semitism has spread to Italy.

man soul, constitutes the beginning of the fulfillment of a two thousand year-old German history and of the longing and striving of the best Germans of these two thousand years of German endeavor. It must become his unshakable conviction that this Third National Socialist Empire, constructed upon fundamental biological laws and embodied in the natural forms of German race and German character, at last re-establishes the purpose of creation, with which the coming into existence of the German people is linked.[8]

The collapse of democracy in Germany appears to be peculiarly puzzling, at least on the surface. It is true that the German people had enjoyed but a brief experience with free institutions. Throughout the recent period of their history they had lived under a limited autocracy and had been pretty thoroughly trained in the virtues and habits of obedience, discipline, and servility. Yet, as autocracies go, the Hohenzollerns with all of their swashbuckling and sense of destiny were unusually enlightened and humane. Their regime had led the world in the establishment of a comprehensive system of public schools, made of the German university a model to be copied in both hemispheres, formulated and propagated the ideal of "academic freedom," promoted the development of the arts and sciences in a measure unequaled elsewhere, made Germany the most dynamic and creative center of culture in Europe. Also under their rule the Reich became the home of socialist thought and of the most powerful labor movement to be found in any country.

It was this people that after an experiment of fifteen years abandoned democratic institutions practically without a struggle and assumed the yoke of an autocracy infinitely more rigorous, merciless, and oppressive than the one overthrown in 1918. Moreover, this people, the most literate of the great nations, elevated to the position of supreme authority a man possessing none of their finer qualities—a foreigner by birth and blood, ignorant, uncouth, demented. That he felt deeply, that he possessed some strange power over the masses, that he was a propagandist of unsurpassed gifts, that he was able to appraise social forces at home and abroad with uncanny precision—all of this must be admitted. And yet there remains something in the situation that seems utterly incongruous to a rational mind, perhaps because the mind of a large fraction of the German people at the time was itself irrational. Little wonder that trained and competent political observers scoffed at the idea that this Austrian housepainter would ever stand in the place of the Hohenzollerns. They scoffed until that day of complete triumph, August 1, 1934, when he stepped into the shoes of the old Field Marshal and proclaimed himself president of the Third Empire. And some of them still scoff, unwilling to believe what they see with their own eyes, even though the course of German policy since his ascension to power has followed with extraordinary fidelity the lines laid down in the ungrammatical paragraphs of *Mein Kampf*.

The rise of this man to the position of supreme ruler of Germany, however, is no miracle. While his personality, twisted by the unsatisfied longings of childhood and youth and by the unnatural exaltation of spirit aroused by the death struggle of the trenches, has undoubtedly given to the Third Reich a peculiarly savage and brutal aspect, National Socialism came because it was desired and nurtured by powerful elements in German society. That these elements might have preferred a finer vehicle for their purposes lies outside the main argument. They but chose from the possibilities that history offered them.

The fact is that Germany was in a revolutionary situation throughout the entire period from 1918 to 1933. At the close of the war the country passed through a deep economic and political crisis. Those revolutionary forces which had been gathering for almost a century came within the narrowest of margins of seizing power and transforming the entire social structure. They did take over the reins of government and write the Weimar constitution; but they left the economic system practically untouched, waiting, as they believed, for a more favorable moment. Thereafter, divided among themselves, they remained relatively helpless. The Social Democrats, the most numerous of the supporters of the republic, compromised again and again with the enemies of democracy, granted unnecessary concessions to the Junkers, refused to convert the army into a defender of free institutions, and courted the leaders of business, finance, and industry. At the same time they cooperated in the ruthless suppression of all movements on the left. Without attempting to assess praise and blame for the situation, it may be said that in Germany, as in Italy, the forces which were committed to the defense of the popular interest were so hopelessly divided that they practically opened the gates of the republic to the enemy.

In the meantime the economy showed increasing signs of decay. Although technological advance continued, the lot of great masses of the people failed to improve. At no time during the years following the war, except briefly in the late twenties, did the number of unemployed fall below the two million mark. The nation passed through the harrowing experience of inflation and deflation which bore most heavily on the middle classes. Then came the great depression with its interruption of production, paralysis of business, mass unemployment, and general insecurity. As the struggle over fundamental economic reform became more and more savage, the population began to drift into two extreme camps— the Communist Party and the Nationalist Party of Hugenberg. But the latter, though powerful from the standpoint of wealth and caste, could not expect to gain support among the broad masses of the people. Consequently, under the free operation of democratic institutions the prospect was ultimate victory by the left and the socialization of large enter-

prise. If the aristocracy was to save itself, heroic measures
had to be taken.

Up to this time Hitler, although his movement dates from
1919, had been unable to secure a mass following. Yet great
leaders of German finance and industry saw possibilities in
the man, his organization, and his program. Beginning in
1928 Hitler began to receive support from these moneyed
interests, and even from the Junkers. With this support he
was able to extend his operations, perfect a national organization, and enroll under his banners discontented and disillusioned members of other parties. Particularly did he address his appeal to the ex-soldiers who for a variety of reasons
were dissatisfied with their status under the Second Reich,
and to the middle classes who had suffered so severely from
the war and its aftermath, were feeling themselves ground
between the upper and nether millstones of capital and labor, and were vaguely longing for a political home of their
own. His poll in the elections now mounted rapidly from
810,000 in 1928, to 6,400,000 in 1930, and to 13,700,000 in
1932, the largest vote he ever received until he actually
achieved power and instituted the practice of the controlled
election. In January, 1933, he was invited to form a government; and shortly thereafter, with the connivance of von
Hindenberg and by perfectly "legal" methods, he destroyed
the republic and inaugurated the reign of the concentration
camp.

In his methods he followed closely the example set by
Mussolini. He gave careful attention to organization, he established military discipline, he armed his followers in the
measure possible, he created special combat detachments, he
provoked violent conflict with his opponents, he intimidated
courts and judges, he received the moral and material support of constituted authorities, he gradually took over the
police power of government. In his campaign for mass support he made the fullest use of symbols, converted political

stage setting into a fine art, employed stirring music and song, developed ritual and ceremony, organized parades and demonstrations, played upon the hopes and fears, the loves and hates, the ignorance and prejudices of his audiences. Utterly incapable of fundamental economic and social analysis, he strove to put the intellectual faculties to rest, to arouse emotional responses, and to generate blind and trusting loyalty to himself. He called his organization the National Socialist German Workers Party—*National* to trade upon the general sentiment of patriotism, *Socialist* to give promise of basic reform, *German* to capitalize upon the open and latent hostility toward other peoples, and *Workers* to break the solidarity of the proletariat—all a device calculated to catch the unwary of every class and to divert "the publick attention" from his real objects by "uttering patriotick words." Although at times he attacked "capitalism" and advocated "socialism," he refused to define either term.

In the early years of the movement, owing to the fact that some persons of ideas had been attracted to it, he did espouse some radical, even if contradictory, measures; but as he came to depend for financial support on the propertied classes he tended to concentrate his venom upon Marxism and the Treaty of Versailles, and upon the Jews as the authors of both. Toward the success of this campaign the champions of the "dictatorship of the proletariat," by their open advocacy of violence and their faith in economic predestinarianism, contributed much. Pointing to their doctrines and certain of their acts, Hitler was able to convince many that he stood for "law and order" and the eternal values. Also those elderly gentlemen who sat in the Hall of Mirrors in 1919 and re-drew the map of Europe and the world placed in his hands an inexhaustible supply of ammunition for use in his "battle"—those self-styled realists who had neither the courage to destroy the German people nor the humanity to make peace with them. The Jews, being a small and helpless minority, were made the scapegoat for these two particular ills and consequently for all the misery the country had suffered. By a process of intellectual legerdemain the enemies of the working classes, here as in Italy, were made to wear the garb of foreign nations, whether they lived within or outside the Reich. Thus were the revolutionary energies of the people deflected from economic reform and harnessed to the construction of what may prove to be the most powerful military machine of modern times. And German democracy was a casualty of the second economic depression since the war.

Spain

The full meaning of recent events in Spain cannot be known today. The civil war now raging must come to some conclusion, and some settlement covering the interests of the great powers involved must be reached before the friends of democracy can draw all the lessons which those events hold. At present altogether too little is known regarding the origins of the struggle to enable anyone to speak with complete confidence regarding its significance. Yet sufficient is already in the record to make possible the perception of a pattern not unlike that followed by the rise of Italian Fascism and German National Socialism.

On July 17, 1936, what appeared to be a military revolt under the leadership of high army officials broke out in Spain. Beginning with the Foreign Legion in Morocco, led by General Franco, the uprising spread rapidly, as if according to plan, to garrisons stationed in the Belearic Islands and on the European mainland. When the first smoke of battle had cleared away it was found that almost the entire army and half the fleet had joined the rebellion, only the small air force and portions of the police remaining loyal. With practically all the arsenals and arms of the country in their hands, the rebel commanders began a concerted assault upon the government to which they had sworn loyalty, with every prospect of a short struggle and a speedy victory. An unarmed people, lacking military experience and knowledge, however brave and determined, could not expect to overcome such heavy odds.

From beyond the borders, moreover, the Spanish people received but little immediate help. Although the Soviet Union championed the cause of the government at all times, it was far away and absorbed in its own tasks and problems. On the other hand, the revolt had the moral support of the two great fascist powers from the first and material support from the moment such support seemed necessary for victory. The heads of the governments of these powers have stated repeatedly that the rebels must and would win, that they would not tolerate a loyalist victory. Whether Italy and Germany were motivated by a desire to encircle France, to weaken the British Empire, to possess the rich mineral resources of Spain, to prevent the spread of democracy in the world, or to achieve several or all of these purposes is not known with certainty. The reasons proclaimed are the same as those given by Theodore Dwight in his attack upon the republicanism of the Jeffersonian era: the protection of the home, the guarding of religion, the preservation of civilization, and the destruction of Bolshevism—the twentieth century version of Jacobinism.

The democracies of the world for the most part passed by on the other side. Indeed they helped to tie the hands of the victim so that the thieves might rob him the more easily. Having no clearly defined policy and fearing above all a general European conflagration, they proposed the plan of non-intervention under which the legal Spanish government was denied a right guaranteed in international law—the right as a legitimate goverment opposing an insurrection of access to the markets of the world for the purchase of the muni-

tions of war. In this case the denial of the right was peculiarly critical because a relatively unarmed people, entitled
to purchase arms abroad, was beset by its own armed forces.
But the explanation of the behavior of the democracies is
not to be found wholly in their lack of policy and their fear
of war. Each of them harbored powerful elements, the Roman Catholic Church and the modern aristocracy of "paper
and patronage," which did not really believe in popular rule,
which placed their privileges above any loyalty to democracy,
which actually desired Franco to win in Spain. The British
ruling class, apparently in considerable numbers, was even
prepared to risk imperial prestige and interests rather than
encourage the threat to property rights which seemed implicit in a victory by the Spanish government.

This brings the analysis to the factors underlying the rebellion. Were the soldiers of the regular army poorly paid
that they should turn against their own government? Were
the officers overworked or badly treated? On the contrary,
the soldiers, particularly the Foreign Legion, which formed
the backbone of the rebel forces in the early days and weeks
of the war, had just been well paid. And the officers formed a
specially privileged class, maintaining numerically the highest ratio to soldiers to be found in any army in Europe.
Obviously the army was but a tool in the hands of the clerical and secular aristocracy of Spain whose members feared
the temper of the rising democracy. Or rather, it should be
said, the military caste constituted an integral part of that
aristocracy and was thus concerned primarily in defending
its own position and vested rights. In a struggle which had
grown increasingly bitter since the World War, involving
the dictatorship of Primo de Rivera established in 1923, the
launching of the republican regime in 1931, the reaction of
1933, and the victory of the "popular front" at the polls in
February, 1936, the issue between left and right became
drawn and the people moved to revoke the long-established

privileges of landlord, army, and Church, and to clip the wings of the rising aristocracy of trade, industry, and finance. Here, as in Italy and Germany, the democracy threatened the rights of property, but with the final outcome as yet undetermined. Under such circumstances it is not surprising that even in America the civil war in Spain has been viewed with mixed feelings.

Yet for the friends of democracy the events in Spain have a positive meaning that should not be overlooked. They show how essential it is that the forces of democracy, in a country with democratic political institutions, move ahead by making full use of those institutions. The Spanish people made one grave, perhaps a fatal, mistake: they failed to take precautions to insure the loyalty of the armed forces of the nation. While, because of this mistake, they have not yet demonstrated the possibility of achieving basic economic reform through the ballot, they have demonstrated pretty clearly the futility of employing any other method. If the forces of democracy in Spain had been outside the law, if they had not been the legally constituted authority, if they had taken the initiative in drawing the sword, in the world as it is constituted today they would have been crushed immediately and completely. It is only the fact that they were the duly elected government that has enabled them to carry on a heroic struggle through the long months. They may go down to defeat; but if they do, they will be vanquished by the armed forces of international fascism.

The Record of Democracy Abroad

The record of political democracy abroad, where it has been put to the supreme test by the forces of revolution, is not reassuring. In Russia, to be sure, the expected happened. But, while the overthrow of an ancient despotism and the ensuing period of internal struggle are in accordance with

the lessons of history, and while the course of the dictatorship has tended to belie its professions of democracy and to
discredit the method of violence in the advancement of popular causes, they cast little illumination on the question of
the efficacy and vitality of democratic government. The developments in Italy, Germany, and Spain, on the other hand,
may be freighted with considerable significance for the
American people. Although the experience of the peoples of
these countries with free institutions had been partial and
relatively brief, the fact cannot be glossed over that the Italians and Germans abandoned a measure of political freedom
for dictatorship. Whether the Spaniards will follow the same
course is being decided now on the battlefields of the Iberian
peninsula and in the chancellories of Europe.

The pattern of events which precipitated the crisis of
political democracy seems to have been roughly similar in
the three countries. As the people threatened to transform
the social structure and achieve control over economic power,
the privileged orders turned to the sword and dictatorship
to protect their interests. In each case the devotion of the
aristocracy to the democratic process was unsubstantial and
entirely secondary to the maintenance of its dominant
status in society. Propertied classes may be expected to
surrender anything but their property. It is not without significance, moreover, that the American aristocracy of the
seventeen-nineties pursued a not dissimilar course in the
face of the rising democracy of Jefferson. Terrified by the
movement of the people toward political power, its members
resorted to a succession of measures which fell short of counter-revolution and the overthrow of the constitution only
by the breadth of a hair. Possibly the knowledge that practically every farmer possessed a squirrel rifle and knew how
to use it deterred them from precipitate action.

In each of the three countries under consideration the
stage for the emergence of a dictatorship of the right was

prepared by the extreme elements of the left. The latter, being enslaved by a body of rigid revolutionary dogma, lost their powers of original social analysis and forced all capitalistic societies into the Procrustean bed of an ossified Marxism. Being incapable of distinguishing between the despotism of the Tsar and the liberalism of the Weimar Republic, between the general cultural backwardness of the Slav and the high cultural level of the Teuton, the extremists in Germany endeavored to impose upon Berlin a pattern fashioned in Moscow. They preached the dictatorship of the proletariat in a country possessing a numerous and powerful middle class; they advocated profound modifications in the family and the destruction of the church in a land where both of these institutions were vital and strong; they proclaimed the totalitarian revolution among a people proud of their traditions and achievements. Also having sung, with the monotony of a Greek chorus, of the inevitability of violence, having taken every occasion to flaunt their potential military strength in the face of their enemies, and having actually resorted to force from time to time in the gaining of ends, they closed every door to the peaceful solution of the social problem and, in accordance with their own dialectical principle, created the conditions which almost of a certainty would generate a counter-revolutionary movement. And in order that this movement might be crowned with success they insured for it mass support by a gross disregard, if not a calculated irritation, of the sensibilities of the middle classes. With the forces of democracy not only divided but even in bitter opposition, the rise of a dictator of some kind was to be expected. In Italy and Spain these same factors were present in some degree.

Perhaps the most alarming feature of the contemporary dictatorships, from the standpoint of the future of democracy, is their popular character. While it is impossible in the nature of the case to know the extent of their support among the people, no one should make the mistake of assuming that the masses of the population are being held in subjection wholly by the machine gun. Unquestionably each of the two great fascist dictators enjoys not only widespread popularity but also the deep loyalty and devotion of millions. This is apparently due to the fact that in a period of economic, political, and moral breakdown, with a feeling of insecurity pervading all classes, these men provided leadership and promised reform. By professing to defend traditional values associated with home, religion, nation, and race they created the comfortable delusion that the future could be reached by retreating into the past and by engaging in foreign adventure. To the standards of such doctrine multitudes can be rallied in any society during periods of general distress. Since the rational processes, upon which democracy depends, are overcome by fear, programs shot through with deep and irreconcilable contradictions may be widely accepted and hailed as roads to salvation. It is not impossible that the American people might be led into the camp of dictatorship flying the flag of democracy.

REFERENCES

1. William Seymour Edwards, *Through Scandinavia to Moscow* (Cincinnati, 1906), 152-154.

2. Quoted in H. W. Schneider, *Making the Fascist State* (New York, 1928), 342.

3. Volt, *Programme della destra fascista*, 154-5. Quoted in *ibid.*, 239.

4. "Fascismo," in *Enciclopedia Italiana* (Milan, 1932), XIV, 850.

5. Emilio de Bono, *La Preparazione E Le Prime Operazioni* (Rome, 1937), 80.

6. Gaetano Salvemini, *Under the Axe of Fascism* (New York, 1936), 3.

7. Adolf Hitler, *Mein Kampf* (Eleventh edition, Munich, 1932), 715.

8. Wilhelm Stuckart, *Geschichte im Geschichtsunterricht* (Frankfurt, 1934), 48.

CHAPTER 8.

A PROGRAM FOR DEMOCRACY

In some form and under some auspices fundamental economic changes are coming in America. This much is clear. The advance of technology has rendered old conceptions and practices obsolete. The failures of the inherited economic system are so manifest and so widely recognized in both conservative and progressive circles that the indefinite maintenance of the *status quo* lies outside the realm of practical considerations. Indeed, the situation is already so fluid that even the definition of a *status quo* to be preserved is quite impossible. In the fascist nations, where reactionary forces have achieved for the moment undisputed control of the state, the economy has been greatly changed. But wherever reform has been carried far, with the possible exception of the Scandinavian countries where the problem is greatly simplified by factors of geography, population, and tradition, attempts to attack the problem fundamentally have been accompanied by a suspension of democratic processes.

In Russia, to be sure, democratic methods had never existed. There the revolutions of the last three centuries—religious, political, and economic—were all rolled into one. Consequently, from that country little can be learned regarding the potentialities of political democracy to grapple with and subdue economic power. Italy and Germany, though differing greatly from the United States in many fundamental respects, present instances of the actual abandonment of popular government. While neither had enjoyed a long and successful experience with democratic institutions, the peoples of both countries surrendered what appear to be precious rights almost without a struggle. In the case of the Germans this was peculiarly alarming because of their exceptionally high level of cultural development and their brilliant and sustained achievements in the sphere of economic, political, and social thought. The war and the grievous injustices of the peace treaties, the widespread feelings of national humiliation, and the extraordinary severity of the accompanying economic distress, undoubtedly created a situation ideal for the practice of the arts of demagogy. But even so, the course of events in these countries reveals how fragile are the foundations of political democracy. When the privileges of the economic aristocracy were seriously threatened and the masses of the people experienced a condition of great economic insecurity, those foundations crumbled and dissolved. And the developments in Spain, though this people has resisted the return of autocracy with heroism and valor, give to the friends of democracy little reason for optimism.

That Germany or Italy, or any European country for that matter, should provide the pattern for the United States to follow is certainly contrary to the convictions cherished by the American people throughout their history. The peculiar character of their heritage and circumstances, as will be pointed out in detail later, gives grounds for the hope that they may follow a different course; that they may succeed in achieving the needed economic reforms under democratic auspices, by democratic methods, and toward democratic ends; that they may fashion an economy of the people, by the people, and for the people. Their victories under Jefferson and Jackson, gained without resort to organized violence, should give them courage and guidance. Also the spectacle of tyranny in those European countries that have abandoned democratic methods and resorted to dictatorship may arouse them to a full appreciation of the worth of political liberty and of the dangers inhering in autocracy. The spectacle of persecution, madness, and tyranny across the Atlantic may cause them to hesitate to abandon rights which were won with the blood of their fathers and which, once surrendered, can be regained only with the blood of their children.

There are no grounds, however, for complacency. In 1800 the American people skirted close to the rocks of counter-revolutionary intrigue and violence; and in 1860 they abandoned legislative halls for the battlefield. If democracy is to be preserved and developed, it will be because the friends of democracy find and practice wisdom—because they find and practice this cardinal virtue while it may still avail. The necessity for haste is imperative; time may prove to be the essence of the matter. The social situation may mature more rapidly than the mind and temper of the nation; the ultimate crisis in democracy may arrive before the population is prepared to meet it successfully. Also the American people must act before they have lost the power to act, before they have lost their democratic spirit under the molding influence of a modern form of feudalism. All of this means that without procrastination they should develop a program based upon the experience of their own past and a critical study of recent events in Europe, designed to preserve democratic values and to make the institutions of political democracy function effectively in the overthrow of that modern aristocracy of trade, industry, and finance which now rules the economy, reaches out increasingly to control the life and thought of the country, and constitutes the only genuine threat to the indefinite perpetuation of free institutions in the United States.

Regarding the content of any program devoted to the purpose of making political democracy work in the present critical age, there doubtless would be considerable disagreement among informed and thoughtful persons. The following nine-point program, however, constitutes an irreducible minimum to which few friends of free institutions could take serious exception; first, the professed friends of democracy must have faith in political democracy; second, the ordinary citizen must obtain the knowledge necessary for a free man; third, the masses of the people must be organized as completely as possible; fourth, government must carry out popular mandates quickly and honestly; fifth, government must maintain a complete monopoly of the military and police power; sixth, civil liberties must be guaranteed to the entire population without fear or favor; seventh, all major campaigns of propaganda must be systematically and thoroughly exposed; eighth, the temper of the democratic process must be conserved and strengthened; and ninth, war must be avoided.

Faith in Political Democracy

Clearly, if the object of the program is to make political democracy work, the most basic and crucial of the nine points is faith in political democracy. Without faith on the part of its supporters, champions, and beneficiaries, no social system can long survive. If an autocrat must believe in autocracy and an aristocrat must believe in aristocracy, so that either order of society may endure, how much more imperative is it that a democrat believe in democracy. Without faith the indispensable orientation and attitude of mind are lacking. If the masses of the American people do not believe profoundly in the potentialities of political democracy, the will to employ and rely upon orderly processes for the settlement of differences and for effecting social changes is paralyzed. If deep in their hearts they harbor doubts and reservations, they will withhold their energies and cripple those processes. Moreover, they will be incapable of testing and releasing the full power of political democracy. Indeed, in such an event they will be a party to the failure of popular rule and the inauguration of dictatorship, should free institutions collapse. Certainly, practical abstention from and even sabotage of the political process by popular groups and parties in both Italy and Germany contributed to the downfall of democracies in those countries.

Friends of democratic political procedure, therefore, whether they stand with the left or the right on the economic or any other issue, should cease playing with the idea of ultimate resort to violence and throw their energies and talents without reserve into the task of upholding democratic methods. They should be prepared to put their loyalty to the process and the general welfare above attachment to any measure or factional interest. Equally they should steadfastly refuse to sit on the side-lines of the social conflict, pedantically debating with one another the efficacy of orderly procedures and pusilanimously awaiting the decision of this issue before committing themselves to the democratic method. The citizen, whatever his motive, who assumes the role of the impartial observer and confines his civic activity to an objective survey of the course of politics, automatically disfranchises himself and becomes a cipher in the current struggle of democracy.

All of this does not mean that these friends of political democracy should bury their heads in the sands, ignore the realities in the social situation, and cultivate a blind optimism to the effect that peaceful methods are certain to prevail. On the contrary they should endeavor to catalog all the hazards above and below the horizon and assess fully and honestly the resources of the adversary, but not for the purpose of deciding when to surrender. A military commander who overestimated his own strength, failed to take precautions against surprise, and neglected to obtain the most detailed and accurate information possible regarding the numbers, armament, and disposition of the enemy would be subject to court-martial and dishonor. Victory in the political struggle, no less than on the field of Mars, depends on accurate, precise, and generally trustworthy knowledge of opposing forces. In either case, the strategist employs his intelligence service, not for the purpose of defining the terms of capitulation, but rather in order to develop a rational plan of action.

Knowledge Necessary for a Free Man

As suggested in the preceding paragraph, faith without knowledge is crippled. While it is true that knowledge cannot avail everything, it is equally true that *ignorance can avail nothing*. A fundamental postulate of the democratic process is an enlightened people. If this is impossible of reasonable attainment, as many profess to believe today, then the entire structure of free institutions must crash to the earth. Without knowledge a people can be herded like a flock of sheep into the fold for shearing or into the abattoir for slaughter. Without knowledge men cannot even know their own interests or recognize their own friends; without knowledge they can be persuaded to shoot and hang their own brothers, to dig their own graves. And all of these things they will do to the tune of sacred music, with such a swelling of the heart, a sense of chastity, and an exaltation of the spirit as moved the knights of King Arthur's court in their quest of the Holy Grail. For knowledge, adequate, precise, and relevant, there can be no substitute.

The dependence of free institutions on popular enlightenment has been recognized by all the great leaders of American democracy from Washington to Franklin D. Roosevelt. But few have seen this relationship more clearly than did a humble New England farmer at the close of the eighteenth century. This man, William Manning by name, completed a manuscript in 1798 entitled *The Key of Libberty* in which he endeavored to show "the Causes why a free government has Always Failed, and a Remidy against it." The document is addressed to "all the Republicans, Farmers, Mecanicks, and Labourers In Amarica" whose "Canded attention is Requested to the Sentiments of a Labourer." In his opening paragraph the author confesses his limitations for undertaking such a task: "I am not a Man of Larning my selfe for I neaver had the advantage of six months schooling in my life. I am no travelor for I neaver was 50 Miles from whare I was born in no direction, & I am no grate reader of antiant history for I always followed hard labour for a living." [1] Although his grammar was bad and his spelling worse, William Manning knew his way about in the difficult field of social dynamics. After giving "A General Description of the Causes that Ruen Republicks," with particular attention to the "Combinations of the few," he concludes that "Learning & Knowledg is assential to the preservation of Libberty & unless we have more of it amongue us we Cannot Seporte our Libertyes Long." He then proceeds to outline the "Knowledge nesecary for a freeman":

The Knowledge nesecary for every freeman to have is A Knowledge of Mankind—A Knowledge of the differend interest that influence all ordirs of men—A Knowledge of the prinsaples of the government & Constitution he lives under—A Knowledge of all the laws that immediately consarnes his conduct & interests—A knowledge that when laws are once constitutially made, they must be obayed, let them be neaver so rong in his mind, and that their is no remidy for greevences but by petitioning the authority that made them & useing his Right in Elections— A knowledge of the true prinsaples, carictor & abilityes of all those he votes for into any kind of office—A knowledge of the existing sentiments wishes & circumstances, of all those of his interest in the town, county, State or Nation to which he belongs, so that he may unite in the choice of the ablest & best men to take care of & defend their interests. Also Unite in petitioning for redress of grevances. Also a knowledge of the moste interesting debates in the Legeslature & the side his own Representitive takes in the desition. He aught to have all this knowledge independant of any ordirs of men, or individuals who may be interested to deceive or misleed him. [2]

It was clear to Manning, as it must be clear to all who are not caught in the academic treadmill, that knowledge, if it is to be politically effective, must be selected and organized in terms of interest, must be relevant to the purposes postulated. He did not believe that free government could be preserved by the general and indiscriminate dissemination of knowledge. On the contrary, he insisted that there were certain special bodies of knowledge which free men should have, if they are to safeguard their freedom successfully. By implication there are other bodies of knowledge which are relatively irrelevant to the task. This does not mean that history and sociology are to be falsified or distorted. To do either would result in harnessing the individual to the purposes of another. But it does mean that in contemporary society the interests of different "ordirs of men" may not be the same and that the "many," composed of "Republicans, Farmers, Mechanicks, & Labourers," must be supplied with those bodies of knowledge which will set *them* free and enable *them* to protect *their* interests. If the schools of the country could give to the rising generation the insight possessed by this untutored Massachusetts farmer, even including with it his grammar and spelling, the future of free government in America would be assured.

How the knowledge necessary for a free man is to be made available is of course a major problem. That the public schools have a heavy responsibility here is self-evident, but the development of this part of the analysis is reserved for later chapters. Here it must suffice to emphasize the urgency of a nationwide program of adult education designed to enroll a large fraction of the population, to make accessible knowledge of the contemporary world, to stimulate the freest and fullest discussion of all the problems and tasks pertaining to the operation of American democracy, and to supply the detailed information requisite to the making of intelligent decisions and choices regarding persons, measures, and programs. Commissioner John W. Studebaker has perhaps seen the need as clearly and stated it as forcefully as anyone of the present generation. He has also conducted practical demonstrations and outlined a comprehensive program which all friends of free institutions should support.[3]

As important and indispensable as government action is, however, complete reliance should by no means be placed upon it. Until the people are sure that they control the government, a condition that does not exist today, they must depend to a large extent on their own efforts. Even then they must take every precaution to insure the integrity of the sources of their opinions, to maintain the highest possible measure of independence from "any ordirs of men, or individuals who may be interested to deceive or misleed" them. The only safe and adequate solution of the problem, according to Manning, is to be found in organization. "As this knowledge cant be obtained," he concluded, "without the expence of a continued sereies of publications that can be red with confidence as to their truth, and as newspaper knowledg is ruened by the few . . . I propose a Sociaty of Labourers." The society would "be composed of all the Republicans & Labourers in the United States who will be at the expense of obtaining the above described Knowledg,"[4] and would provide a "Magazein" which could be read and trusted by the many because it would be under their control and devoted to their interests. This horny-handed farmer, moreover, who had "always followed hard labour for a living" and who had never been fifty miles from where he "was born in no direction" envisaged his organization of working people extending beyond the boundaries of nations. "And I have often had it impressed on my mind," he wrote, "that in some such way as this Society might be organised throughout the world as well as government, & by sotial corraspondance & mutual consestions all differences might be settled, so that wars might be bannished from the

Earth." [5] If the existing powerful organizations of laborers and farmers would listen to the advice of this eighteenth century tiller of the soil and devote a larger portion of their energies to the dissemination of knowledge necessary for a free man, they would contribute mightily to the advancement of the cause of democracy.

Organization of the Many

The masses of the people must be organized as completely as possible, not only for the purpose of promoting their own enlightenment, but also for the immediate defense of popular interests and rights and for the formulation of far-reaching policies and programs. In view of the concentration of economic power in the hands of a small minority of the population and the combination of this minority in chambers of commerce, associations of manufacturers, and bankers' associations, the democratic elements, if their efforts are not to be dispersed and rendered ineffective, must unite their forces and secure concerted action. This was found necessary in the great battles for democracy at the end of the eighteenth century. In the seventeen-nineties, as already noted, democratic clubs sprang up all over the country from Georgia to Massachusetts and took an active part in the struggle for the triumph of republican principles. The fact that the aristocracy of that time feared them and sought to destroy them is perfect testimony to their worth. The many can oppose the few successfully only if they make full use of their numbers.

The natural and most basic pattern of popular organization in contemporary society follows the lines of production. Already this type of combination either in its industrial or craft form is well advanced through labor unions, farmer organizations, and numerous bodies of technical and professional workers. The experience of both Europe and America

demonstrates fully that these organizations, and particularly
the unions of manual workers, are the democratic clubs of
the present day, the defenders of popular rights, the foes of
aristocracy, the most powerful bulwark against the resurgence of autocracy. Moreover, in the current age of large-
scale economic operations and separation of the workman
from the tools of production the individual can gain that security necessary for a free man only through association and
combination with his fellows. But the movement toward organization, though growing rapidly and greatly stimulated
by the policies of the Roosevelt administration, is still in its
beginnings and should be pushed until it embraces not only
the great majority of the laboring and farming population,
but also a large proportion of the clerical, technical, and professional people. All those whose position in society is dependent primarily upon the labor they perform, whether
factory operatives, longshoremen, independent artisans, freehold farmers, stenographers, journalists, teachers, engineers,
physicians, or even small business men, should organize and
bring their combined strength to the task of promoting and
advancing the cause of democracy. Certain of these elements,
because of tradition, association, snobbery, or calculated self-
interest, will doubtless continue to serve the aristocracy; but
their numbers, once the issue is clear, should be smaller in
America than in any country of the Old World.

While the organizations of producers may be expected to
manifest the highest degree of solidarity and militancy, the
people should also combine as consumers according to the
Rochdale plan. How effectively the cooperative movement
may contribute to the campaign to break up the great con-
centrations of economic power in America is uncertain. It
is only well launched on this side of the Atlantic; but its
achievements in the Scandinavian countries suggest that it
might become a powerful arm of democracy. In its ideals it
represents the cooperative commonwealth toward which the

prophets of mankind have aspired and struggled through the ages. As it grows it weans its members from the law of the jungle, spreads more humane values through the culture, and provides a training ground for leadership and technical talent devoted to the promotion of social ends. Finally, because of its general appeal to consumers regardless of occupational affiliation, it softens the acerbities of the class struggle and provides an opportunity for members of the aristocracy possessing a social conscience to participate in the reconstruction of the economy.

The organization of the people should also assume a political form. It has been apparent for at least a generation that the major opposing parties in the United States bear little relation to the realities of American life, that those parties at best are the instruments of conflicting factions of the aristocracy, that from the standpoint of the many the recurrent political campaigns with their unsurpassed fanfare and ballyhoo are essentially sham battles. There is reason for believing, however, that the old lines, formed by issues long since dead, are disintegrating and that a new alignment of forces is on the way. The natural and necessary foundations for a true party of democracy in the age of industrialism, a party representative of and sensitive to the interests of the great majority of the people, are the occupational and co-operative organizations now developing. If a new aristocracy has emerged, a fact which is patent to anyone who cares to use his eyes, it can be successfully opposed only by the most powerful possible combination of the democratic forces of the country. This is the simplest of political maxims. If free institutions are to be preserved and employed in social reform, the people must capture the state.

The point cannot be too strongly emphasized that the organization of the people, as producers, consumers, and citizens, should be promoted on the broadest possible basis. No one of the major occupational categories embraces a suffi-

cient number of members to achieve power by democratic
methods. The most numerous of them, the industrial wage-
earners, included in 1930 but 37.9 per cent of the total gainfully employed. This group does indeed constitute a large
proportion of the population, but it could scarcely hope by
itself to rebuild the economic foundations of democracy,
particularly since it could never organize its entire membership. Moreover, due to the growing mechanization of production, its relative strength actually decreased four and
one-half per cent during the decade from 1920 to 1930, to
reach a position slightly below that occupied in 1910. Since
the introduction of automatic machinery can be said only
to be well begun, the representation of industrial wage-
earners in the population may be expected to decline further
in the years ahead. If, according to Sogge, a value of 100 is
assigned to each of his occupational groups in 1870, it is evident that the professional service and lower salaried workers
have been increasing most rapidly, and much more rapidly
than the manual workers of industry. For the professional
service the figure rises more or less steadily to 239 in 1930,
and for lower salaried employees to 584; while in the case of
industrial wage-earners it advances to 159 in 1920 and re-
cedes to 142 in 1930. Only if the object is to seize power by
force and establish a dictatorship through a relatively small
disciplined group can the appeal be addressed to the so-
called proletariat.[6] Certainly the success of the democratic
method demands a broad popular base.

The objection that will be raised to the foregoing proposals for the organization of the people, indeed the objection that has been raised to it, is that it arrays class against
class and destroys the unity of the nation. But this should
arouse anxiety in no real friend of democracy. It is the ancient bogey that has been invoked by every aristocracy when
threatened by a popular uprising; it is the time-worn watch-
word that has been employed by the few to damn every for-

ward step by the many. It was raised in horrendous tones by Theodore Dwight and his companions in politics in an effort to destroy the movement that eventually brought political democracy to the United States; it was raised by the American Liberty League, one of the most class conscious bodies ever to appear in the country since the days of Federalist rule, in its attacks on the Roosevelt administration in 1936; it is raised today by every spokesman of privilege whenever anyone proposes to bring economic power under popular control or even to ameliorate somewhat the present great disparities of income and fortune. To the informed, the cry from the friends of aristocracy that class antagonisms are being aroused is perhaps one of the surest indications that democracy is really on the march. William Manning, anticipating the response of the privileged "ordirs" to his proposal for the establishment of a "Society of Labourers," disposes of their criticism in a manner that would be wholly fitting today:

As all new things make a grate stir at first, so it may be expected this will, & many objicttions raised against it. The ordirs of the few may denounce it as daingerous to Government. But if all the powers of Hell should rise up & assume the wisdom & grateness of Angels & try to overthrow it they aught not to be heard to nor minded, for it is perfectly Constitutianal, & what all the ordirs of the few have practised upon (as I have before shewen) & their oposition to it arises holly from selfeish vues. Therefore I will not say much on this objection.[7]

There should of course be no desire on the part of the champions of democracy to arouse sharp antagonisms among the various elements composing American society. Without indulging in vapid sentimentality, the friends of democracy should devote their energies to the positive reconstruction of the economy in terms of the long-time interests of all rather to the satisfaction of a vengeful spirit or the enforcement of the barbaric *lex talionis*. The appeal to hatred is always a dangerous expedient and should never be undertaken lightly, lest it release destructive forces which may pass beyond the bounds of peaceful procedure. All who have been nurtured on the great humanistic tradition out of which modern democracy springs can only lament that inhumanity of man which has so frequently blackened the pages of history. But as long as society contains within itself the seeds of class war—privation, misery, insecurity, injustice, denial of opportunity, and autocratic rule in government or economy —just so long will those bitter struggles recur which give to the face of civilized man the grim and brutal visage of the savage. Those who would outlaw the rule of force will band together to bring into the service of all that fabulous power which modern technology has given the world.

In this struggle for democracy, for such it is, individuals will be drawn from all ranks of society, even from the aristocracy. Enlightened and humane offspring of caste and privilege have in all ages devoted their talents and their fortunes to the cause of popular liberation. And in contemporary America, for reasons to be presented later, the number of such men and women should be greater than elsewhere and in other times. Yet the fact remains that an aristocracy as a class has never voluntarily surrendered power and privilege. The major appeal, therefore, as Abraham Bishop clearly saw, must be directed to the masses of the people—to "weak men and fools" whose self-interest, as well as humane sentiments and loyalties, can be counted upon to motivate and sustain action. If the few continue to oppose the general welfare, as they doubtless will, then by supporting the interests of a portion against the interests of the whole they must bear the onus of introducing the struggle of classes into American life.

The chief danger in the situation lies in the possible and even probable division of the democratic forces. "Divide and conquer" is a principle of warfare that has been employed from the beginning of time, not only by military commanders, but also by oligarchies and tyrants in their efforts to achieve and to hold power. It is being used today in America. If the people were united, nothing could halt their attack upon the economic problem. This the aristocracy realizes full well and strives constantly to introduce divisions into the ranks of the many by raising false issues and by turning against the people those fine humane sentiments which the great majority possess and cherish. And in this process of obfuscation it is aided by the personal ambitions and rivalries of popular leaders and the tendency toward sectarianism and the servitude of orthodoxy which appear in all mass political movements. It was one of the tragedies of the Italian, German, and Spanish democracies that in the face of the rising threat of dictatorship persons and organizations professing the same ideals were unable to compose their differences and present a common front to the common enemy. It is one of the tragedies of American democracy today that the ranks of organized labor are split to the bottom by the failure of an old leadership to adapt itself to changed conditions and to take advantage of a heaven-sent opportunity to erect an insuperable barrier against the advance of fascism. Equally tragic are the lines which divide farmers from urban dwellers, manual from "white-collared" workers. Men sometimes seem to be driven by a strange perversity to hate their closest friends more ardently and steadfastly than their most dangerous enemies. If democracy is to survive, this must not be permitted to occur in America.

Efficient Execution of Popular Mandates

Government must carry out the mandates of the people quickly, efficiently, and honestly. The surest way to discredit any government is to render it impotent in times of crisis when action is required and the people are aroused. And this is particularly true of democratic government because of its dependence on popular sentiment. If elections won at the polls are lost in the machinery of government, if the will of the people is frustrated by checks and balances, by inefficiency in administration, by cowardice or dishonesty in leadership, popular faith in free institutions will be destroyed. Then the opportunity of the irresponsible demagogue appears and the road to dictatorship is laid open. This is one lesson that the experience of post-war Europe teaches unequivocally. Before democracy crashed in both Italy and Germany large elements had already shifted their loyalties and had accepted the judgment that parliaments are merely debating societies, incapable of upholding the interests of the nation. Where democratic institutions have been forsaken without a struggle, they first proved themselves to the satisfaction of multitudes unable to relieve distress, introduce needed reforms, and provide honest, effective, and enlightened leadership.

The essential soundness of this position is amply demonstrated by the response of democratic peoples throughout the world to the early years of Franklin D. Roosevelt's first administration. The courage and despatch with which he met the economic and political crisis, even though some of his measures were patently inadequate or badly conceived, gave courage to the friends of popular government everywhere. It began to appear that a political democracy need not suffer from a state of perpetual paralysis. But as the depression receded and the "aristocracy of paper and patronage" recovered from fright, a campaign of abuse, misrepresentation, and sabotage was launched against the President and his administration which succeeded in halting almost his entire program of reform. This campaign succeeded, moreover, immediately after he had received the greatest popular endorsement since the election of James Monroe in 1820. The special session of the Seventy-fifth Congress which he called to deal with emergencies in both domestic and international affairs met, deliberated, and adjourned without having passed a single important measure. Its total achievement embraced the appropriation of $225,000 for the traveling expenses of Congressmen, the authorization of the loan of four paintings to the Constitutional Sesquicentennial Commission, a minor amendment to the Co-operative Credit Union Act, the appropriation of $12,000 for the payment of the Congressional page boys, and the authorization of a time extension for the completion of a bridge over the Tennessee River. And the succeeding regular session of the same Congress was reduced to a condition of suspended animation for a month by a minority engaged in a filibuster against the passage of the anti-lynching bill. Those who led the attack upon the President and his program pretended to be defending the "American system of government." Anyone who has followed the course of democracy in Europe knows that they struck a deadly blow at the perpetuation of free institutions on this continent. An election won overwhelmingly at the polls was lost in the machinery of government. Prospective dictators could ask no more.

If the American people would save democracy, they must learn to distinguish clearly between dictatorship and efficient government. The two are by no means identical, as the friends of aristocracy would have the electorate believe. On this point there seems to be much confusion in the public mind. At any rate the charges of dictatorship which have been constantly hurled at the President, because of his attempts to make the federal government efficient and sensitive to the popular will, either reflect confusion or are calculated to create confusion. Whether those making the charges are lacking in political knowledge or are engaged in deliberate misrepresentation, the problem remains much the same. In either event, vast numbers of citizens, genuine friends of democracy, have apparently become convinced that the President is pursuing the model of a European dictator. This of course is utter nonsense. And one does not have to dwell long in a land of tyrannical rule in order to detect the falsehood of such charges—charges which contain about as much truth as the accusation of Theodore Dwight that the ultimate object of the advance of political democracy under Jefferson was "to destroy every trace of civilization in the world and to force mankind back into a savage state." The essence of dictatorship is the suspension of civil liberties and rule by police power. Of this Franklin D. Roosevelt has shown not the slightest trace. In fact he has been far less guilty here than many of his predecessors.

Competent government is necessary in these times, partly because of the social crisis and partly because of the increasing burdens which have been placed upon public agencies. The latter constitutes a long-time trend that reaches back a hundred years and represents a response to the advance of industrial civilization. Moreover, owing to the increasing integration of American life and economy, the major problems of the age are national in scope and cannot be confined or solved within state boundaries. This accounts for the fact that the attention of the citizens is being shifted more and more from locality and state to the nation. It is therefore peculiarly necessary that the federal government be efficient and capable. Such a condition is likely to continue until some new pattern of decentralization, based not on geography but on the functional divisions of the economy and congenial to the structure and spirit of a closely integrated society, is developed. In the meantime and in contrast with the past the American people are going to have relatively strong government. The only question is whether it will be achieved under the auspices of democracy or dictatorship.

It is interesting to note that American privileged orders have not always feared strong government. During the early years of the Republic, in the Constitutional Convention and under the banner of Federalism, they fought for it valiantly and successfully. Writing in defense of the new constitution in the first number of *The Federalist,* Hamilton commenting on the perversities of human nature observed that, whereas "vigour of government is essential to the security of liberty," an "enlightened zeal for the energy and efficiency of government will be stigmatised as the offspring of a temper fond of despotic power and hostile to the principles of liberty."[8] Was Hamilton foreseeing and attacking his spiritual descendants in the American Liberty League? Or has the aristocracy experienced a change of heart and with increasing wisdom accepted the principles of Jefferson? Neither explanation seems adequate. The fact is that in the seventeen-eighties and nineties men of birth and property feared state government because it was relatively close to the people and responsive to the popular will, while they looked with favor on the federal authority because they thought they could control it. They wrote provisions into the constitution which were carefully designed to keep all three branches of the national government in their hands.

Today the tables are turned. By constitutional amendment and the gradual extension of political democracy, the legislative and executive branches of the federal government have been brought within the reach of the people. The provisions calling for the indirect election of president and senators, intended to serve as a bulwark against popular encroachments, have been abrogated. Only the federal judiciary, and particularly the Supreme Court of the United States, remains as a dependable guardian of the vested interests of the aristocracy. That the "ordirs of the few" should resist to the last the current attempt on the part of the many to capture this last citadel of privilege in the federal government is inevitable. Since the Civil War the Supreme Court, by declaring unconstitutional acts of the Congress and state legislatures aimed at the control of corporate wealth, has beaten back and dissipated wave after wave of popular protest against the concentration of property. Through its "tortured interpretations" of the constitution it has created a vast domain from which both state and national governments are barred—a great "no-man's land," as someone has said, thickly inhabited by corporations. If the Supreme Court should go over to the side of democracy, or even remain neutral, the struggle for the control of economic power would be fought in the open and the fortunes of battle could be gauged by the counting of ballots. The appeal to revolutionary violence would then lose all support in reason.

In concluding the argument the point should be emphasized that men do not naturally fear vigorous and efficient government. Certainly there is no instance in American history of a faction fearing a legislature, an executive, or a judiciary, however strong and determined, that served its interests and purposes. In a word men do not fear themselves. Large business enterprise in the United States, though always loudly professing its allegiance to the principle of *laissez faire,* has consistently and for the most part successfully demanded a government capable of performing the services it desired to have performed. The current protest of the aristocracy against the intrusions of government is in fact a protest against the intrusions of the people. They fear a government that will not be amenable to their wishes, a government for example that will not employ the armed forces of the nation in the breaking of strikes, in the enforcement of the foreclosure of mortgages, or in the defense of investments abroad. The great body of citizens, if they are capable of self-government, will welcome the anxious cries of the privileged minority as clear evidence that the state is guarding and advancing their interests. They should know that, if government deals effectively with the issues of the times, it will arouse the most bitter opposition and denunciation. Instead of becoming alarmed at such manifestations of hostility, they should note the source from which they proceed and thus obtain guidance for the further prosecution of their campaign.

Government Monopoly of Military and Police Power

Government must maintain a complete monopoly of the military and police power. No government that fails in the discharge of this basic obligation can be regarded as authentic, for in the last analysis here is the ultimate foundation of government. Although the state may appear to rule wholly by custom, persuasion, and consent, the final test of its power to govern is its ability, if the situation requires it, to command the forces and instruments of physical coercion. And this test comes in those periods of deep national crisis when great issues are at stake, passions are inflamed, men become desperate or frightened, and the spirit of revolution broods over the land. It is particularly necessary in a democracy that the role of police and military power in government be thoroughly understood. While the democratic method substitutes the ballot for the sword, the verdict of the ballot, if threatened by the sword, must be upheld by the sword. A democracy, no more than an autocracy, can permit its decisions to be flouted and its authority defied. As Elihu Root said in an address before the New York State Legislature in 1909, "the only way to maintain the powers of government is to govern." [9]

That American democracy is threatened at this point is indicated by a long record of private violence and a general disrespect for constituted authority. As will be pointed out in some detail in the next chapter, armed mobs and bodies of irate citizens, sometimes to enforce and sometimes to subvert justice, have taken the law into their own hands in practically every state of the Union. While much of this violence has been without political motive, under the cover of this old tradition a situation is developing which in the course of time might assume the aspect of widespread civil war. The subcommittee on civil liberties of the Committee on Education and Labor of the United States Senate, headed by Senator Robert M. La Follette, has revealed a condition that threatens the authority of government—the general use by employers of armed men and munitions of war in the breaking of strikes. In fact the Committee has shown that a profession of strike-breakers, recruited from thugs and hoodlums, has become one of the adjuncts of large-scale business enterprise in the United States. Moreover, in many communities private policemen and detectives surpass in number the official guardians of the law. All of this constitutes a dangerous usurpation of the functions of government on the part of private citizens. If long continued, it might easily undermine the confidence of the ordinary man in the integrity and authenticity of constituted authority.

If the experience of Europe means anything for the United States, the deliberate arming and disciplining of a political party is far more serious than sporadic resort to violence in the economic struggle and even the employment of private police in the settlement of civil disputes. Clearly the intent of such a movement is the repudiation of the ballot and rule by the sword. The organization for political purposes of armed forces and bands and the promotion of military training and mentality by political movements are incompatible with the principles of free government. Wherever these tendencies appear, stark dictatorship may be seen in embryo. This was certainly the road traveled by the rising dictators in both Italy and Germany. If government does not govern, then the forces possessing the will to govern will become the government. And government that permits the police power to slip from its grasp, however pure its motives, has already lost its ability to govern, and its right to respect. Also, as the

Spanish tragedy demonstrates, a government that fails to keep command of the army may awake some morning to discover the army in command of the government.

Lest there be confusion, the point should be made that government does not maintain its authority by exercising the police power under the coercion of a body of private citizens. Thus, if the state lynches the victims of a mob in order to appease the mob, it does not thereby uphold the majesty of the law. A most impressive instance of this general type is to be found in the formation on July 15, 1937, at Johnstown, Pa., of a national organization dedicated to the preservation of the "inalienable constitutional right to work." The words of dedication suggest that the membership is going to devote itself to the great and humane task of finding work for the six to ten millions of unemployed in the country. But a careful reading of the proceedings of the meeting, as reported in *The New York Times,* indicates that the object of the organization is to compel government to support the interests of the "ordirs of the few," to halt the movement for the organization of labor, and to make the steel industry safe for such men as Mr. Tom Girdler. "As loyal American citizens," runs the preamble to the resolutions adopted, "we feel it is our patriotic duty to perfect a nation-wide organization whose function it shall be to restore and protect those constitutional rights that have been taken from American citizens by certain unworthy officials." [10] According to the findings of the La Follette committee, "a handbook of vigilantism" was recently prepared under the auspices of powerful employer interests and distributed in thousands of copies. This pamphlet, "in the guise of reporting on developments in labor disputes in numerous cities in three States, outlined the forms of organization, the 'principles' and newspaper advertisements, and the overt acts of a number of bodies called citizens' committees, 'law and order leagues,' business advisory councils, emergency committees, etc." [11] The democracy must learn to distinguish between the actual abandonment of the police power and the refusal of the government to employ that power in the interest of some powerful and vociferous element in the country.

From the standpoint of the preservation of free political institutions, the question of the control of police and military power has become extremely grave because of changes in the instruments of warfare. It has been observed that the rise of democracy in the western world went hand in hand with the advance of the infantry. During feudal times the accouterments of the warrior were so expensive that only the few could possess them. And possessing them, they held a practical monopoly of military power and were enabled to impose their will upon society. The invention of firearms was one of the greatest leveling forces in history. With a musket in his hands the plowboy or tradesman stood eye to eye with the armored knight on his steed. Certainly the part played by this invention in the development of democracy in the United States, where practically every citizen was skilled in its use, has never been fully recognized. Fanny Wright commented on the fact that the ordinary American was "not only regularly trained" to the musket "as a man, but practised as a boy." [12] It must not be forgotten that in the time of Jefferson and Jackson men were roughly equal in the most fundamental sense—in the power to take human life. At any rate class distinctions had little significance on the field of battle. When the principle of manhood suffrage was established, the political formula read, not one man—one vote, but one man—one rifle—one vote.

Today the middle term of this formula has practically disappeared. This is not to say that great numbers of American citizens are not practiced in the use of firearms. As a matter of fact they are so practiced to a large extent, even though the growth of cities has doubtless greatly reduced the proportion. But the crucial consideration is that the arms which they own and with which they are familiar are but popguns alongside modern instruments of warfare. Although the chief of staff of the United States army has said recently that the infantry is still supreme, broadly speaking the foot soldier of tradition is in retreat before the advance of machine guns, tanks, airplanes, poison gas, and other mechanized means of conducting war. The full meaning of this change is not known today; but it seems probable that an era is opening in which the common man will be at great disadvantage in any trial of military strength. Can it be that democracy will retreat, as it advanced, with the infantry? Whether such an extreme conclusion is justified or not, the perpetuation of popular rule would appear to rest upon the ability of government to achieve and maintain a complete monopoly of the police and military power. To insure such a monopoly untiring vigilance on the part of all friends of democracy is mandatory.

Guaranteeing Civil Liberties

Civil liberties must be guaranteed to the entire population without fear or favor. If there is a touchstone by which the rise and fall of political democracy is to be judged, here it is. These great liberties written into the constitutions of state and nation—the rights of freedom of speech, belief, press, assemblage, petition, and security of person—constitute the essence of the democratic process—a priceless heritage to be guarded and cherished. Deny these rights to any section of the people, and those affected will be forced beyond the pale of politics; curtail or abolish them generally and the stern visage of dictatorship appears at the head of the state. Then and only then can it be said with certainty that popular rule has given place to autocracy and government to brute force assisted by organized propaganda. Without civil liberties political discussion is reduced to talk about the weather, and public opinion becomes but an echo of the dictator's voice;

without civil liberties the counting of ballots is a farce designed to deceive the untutored—a fraudulent concession to the conscience of mankind.

As the exercise of civil liberties is of the essence of democracy, so the suppression of these liberties is of the essence of dictatorship. The American aristocracy of the early years of the Republic, fearing the rise of the common man, passed the Alien and Sedition Laws, jailed newspaper editors, and endeavored to limit the rights of free speech and assemblage. In contemporary Europe the new autocracy, as Mussolini boasted, walks over the prostrate body of the goddess of liberty: it mocks the very idea of free speech, smashes all political opposition, establishes a new orthodoxy and priesthood, engages in a perpetual heresy hunt, spreads terror of opinion throughout the population, jails, tortures, and murders its critics and opponents, and sanctifies the whole process of suppression with some mystical doctrine propagated by the unified and coordinated voice of the entire cultural apparatus—press, school, radio, cinema, theater, and church. Security of the flesh is bought at the price of damnation of the soul; and salvation of the soul is purchased by torture of the flesh. And the road back to the great heritage of individual freedom and integrity—the highest spiritual achievement of the western world—can be opened only with the sword and at the price of unutterable misery. "Man once surrendering his reason," wrote Jefferson near the close of his life in 1822, "has no remaining guard against absurdities the most monstrous, and like a ship without rudder, is the sport of every wind." [13]

The task before the American people leaves no room for complacency. While they have fought for civil liberties at various times with courage and understanding, the enemy is always at the gates ready to take advantage of the slightest relaxation of the watch. At no time in their history has the ideal been completely realized: at every period the full protection of the bill of rights has been denied various groups—oppressed classes, certain racial, national, and religious minorities, and generally all who have been deeply critical of inherited institutions or have challenged the rule of privileged classes. Today men languish in prison in the United States because of the unequal administration of the laws. The record of violation of civil liberties on the part of American business disclosed by the La Follette Committee is both nauseating and terrifying. Among other things the Committee finds that the practice of spying on its employees is an "almost universal practice in American industry." The following quotation transmits to the reader some of the more significant passages from a report presented to the Senate on December 21, 1937:

The known total of business firms receiving spy services from these enumerated agencies is approximately 2,500 . . . The list as a whole reads like a bluebook of American industry . . . The names and distribution of these firms conclusively demonstrate the tenacious hold which the spying habit has on American business. From motion-picture producers to steel makers, from hookless fasteners to automobiles, from small units to giant enterprises—scarcely an industry that is not fully represented in the accompanying list of clients of the detective agencies . . . Large corporations rely on spies. No firm is too small to employ them. The habit has even infected the labor relations of noncommercial, philanthropic organizations.[14]

The battle for civil liberties goes on with varying fortunes: one year the record improves; the next it grows worse. The number of cases serves as a kind of inverse barometer of the economic and political struggle, rising as the struggle sharpens and falling as it moderates. On the side of those who would destroy this heritage of freedom are not only the "ordirs of the few" whose interests may be placed in jeopardy by social change, but also practically every one of the self-styled patriotic organizations from the National Society of the Descendants of the Signers of the Declaration of Independence, to the American Legion composed of veterans of the war "to make the world safe for democracy." A sense of humor on the part of the members of such organizations would seem to be sufficient to expose the utter incongruity and absurdity of this whole business; but they go blithely on their way militantly proclaiming their intention "to preserve and protect our Constitution and our American institutions" while they trample under foot the bill of rights. One can only conclude that they are either stupid, dishonest, or the tools of vested interests. It must be left to the spiritual rather than the lineal descendants of the signers of the Declaration of Independence and the other great papers of American democracy to carry on the battle for free institutions today. Perhaps the most effective method of participating in the struggle is to lend vigorous support to that old and tried champion of popular rights—not The American Liberty League, but the American Civil Liberties Union. Also the subcommittee on civil liberties of the Senate should be established as a permanent organ of American democracy.

Exposure of Political Propaganda

All major campaigns of political propaganda must be systematically and thoroughly exposed. There is no suggestion here, of course, that such campaigns should be prevented or outlawed, for complete freedom of propaganda is essential to democracy. It is merely proposed that secrecy, deception, and manipulation be removed from the process as thoroughly as possible; that measures be undertaken for redressing the balance between the few and the many which arises out of the mal-distribution of economic power; that every campaign of propaganda be made to appear in the arena of politics under an honest and adequate label.

It might be expected that this end would be achieved

automatically through the protection of every citizen in the exercise of his civil liberties. And such was the expectation of the early advocates of political democracy. Government would be guided by public opinion, so the argument ran; and public opinion would be constantly purified by the free play of inquiry and intelligence guaranteed by the bill of rights. Jefferson made the classical statement of this faith of American democracy: "truth is great and will prevail if left to herself. . . . she is the proper and sufficient antagonist to error, and has nothing to fear from the conflict unless by human interposition disarmed of her natural weapons, free argument and debate; errors ceasing to be dangerous when it is permitted freely to contradict them." [15] The present difficulty resides in the fact that, because of the concentration of economic power, the contest between truth and error in the political sphere may be very unequal and truth may be "disarmed of her natural weapons" by "human interposition." Such is peculiarly the case when deep economic issues are at stake. Error can scarcely be expected to sit in judgment on itself. If the democracy is to function effectively, this condition will have to be corrected and the sources of knowledge concerning current questions relieved of corruption and the bias of privilege.

One of the most ancient modes of autocratic rule has been the careful selection and preparation of the mental pabulum on which the people are nourished. Abraham Bishop in his discussion of the nature of political delusion exposed methods of propaganda which have been employed by ruling classes throughout the ages. John Taylor showed how the new "aristocracy of paper and patronage" creates the intellectual and moral atmosphere which the people breathe. "Solomon said, Train up a Child in the way he should go," observed William Manning, "& when he is old he will not depart from it. And it is as true that if a child is trained up in the way he should not go, when he is old he will keep to it." [16]

This Massachusetts farmer then points out that "despotick government" and "grate men" endeavor to "train up" the many in the way they "should not go." Thus do the few rule the many by peaceful means.

What the future may hold is suggested by the experience of the American people in 1800 and in recent years. Let any political party or leader threaten ever so lightly the position of the aristocracy, and a nation-wide campaign of misrepresentation, villification, and intimidation will be launched. It will be represented that the advocates of fundamental reform are seeking to overturn the work of the fathers, scrap the constitution, desert the American system, foment class warfare, destroy the Republic, betray the national interest, import foreign ideas, and set up a dictatorship. If this is not sufficient to frighten the timid, it will be declared and proved that the apostles of change intend to destroy the home, legalize rape and arson, glorify robbery and murder, convert vice into virtue, abolish religion, and desecrate all the altars of God. Whether any of the propagandists for aristocracy will rise to the heights of Theodore Dwight and charge the champions of economic democracy with designing to flay their victims "in order to procure leather for the use of the army," only the event will reveal. That individual character will be blackened, assassinated if possible, is certain. All of this may well be done in the name of Thomas Jefferson, the great philosopher of the people and the rights of man. At the same time the real issue—the control of economic power —will receive the treatment of silence and evasion.

The innoculation of the American people against this virus requires various measures. It is partly a responsibility of the school, a subject reserved for a later chapter; but since this institution deals primarily with the next generation, it can only lay the foundations in knowledge and thought for the detection of propaganda. It is also a responsibility of the agencies of adult education which should be devoted largely to the spread of civic enlightenment and understanding. The more immediate task, however, is to subject to constant scrutiny those modern and far-flung organs of news, opinion, and political indoctrination—the press, the radio, and the cinema —and those professed artists and purveyors of propaganda —advertising firms and public relations counsellors. This might be accomplished in some measure through liberal newspapers and periodicals, a number of which are already in existence, but much more is needed. Perhaps the most promising suggestion is the establishment of a powerful bureau or institute under wholly independent and trustworthy auspices whose function it would be to trace to its sources every important campaign of propaganda, thoroughly exposing the personalities, organizations, and interests involved —their methods, their purposes, and their economic, social, and political affiliations. Also from the standpoint of truthfulness, balance, fairness, and general integrity it would appraise at regular intervals the great dailies, periodicals, news services, broadcasting chains, columnists, commentators, and moving picture producers and productions. Its findings would go directly into all channels of publicity and particularly to the schools, colleges, forums, churches, civic clubs and societies, and to all organizations of farmers, laborers, professional workers, students, and consumers. The support of such an institution might come from the pooled resources of many persons and associations or from the benefactions of some individual of great wealth able to detach himself from his class and think wholly in terms of the general welfare. A beginning has already been made by the late Edward A. Filene in the launching of The Institute for Propaganda Analysis.

Conservation of the Democratic Temper

The temper of the democratic process must be conserved and strengthened. Free institutions do not function automatically. Their successful operation depends upon certain habits and qualities of mind: a readiness to abide by the rules of the game, to accept the verdict of the polls, to admit the fallibility of both personal and party judgment, to be suspicious of sectarian dogma, to place the welfare of the nation above the interests of a faction, and to devote time and energy to the advancement of the common good; the ability to hold passion in leash, to refrain from mob behavior, to respect honest opposition, to know when to compromise, to conduct the political struggle with some sense of proportion, to accept defeat as well as victory with composure, to sense sincere and competent leadership, and to feel social injustice deeply; a desire to get all the relevant facts, to understand the position of opponents, to obtain a peaceful solution of an issue, to make democratic methods prevail, to maintain a measure of unity in a society marked by diversity and conflict.

That the various peoples of the world, due doubtless to a combination of geographical and cultural factors, have possessed these qualities in varying degrees seems to be demonstrable. Undoubtedly the English have exhibited them in unusual measure during the past century or so. Lord Balfour, in considering the possibility of the spread of parliamentary institutions to other countries, placed large emphasis on the peculiar temperament of the English people among whom the institutions developed. "It matters little," he wrote toward the end of his life, "what other gifts a people may possess if they are wanting in those which, from this point of view are of most importance." He then proceeded to indicate the traits which place success in jeopardy: "If, for example, they have no capacity for grading their loyalties as well as for being moved by them; if they have no natural inclination to liberty and no natural respect for law; if they lack good humour and tolerate foul play; if they know not how to compromise or when; if they have not that distrust of extreme conclusions which is sometimes misdescribed as want of logic; if corruption does not repel them; and if their divisions tend to be either too numerous or too profound, the successful working of British institutions may be difficult or impossible." [17] Certainly wherever dictatorship has appeared or assumed extreme forms in the contemporary world, these powers have been lacking or very meagerly distributed through the population.

To what extent the American people possess the democratic virtues as here outlined is by no means clear. Their record is far from reassuring. Unquestionably, as will be pointed out later, they seem to have a strong predilection for violence, mob behavior, and extreme conclusions. They are a nation of "one-hundred-percenters," a phrase of their own coinage and expressive of their mentality. Michael Chevalier during his visit to the United States in the eighteen-thirties, as the slavery issue was beginning to sharpen, noted the overwhelming power of the mob as it affected the newspapers:

The press, which is here so outrageously violent and brutal in its treatment of members of congress belonging to the opposite party, is, on the other hand, more cautious and reserved in regard to the multitude. The American press is free in so far as it gives no bonds and pays no stamp duty, but it is dependent on a capricious, despotic, and not very enlightened public opinion, which requires it to flatter the passion of the hour, and does not look to it for lessons of morality. The public opinion of the democracy is a master who is easily offended, and who quickly shows his displeasure. The American journalist is well aware that for the slightest display of boldness he will be deserted; and since the late events, this is not his only fear, for he knows that if his enemies should choose to brand him as an abolitionist, for example, it would be easy to raise a mob of vagabonds, who would pillage and pull down his house, tar and feather his person, and drive him from home without any interference by the public authorities. He is therefore exceedingly circumspect. In a word, the *reign of terrour* is begun in the United States.

Men of courage and devotion to the cause of law have no rallying point in the press; and even when the public authority would be disposed to support them, it proves insufficient, either through fear, or concern for party interests, or want of physical force.[18]

To ask the American people to display the rare and immaculate virtues of political democracy during a period of deep economic and political struggle reminiscent of the conflict over human slavery may seem a counsel of perfection. Perhaps it is. Certainly it would be, if there were any expectation that the habits and qualities of mind enumerated must be the possession of the entire population. Great numbers from all classes and groups in any society, even the freest and wisest, will doubtless prove too weak to live by the democratic faith. Yet, by taking thought and shaping the educational processes in time, the proportion might be so increased as to give free political institutions an opportunity to show their worth and power. If the differences now emerging are to be settled by peaceful means and the road to dictatorship avoided, such an achievement would appear to be necessary.

Avoidance of War

War must be avoided if possible. This scourge constitutes the greatest danger to free institutions everywhere. It tends to destroy those habits and qualities of mind necessary to the successful functioning of democratic processes. The conduct of war, which of necessity is barbarous in nature, demands a general retreat from the behavior and mentality of civilized and humane existence. It requires the establishment of a kind of economic and cultural dictatorship; it requires the exaltation of passion, the spread of suspicion, the arousal of fear and hatred, the propagation of falsehood, the inauguration of a system of espionage, the regimentation of opinion, the interruption of critical thought, the suspension of constitutional guarantees, and the general triumph of the military mind. The history of the American people amply demonstrates that military conflict, whatever its leadership and professed auspices, leads inevitably to political reaction and the postponement of the consideration of domestic issues. Under the hysteria and madness of the battlefield, magnified and extended to the entire population by modern engines of warfare and propaganda, even a consideration of the aims of the struggle is proscribed and everything subordinated to the task of "winning the war."

The fortunes of the democratic process and the course of social demoralization attending the launching and prosecution of military conflict were described by Mark Twain with complete realism and integrity. The following lines were composed before the emergence of the concept of the "totalitarian war" already written into history by fascist and quasi-fascist states:

There has never been a just one, never an honorable one—on the part of the instigator of the war. I can see a million years ahead, and this rule will never change in so many as half a dozen instances. The loud little handful—as usual—will shout for the war. The pulpit will—warily and cautiously—object—at first; the great, big, dull bulk of the nation will rub its sleepy eyes and try to make out why there should be a war, and will say, earnestly and indignantly, "It is unjust and dishonorable, and there is no necessity for it." Then the handful will shout louder. A few fair men on the other side will argue and reason against the war with speech and pen, and at first will have a hearing and be applauded; but it will not last long; those others will outshout them, and presently the anti-war audiences will thin out and lose popularity. Before long you will see this curious thing: the speakers stoned from the platform, and free speech strangled by hordes of furious men who in their secret hearts are still at one with those stoned speakers—as earlier—but do not dare to say so. And now the whole nation—pulpit and all—will take up the war-cry, and shout itself hoarse, and mob any honest man who ventures to open his mouth; and presently such mouths will cease to open. Next the statesmen will invent cheap lies, putting the blame upon the nation that is attacked, and every man will be glad of those conscience-soothing falsities, and will diligently study them, and refuse to examine any refutations of them; and thus he will by and by convince himself that the war is just, and will thank God for the better sleep he enjoys after this process of grotesque self-deception.[19]

The final degradation of the human spirit, the ultimate crucifixion of ethical values which war invariably exacts of its votaries was etched with terrifying veracity in another passage from the pen of this bard from Missouri. The scene is that of a nation at war; the "holy fire of patriotism" is burning in every breast; the battalions are about to leave for the front; the people gather in the church to invoke the blessing of God; the minister prays eloquently for success on the field of battle. At the close of the supplication a stranger in the form of an old man mounts the pulpit, and proclaims himself a messenger from "God the Father." After obtaining permission to explain the full import of the petition which he has just heard, he proceeds in the following "War Prayer" to render explicit what has been implicit in practically every appeal from the beginning of time for divine favor in military combat:

O Lord our God, help us to tear their soldiers to bloody shreds with our shells; help us to cover their smiling fields with the pale forms of their patriot dead; help us to drown the thunder of the guns with the shrieks of their wounded, writhing in pain; help us to lay waste their humble homes with a hurricane of fire; help us to wring the hearts of their unoffending widows with unavailing grief; help us to turn them out roofless with their little children to wander unfriended the wastes of their desolated land in rags and hunger and thirst, sports of the sun flames of summer and the icy winds of winter, broken in spirit, worn with travail, imploring Thee for the refuge of the grave and denied it—for our sakes who adore Thee, Lord, blast their hopes, blight their lives, protract their bitter pilgrimage, make heavy their steps, water their way with their tears, stain the white snow with the blood of their wounded feet! We ask it, in the spirit of love, of Him Who is the Source of Love, and Who is the ever-faithful refuge and friend of all that are sore beset and seek His aid with humble and contrite hearts. Amen.[20]

The author adds an appropriate finishing touch in these words: "It was believed afterward that the man was a lunatic, because there was no sense in what he said."

If sufficiently severe and prolonged, war might easily lead to a complete overthrow of democratic institutions and the establishment of dictatorship. The destruction of whatever moral order men had achieved through the centuries and the emergence of the tyrannical systems which now seek to conquer the earth were a product of the first world war. But in case the struggle should fail to bring such extreme consequences to the American people, its reactionary and repressive tendencies would certainly continue through a post-war period of longer or shorter duration, impound the energies of social change, and pave the way for violent revolution. As Charles A. Beard has pointed out, the wars of 1812, 1861, and 1917, not to mention the minor conflicts in which the nation has engaged, all strengthened the power and rule of the economic aristocracy.[21] The war which was waged to "make the world safe for democracy" threatened to destroy democracy at home. Liberal forces which had been gathering for a generation and which gave some promise of fundamental reform were divided and scattered; and under the Harding administration the civic life and conscience descended to depths that had been approached only during the presidency of Grant immediately following the Civil War. It was not until the onset of the 1929 depression that the nation regained the level of political morality and intelligence of 1914 and returned to a consideration of those pressing domestic problems which it had abandoned in order to wage war.

If war could be avoided, American democracy could face the future with some equanimity and confidence. But the road to peace is beset with all but insuperable obstacles. No one with any knowledge of international affairs can pretend to have an infallible remedy for this most deadly of social maladies. The world is habituated to war by its past; it is organized for war today; it is moving inexorably toward war tomorrow. The great opportunity which came to men in 1918 to liquidate the heritage of hatred and injustice among the nations and to make a fresh start along the paths of peaceful cooperation was mocked at Versailles. When that opportunity will return seems to be in the lap of the gods.

There appear to be four realities in the international situation today which must be taken into account by anyone who would consider the relation of democracy to war. In the first place, the disposition of peoples over the earth bears little relation to the distribution of natural resources. Huge populations are confined within narrow quarters; small populations enjoy the riches of continents. Moreover, the boundaries of nations and the titles to territory, expressive of the dynamics of a past age, are out of harmony with the present and emergent balance of forces and interests. In the second place, under the aegis of extreme nationalism a spirit of calculated aggression, far more determined and desperate than the imperialism of the eighteenth and nineteenth centuries, which reflected the energy of a rising and vigorous capitalism, is spreading through the world. Three powerful nations—Germany, Italy, and Japan—supported by a growing number of smaller states, have served notice on all peacefully disposed countries and peoples in the unmistakable language of the deed that they will respect no treaties, acknowledge no accepted principles of international law and morality, and make no concessions to the opinion of mankind. That this spirit of aggression will be checked before it is destroyed by superior armed forces or has redrawn the political boundaries of the earth seems improbable. In the third place, because of the advance of technology, the world has become one. Through lines of communication, economic and cultural ties, and even the instruments of warfare, all races and peoples seem to be irrevocably bound together and compelled to share a common destiny. The battles of American democracy may be fought in what were once remote corners of the planet—in Ethiopia, in Spain, in China, in Brazil. In the fourth place and in summary, the inherited institutions and arrangements, both within and among the nations, manifest a high degree of instability. Internal economy is shaken periodically to its foundations; political divisions for the most part are too limited in scope and resources to utilize the potentialities of technology; and neither privileged classes nor favored countries are prepared to make substantial concessions in the interests of either domestic or international peace and harmony. Such disturbing facts must be included in any honest picture of the contemporary world.

American democracy faces a harsh and implacable dilemma. If it should assume the responsibility of defending justice abroad, it may destroy freedom at home; if it should strive to isolate itself completely from world conflict, it may become the ultimate victim of an all-powerful fascist bloc. Furthermore, if America should endeavor to remain neutral when the peace of the world is outraged, she may actually throw her great strength to the side of the aggressor; but if in a given case she should enter the struggle, it is by no means certain that in the final analysis she would find herself fighting in the cause of justice and freedom in the world. Lacking a clear-cut policy conceived in terms of the abiding interests of her people, she might easily be made the in-

strument for protecting and advancing the exclusive interests
and vested privileges of her own aristocracy or even of the
ruling class of some European or oriental state. Apparently,
if democracy is to be preserved in the United States, the
country dares neither to enter nor to keep wholly aloof from
the rising conflict among the nations. Equally logical is the
inference that in the long run it will not and cannot withdraw completely from the world and pursue a life of national
monasticism on the North American continent. Little wonder that men of peace, good will, and courage fail to agree
on the course to be espoused. Manifestly, there is no rational
justification for that dogmatism and imputation of bad faith
to opponents which tend increasingly to mark the conduct
of the controversy.

In view of the foregoing facts and considerations the problem of avoiding war, either today or tomorrow, seems practically insoluble. Any possible line of action, whether
negative or positive, is replete with hazards for American
democracy. The simple truth is that the people of the United
States do not hold in their own hands all the vital and controlling factors in the situation. Nevertheless the formulation
of policy, based upon wide popular understanding, is preferable to blind drift—a policy which would be designed to
deal only with those conflicts arising out of the deliberate
and clear violation of the laws of nations and tending to increase the power of aggressive states.

It is proposed here that such a policy should embrace at
least nine points. First, the government of the United States
should recognize the distinction in moral position between
the states in conflict and employ its diplomatic power in
support of the victim of aggression. This it should do either
alone or in concert with other nations. Second, it should
place an embargo on all trade with the aggressor and thus
refuse to be a party to the violation of international law and
treaties to which it is a party. The costs of the embargo

should not be borne by the business enterprises and work-men immediately concerned but by society as a whole. Third, it should permit its citizens to aid the country attacked in every possible way. Whether this assistance is given through granting of credit, voluntary enlistment in armed forces, or in the sale or contribution of needed commodities; or whether it is motivated by desire for material profit, love of adventure, or devotion to the ideals of freedom and justice is a matter to which the government should be indifferent. Fourth, it should withdraw its own armed forces entirely from the area of conflict and place upon the private citizens concerned all the risks involved in residence in the countries at war or in participation in the struggle. The principle should be made perfectly clear that the flag will follow neither the dollar nor the passport into the troubled region. Fifth, it should steadfastly refuse to be drawn into the war by any of those "incidents" which in the past have commonly led to such action. That incidents of this character would arise in considerable numbers is inevitable. But in the interest of maintaining peace the American government should be ready to tender "apologies," to suffer "humiliation," to endure "insults," and even to see the "national honor" profaned. Sixth, it should so organize the internal economy and so control foreign trade that the country would be able to bear the economic dislocations flowing from the shocks of international struggle. It should center its attention on the development of the home markets and the increase of the purchasing power of its own population. Seventh, it should strengthen the military defenses of the nation so that a successful attack from without would be impossible. This should be undertaken without any intention of protecting distant possessions and economic interests. Eighth, it should individually and in cooperation with nations desirous of peace initiate and support all practicable measures designed to remove the present injustices in the distribution of the natural resources of the world. At no time should it permit itself to be drawn into an alliance intended to maintain the *status quo.* Certain of the aggressive nations have just grievances which can be disregarded only at the peril of war and the perpetuation of free institutions. Ninth, and most important of all, the American people should devote their energies to the establishment of such a reign of social justice at home that no political adventurer would be tempted to escape domestic difficulties by engaging in foreign quarrels. It is also well known that the most effective means of defense is that solid and reasoned loyalty of the masses of the people which is derived from a knowledge of the just and efficient operation of social institutions.

That the policy outlined is fraught with great danger must be admitted. But the same may be said regarding any possible alternative. A major strain would doubtless be placed upon the intelligence of the American people. The inevitable "incidents," exploited by press and radio, might easily generate popular passions which would override all counsels of sanity and drive the nation into war. This must be admitted. But the admission merely means that the ordinary individual is unprepared today to bear the responsibilities of citizenship in the "great society" from which he cannot escape and in which he must live. It means that the task of civic education, toward which the entire discussion of this volume is pointed, is only beginning to be sensed. Democracy, as distinguished from other forms of society, rests upon the enlightenment of the entire population.

REFERENCES

1. William Manning, *The Key of Libberty* (Billerica, 1922), 3.
2. *Ibid.,* 61.
3. See John W. Studebaker, *The American Way* (New York, 1935) and *Choosing Our Way* (Washington, 1937).
4. *Op. cit.,* 61-62.

5. *Ibid.*, 66.

6. *Op. cit.*, 203.

7. *Op. cit.*, 62.

8. Alexander Hamilton, *The Federalist* (Everyman's Library edition, New York, 1929), 3.

9. Elihu Root, *Addresses on Government and Citizenship* (Cambridge, 1916), 252.

10. *The New York Times* (July 16, 1937).

11. Senate Committee on Education and Labor, *Interim Report* (Washington, April 15, 1938), 3.

12. Fanny Wright, *Views of Society and Manners in America* (New York, 1821), 211.

13. Thomas Jefferson, *The Writings* (Washington edition, New York, 1854), VII, 270.

14. *The New York Times* (December 22, 1937).

15. Thomas Jefferson, *The Writings* (Ford edition, New York, 1893), II, 239.

16. *Op. cit.*, 19.

17. Earl of Balfour, "Introduction" to Walter Bagehot, *The English Constitution* (The World's Classics edition, Oxford, 1928), xxii.

18. Michael Chevalier, *Society, Manners and Politics in the United States* (Boston, 1839), 391-392.

19. Mark Twain, *The Mysterious Stranger and Other Stories* (New York, 1922), 119-120.

20. Mark Twain, *Europe and Elsewhere* (New York, 1923), 398.

21. Charles A. Beard, "National Politics and War," *Scribner's Magazine.* (February, 1935), 65-70.

CHAPTER *9:*

SOME LIABILITIES

THE achievement of the program suggested
in the previous chapter would insure the peaceful reconstruction of the economic foundations of democracy. Such
achievement, however, can by no means be assumed as certain, even though the friends of popular liberty possess the
best intentions in the world. Doubtless much depends on
the unfoldment of the historic process over which the masses
of the people can have only limited control—the emergence
of gifted leadership, the movements of mob psychology, the
involvement in a great international conflict, the hapless
succession of incidents. Also in every society may be found
relatively abiding elements and factors which are favorable
or unfavorable to the successful operation of free political
institutions—geographical, historical, cultural, psychological.
In some the favorable will appear to outweigh the unfavorable, while in others the reverse will be true. It is proposed
here to examine the resources of the American people and
to assess the liabilities and assets with which they enter what
may prove to be the greatest struggle for democracy since
1776. In the present chapter the liabilities will be passed in
review.

The liabilities in the American cultural heritage and
social structure are many and severe. The fact should be
faced squarely and honestly by all citizens, at least by all who
place the welfare of their country above the interests, privileges, and prejudices of any faction. If they are to be intelligent actors on the present stage of their history, they must
demand, in the words of Abraham Bishop, that the picture
be "drawn truly and without flattery," refusing to gloss over
the unpleasant features of their life and institutions. While
216

the liabilities are probably not all known today, some waiting to be revealed by the course of events, and while certain
others might be subject to dispute, it would seem that no
informed observer could omit any one of the following from
the catalog: the concentration of economic power, the complexities of industrial society, the heterogeneity of the population, the legacy of economic individualism, the symbols
and loyalties of a great heritage, the spread of spectacles and
circuses, the rise of chronic unemployment and relief, the
long tradition of violence and intolerance, the system of
checks and balances, and the failure of organized civic education.

Concentration of Economic Power

The greatest liability of all is of course that essential negation of democracy in the social structure, that concentration
of economic power in a few hands which has accompanied
the rise of industrial capitalism in America. In fact, as pointed
out in an earlier chapter and as far-sighted men and women
have foreseen since the days of the founding fathers, the
current threat to democracy comes from this quarter. A new
aristocracy, already deeply rooted in the past, founded on
long cherished ideas and practices, and entrenched behind
custom, legislation, and judicial interpretation, has steadily
and rapidly achieved control over the citadels of substantial
authority and power in the nation. Sustained by premises
widely accepted in society and preaching doctrines harmoni-
ous with popular prejudices, it has subdued its rivals and
today can be challenged successfully only by the organized
opposition of an informed and united people.

John Taylor, viewing this aristocracy in its early stages,
predicted that "the more oppressive it shall become, the
greater will be the difficulty of discovering its existence."
And so history has demonstrated. This is due to the fact that
as it has grown, it has succeeded in pervading the social

structure and molding both men and institutions to its pattern and outlook. Controlling the sources of livelihood, it has been able to attract talent to its banners; and talent has looked to it for opportunity and patronage, whether in the field of business, government, the law, the arts, the sciences, or even organized religion itself. It has been able to do this the better because it can rule without appearing to do so. It carries no sword and wears no physical emblem of caste, not even a badge or distinctive dress. Standing at strategic points in the economic system, acquired through inheritance or chance, or won by personal daring, initiative, shrewdness, rapacity, or some special ability, its members make their exactions generally under conceptions of legality which they as well as the population as a whole regard as derived from a natural economic order.

In the sphere of government the translation of economic into political power assumes many forms. William Manning's development of this subject in a short paragraph on elections leaves little to be added:

This is a grate object with the few, to carry their points in elections, this being the ondly meens by which the Many can seporte their Rights. Consiquently the few all unite in extoling the goodness & abilityes of their candidates, & of runing down & blackgarding the candidates on the other side. Also they will appeal to the electors in a veriaty of ways. Some they will flatter by promises of favours, such as being customers to them, or helping them out of debt, or other difficultyes; or help them to a good bargain, or treet them, or trust them, or lend them money, or even give them a little money, if they will vote for such & such a man. Others they will thretten, 'if you dont vote for such & such a man,' or 'if you do' &cc, 'you shall pay me what you owe me,' or 'I will sew you'—'I will turne you out of my house' or 'off of my farm'—'I wont be your customer any longer'—'I will wager a ginna that you dare not vote for such a man—if you do you shall have a bloody nose for it,' Or they will hire some body to communicate these things to the electors. Also they will hinder votes from being counted or returned right, & often will themselves (or hire others to) put in two or three votes apeace. All these things have bin practised & may be again.[1]

The more obvious method of translating economic into political power, direct control of elections by purchase of votes and bribery of officials, though often employed, is perilous and far less important than the method of indirection—the molding of opinion and the shaping of civic attitudes. Daniel Webster observed that "universal suffrage . . . could not long exist in a community where there was great inequality of property. The holders of estates would be obliged in such case either in some way to restrain the right of suffrage, or else such right of suffrage would ere long divide the property." Just what Webster meant by "restrain the right of suffrage" is not altogether clear. If he meant the actual denial of the voting privilege to some element in the population, "holders of estates" have indeed contemplated such a measure in recent years. At any rate the New York State Economic Council, representing the great propertied interests of the richest state of the Union, did propose in 1934 the disfranchisement of all persons on relief.[2]

But the right of suffrage is also restrained by other means. With great economic resources the aristocracy can organize and conduct nationwide campaigns of propaganda in support of its candidates and measures. It can purchase brains, speakers, writers, editorials, newspaper space, radio broadcasts, moving pictures, and public relations' counsellors. All of this was done by the power companies, as shown by the investigation of the Federal Trade Commission, in their effort to halt the march of government ownership. On a much larger scale it is done in every presidential election, if the choice of one of the candidates would seem actually to endanger the system of property relationships ever so slightly. Whenever any person or group seriously challenges the rule of the few, the pattern of denunciation and vilification so highly perfected by Theodore Dwight in the attack on Jeffersonian democracy is taken from the political arsenal, oiled, polished, and put to use. It was employed unsuccessfully in the presidential campaign of 1936 and successfully in the discrediting of Roosevelt's Supreme Court proposal in 1937. That the latter proposal, if adopted, would have had the dire effect on the course of American history predicted, is unthinkable. It would, however, have removed for a time one of the bulwarks behind which the aristocracy has grown to maturity. Whatever may have been the motives of the Senators and Congressmen who opposed it, the center and source of opposition were unquestionably located in New York rather than Washington.

The task of the democracy, however, would be far easier than it is, if the forces of privilege in the nation were compelled to purchase in a free market the services of the engines of opinion and propaganda. The newspapers may be taken to illustrate the principle. In the very nature of the case the American press is at bottom on the conservative side of the political argument. Though, taken as a whole, it is admittedly superior to the press of any other country, it can scarcely be said to represent the entire people. The newspapers of the United States, with very few exceptions, are great business enterprises run by business men for business purposes. At least this is the framework in which they operate; and very few of them are able to transcend that framework, even though they may strive earnestly to do so. The editors of the great journals and chains are bound by their associates and stockholders, by the logic of the system of which they are a part, by conceptions of general welfare rooted in the interests and outlook of a privileged class. A baseball game, a prize-fight, or even an ordinary murder is commonly reported with admirable objectivity and balance of detail, but the same cannot be said regarding a strike, a presidential election, or a struggle over a constitutional issue involving the rights of property.

In the second election of Roosevelt, as will be seen in more detail later, more than seventy per cent of the great dailies of the country supported Landon, a number of old Democratic papers deserting to the Republican side as it became evident that the President, if reelected, would continue the struggle to emancipate the federal government from its long bondage to large property holders. Where today are the *Auroras* and *Republican Watch-Towers* which fought the battles of democracy in the days of Jefferson? The answer of course is that with a very few honorable exceptions they have grown fat and serve the cause of the contemporary aristocracy. To say in self-defense, as they do, that the news columns are uninfluenced by the editorial page, is to pay tribute to a great ideal, but one which is literally impossible of fulfillment. Even the learned and disciplined justices of the supreme bench have been known to permit their economic and political predilections to affect their interpretations of the fundamental law of the land. The most elementary understanding of the psychology of personality and the sociology of knowledge and inquiry must lead one to doubt the complete separation of editorial opinion from the reporting, selection, and printing of the news. And what has been said of the press may be applied with equal force to the radio, the cinema, and other organs of opinion and propaganda.

A struggle is going on within the press, however, which may alter the above picture considerably and which the friends of democracy should follow closely. The newspaper workers, organized under the American Newspaper Guild, are beginning to demand a voice in the determination of newspaper policy. They have formulated a professional code of ethics to guide them in reporting and writing, particularly in the field of economic, social, and political controversy. For the most part the Guild has encountered the hostility of newspaper owners, partly on the grounds that the affiliation of the Guild with organized labor will tend to destroy objectivity of reporting and give to the news a serious bias. In support of their position the publishers have appealed to the public in the name of one of the most glorious ideals of democracy—freedom of the press. If some of these gentlemen had not opposed the regulation of hours and wages of newsboys in the same terms, their alarm might merit more sympathetic consideration.

There seems to be an inclination among them to seek shelter under the ample folds of this great ethical and political conception whenever their profits are endangered. The issue of a free press is so crucial in these difficult times, however, that the question raised by the publishers should not be dismissed lightly. To the extent that the dissemination of news and opinion is fettered the foundations of popular government are impaired. But the citizen should know that since the right of freedom of the press was written into the constitution the character of the newspaper has been transformed. In the eighteenth century men struggled for this right in order that the press might become a vehicle for the uncensored criticism of political measures and personalities and the unrestrained publication of the observations and views of men who thought they had something to say. Newspapers were small undertakings, like most business of the time, with owner, editor, reporter, and printer all represented in one person and sometimes a few helpers. Today, unless some form of authoritarian state appears, the only danger to a free press in the original sense comes not from government but from newspaper owners; and the fight for a free press must be carried on against the dictation of the dominant property interest. The people who should be free to write without censorship are those who see events and think about them. The very thought that a person holding title to a great newspaper or a great chain of newspapers has the right to command and direct the talents of reporters, editors, and feature writers is repugnant to the entire spirit of freedom of the press. The fact that publishers dare to make public claim to such a right shows how far the American people have gone in accepting the rule of the "aristocracy of paper and patronage." The press will be free in the original meaning of the term only when its columns are open to all legitimate interests and positions and when those who write for it possess such economic security that they can enjoy the luxury of honesty and sincerity. The struggle of the Guild to organize newspaper workers should be judged from this standpoint.

One final manifestation of economic power in politics must be noted. A number of the great leaders of the early years of the Republic, notably Madison and Webster, feared the granting of the right of suffrage to the propertyless because men without property cannot be free and independent in their political convictions and actions. Jefferson placed his confidence in the freehold farmer for the reason, in part, that the latter was beyond the reach of economic pressure. "In the general course of human nature," wrote Hamilton in advising a fixed provision for the support of judges, *"a power over a man's subsistence amounts to a power over his will."* [3] The matter could not be put more plainly. Clearly if a man is to be master of his own soul, he must have economic security, he must not be dependent on another for his bread. By any such standard the proportion of free men in the United States today is extremely small. In the case of the great majority of the population, the individual is dependent for simple employment and promotion on some one above him. The average American citizen of today is trained to say "yes" from the time he obtains his first job to the day he is claimed by old age. There is much evidence, moreover, that his advancement to the more preferred positions requires political conformity. And it is well known that employers often endeavor to intimidate workmen by threats of unemployment or wage reductions into voting for the representatives of property. The concentration of economic power constitutes a dangerous threat to the integrity of the democratic political process.

Complexities of Industrial Society

If the road of political democracy looked difficult and hazardous in the closing years of the eighteenth century, how much more so must it appear today. Then life was lived for the most part in families and rural neighborhoods, in face-to-face groups in which the citizen saw at first hand much of what went on in his world; today life is carried on in a society of almost incomprehensible vastness and intricacy, embracing the whole nation and reaching out to the uttermost ends of the earth, in which the individual can observe directly only the smallest fraction of the events which may profoundly affect his fortunes. Never before in history has man had experience in such a far-flung empire bound together in intimate interdependence by the fruits of science, technology, and invention, by railroads, steamships, automobiles, and airplanes, by telegraph, telephone, and radio—an interdependence so delicate that the Kansas farmer or the shoe-clerk in Chicago may feel almost immediately repercussions from a war in China, a rebellion in Spain, a drought in Australia, or an invention in Germany. Events occurring far beyond his range of vision or knowledge may influence his life more than the happenings of his immediate neighborhood.

This great society, created through the generations by the uncoordinated efforts and discoveries of multitudes of individuals, without intention or conscious design, seems to place an insuperable burden on human attention and understanding. As it plunges ever more deeply into crisis men and women find themselves driven onward by forces which they seem unable to control. War and peace alike, economic catastrophe and prosperity, overtake them as if propelled by the capricious will of an inscrutable fate. As they contemplate the complexities of the contemporary world they feel themselves confused, overwhelmed, and impotent. How can the ordinary citizen, limited in talents and busy with the immediate demands of family, occupation, and amusement, be expected to make intelligent decisions on the countless political issues that confront him from day to day? Even great scholars, who have devoted their lives to the study of society, disagree in their diagnosis of both good and evil fortune. Jefferson's freehold farmer, if he had survived to the present time, would certainly be asked to discharge responsibilities that were never envisaged by the father of American democracy.

The situation is made to order for the demagogue, the charlatan, the adventurer, the madman. In times of quiet, peace, and contentment the citizen goes his way under the pleasing deception that the world was made for him and that the voice of the people is in truth the voice of God. But when disaster descends upon him, taking away his job, consuming his property and savings, threatening him with sickness and pauperism, and perhaps sending him and his sons to distant battlefields, he loses his bearings, or rather for the first time becomes aware of the fact that he never had any dependable points of reference. It is then that he begins to abandon his faith in the democratic process and to listen to the siren song of mysticism, authoritarianism, and dictatorship. Not having the slightest understanding of the forces of which he is the victim, he is in a mood to follow any leader who will but appeal to his deep-seated prejudices and promise an easy road to social and economic salvation—a Mussolini who counsels a return to the glories of ancient Rome, a Hitler who traces all misfortunes to the machinations of the Jews, a Huey Long who proposes a "share-the-wealth" picnic, a Doctor Townsend who promises an old-age pension of two hundred dollars a month, or a Father Coughlin who with great solemnity shouts *nothing* through the microphone. If the democratic process fails to cure the deeper ills of industrial civilization before popular confidence is destroyed, that process will be abandoned under the impact of some great social crisis. The extreme complexity of society and the vast knowledge necessary for its direction must arouse in the mind of every informed friend of democracy a profound sense of the magnitude of the educational task which lies ahead.

Heterogeneity of the Population

The success of the democratic process is further imperiled by sectional, racial, national, and religious differences. With an area almost as large as the whole of Europe, the country is naturally divided into great regions, each distinguished by certain peculiarities of history, culture, and economic interest. While these differences have been greatly moderated by the integrating influence of technology, it must not be forgotten that sectionalism has played a large role in American politics and in more than one instance has threatened to disrupt the Union. The inhabitants of this huge empire, though undoubtedly bound together by a deep love of a common country, are also divided into innumerable groups by reason of origin, psychology, doctrine, and outlook.

To the original settlements of Englishmen, supplemented by Swedes, Spaniards, Frenchmen, and Hollanders, there have been added through the generations contingents from all the races and nations of Europe and from many of the peoples of Asia, Africa, and the islands of the seas. According to the federal census of 1930, almost fourteen million persons out of a total population of approximately one hundred and twenty-three millions were classed as colored—Negroes, Mexicans, Indians, Japanese, Chinese, and Filipinos. Of the whites more than twenty-five million were of foreign or mixed parentage, while an additional thirteen million were foreign born. Only seventy million, about fifty-seven per cent of the whole, were both white and of native parentage. And of this dominant element a large portion was derived from non-English stock. In addition, fifty-five per cent of the people of the United States thirteen years of age and over are separated by religious creed into more than two hundred denominational bodies, twenty-four of which claim at least two hundred thousand adult members each. Of the total adult church membership approximately sixty-five per cent are Protestant, thirty per cent Roman Catholic, and five per cent Jewish.

These diverse elements of the population are not only separated by differences in ancestry, doctrine, and color of skin; they are also divided more or less by prejudices and antipathies, fears, hates, and jealousies which have been accumulated during the thousands of years that farmer and city dweller, oriental and occidental, white and colored, Roman and Teuton, Englishman and Frenchman, Jew and Gentile, Catholic and Protestant, have met in the markets, on the seas and battle-fields, and in the prisons and torture-chambers of the world. And the history of the United States is by no means bereft of evidences and instances of this endless struggle of sects and peoples. The original stock, overwhelmingly Protestant in religion, has ever looked with distrust on all who owe allegiance to the Roman pontiff. Americans generally have feared and disliked aliens, particularly those of a markedly different race, culture, or standard of living when competing in the labor market. They have had their alien laws, their Know-Nothing Parties, their Ku Klux Klans, their Black Legions, their race riots, their persecutions of foreigners, their campaigns of "one-hundred per cent Americanism." Also the country has ever been suspicious of the town, the "hayseed" of the "city feller."

Deeply embedded in the mores of the American family and in the breast of the ordinary citizen there slumbers a heritage of passion and prejudice which would burst into flame with the first breath of air. Here is a field of almost unimagined riches to be exploited by some unprincipled leader who might appear in time of severe crisis. What an opportunity for an American Hitler! By playing upon the strands of this heritage as a virtuoso plays upon the strings of his violin he could divert the attention of the people from the real causes of their distress and divide them into warring camps. He could turn farmer against laborer, native against alien, white against black, Protestant against Catholic, and Christian against Jew. He could implant in mulitudes the conviction that the source of their troubles is located in Rome, Moscow, Tokyo, or Jerusalem and lead them in a holy crusade to deport foreigners, lynch Negroes, break strikes, and send Catholics or Jews to concentration camps. American history, the social composition of the population, and the recent experience of other countries would seem to indicate that democracy in the United States is peculiarly vulnerable to an attack of this character.

Legacy of Economic Individualism

The old American democracy was founded on economic individualism or familism, on private ownership and management of small productive property; the new democracy, if such an order of society is to survive in any form, will be based in considerable measure on some kind of social ownership, management, and regulation of large productive property. The great majority of the population, having lived in the relatively recent past under the system of freehold farming, are the possessors of a legacy of ideas, attitudes, and loyalties which unfits them for building the only type of democracy possible under the conditions of industrial civilization and makes them an easy prey for those representatives of the aristocracy who would thwart all popular efforts to gain control of economic power.

While the individualistic tradition in economy has had its harsher features, it has been an authentic element of American history and has given meaning to American life. If it has led to pitiless exploitation of both natural and human resources, it also has glorious achievements, spiritual as well as material, to its credit. It served to break the chains of caste, release the energies of the common man, give hope to the oppressed of many lands, and encourage the growth of a spirit of independence and dignity among the people. Men and women who had been serfs, bond servants, and slaves under the exactions of ancient custom and law found themselves in a world of opportunity where industry and ambition were wont to receive their just rewards. The story of the poor boy who by dint of hard work and careful management in the pre-industrial era carved a farm out of the wilderness and in a later day achieved a fortune or rose to high political office became the epic of American life.

This phase of economic individualism was taught to two generations of Americans in the McGuffey Readers and was celebrated in the famous Horatio Alger stories so popular a few decades ago. It is recorded in the lives of Franklin, Jackson, and Lincoln, and more recently in the careers of Thomas Mellon, John D. Rockefeller, and Henry Ford. The case of Mellon, the founder of one of America's wealthiest families, illustrates perfectly the "heroic" side of the tradition. Born in Ireland in 1813, he came to the United States at five years of age and settled with his parents on a farm in Pennsylvania where during childhood and youth he felt the bitter pinch of poverty. When nine years old, with ninety-nine cents in his pocket, he set out on foot to visit the "great city of Pittsburgh." On the way he passed through East Liberty Valley where, as he gazed in awe and admiration on the Negley estate with its mansion, its outbuildings, its broad and well-tended acres, he sensed for the first time the power and promise of riches. "The whole scene was new to me," he wrote sixty years later in his autobiography. "I remember wondering how it could be possible to accumulate such wealth, and how magnificent must be the style of living and what pleasures they must enjoy who possessed it. I remember also of the thought occurring whether I might not one day attain in some degree such wealth, and an equality with such great people." [4] Later he was to marry one of the Negley girls, march from one economic triumph to another, and lay the foundations of a fortune with few rivals in history.

The tradition of economic individualism is true enough. At one time the vast majority of the American people practiced it. But it is essential to know that it existed in two forms so different in spirit and social implications that the same word would seem to be incapable of embracing them both. One was the individualism of Jefferson's freehold farmer, who, standing on his land and conducting a relatively self-contained economy, issued a declaration of independence from organized society and without fear or favor carried on the hard struggle with the elements. This was an individualism of the many and formed the economic basis of democracy. The other was the individualism of the merchant, the enterpriser, the capitalist, who with his eye on the market and money profits made organized society the scene of his operations and lived by the celebrated maxim of *caveat emptor*. This was the individualism of the few which with the rise of industrial society led to the ever increasing concentration of wealth, destroyed the individualism of the many, and made possible the aristocracy of today. "We may trace the contest between the capitalist and the democratic pioneer," says F. J. Turner, "from the earliest colonial days." [5]

If the American people are to bring economic power under social control, they will have to learn to distinguish between these two types of economic individualism. Until they have succeeded in this, they will be the easy victims of a fraud founded on ignorance and noble sentiments. Peculiarly subject to such fraud will be the farmers who throughout the greater part of their history lived under the democratic version of individualism and who today, while still grasping in their clutched fingers the lifeless forms of the older economy, have no experience with its substance. Though they may hold title to a bit of landed property, the rise of the pecuniary system has made them only less dependent on society at large than the factory worker. If they fail to realize their changed status, unwittingly they will be a party to destroying that American democracy which in an earlier age they conquered with their sweat and blood; they will follow the deceptive leadership of such organizations as the American Liberty League and thus embrace the foe which they have fought consistently from generation to generation under such leaders as Jefferson, Jackson, Lincoln, Bryan, Theodore Roosevelt, Wilson, and La Follette. Like the peasants of Europe, they might even become the gendarmery or cossacks, the black shirts or brown shirts, of profound reaction.

Symbols and Loyalties of a Great Heritage

The foregoing analysis suggests that a nation may become enslaved by its own achievements, by a great moral and political heritage. That the American people possess such a heritage cannot be disputed. Through their revolution they proclaimed to the world ideas of popular liberty and conceptions of government which rocked the foundations of autocracy in the countries of Europe and kindled a spirit of revolt in masses of ordinary men and women in many lands. Then under the great leaders of democracy they advanced from victory to victory and demonstrated their ability to govern themselves, if not to the complete satisfaction of their friends, at least to the severe discomfiture of their enemies. Throughout most of the nineteenth century America was the symbol and champion of the democratic principle in human society. The average citizen, convinced that the United States has marched in the vanguard of the struggle against tyranny, is proud, and rightly so, of his country's history. He is therefore deeply patriotic and easily roused to anger by any attempt to tarnish the glory of his fathers.

In the present critical period this great heritage is both a liability and an asset. It is an asset, if the American people understand it and remain loyal to its spirit; it is a liability, if they attach their allegiance wholly to its historic symbols. It is an asset, if those who are fighting the battles of democracy today make it their own and build upon it; it is a liability, if they repudiate its substance as well as its outworn forms and thus permit the opposition to assume undisputed guardianship over a glorious past. Only by working in this tradition can the forces of progress prevent ultimate resort to revolutionary violence. By rejecting it they place in the hands of reaction the one weapon by which it can certainly achieve power, consolidate its position, suspend parliamentary procedures, establish rule by force, proclaim some brand of American totalitarianism, and accomplish all of this without transcending the bounds of legality. The overthrow of such a regime by the people might require generations of bitter struggle and would probably be achieved only in some catastrophic war or after the complete decay of the new autocracy.

The necessity of appealing to the democratic heritage has been recognized by the privileged classes ever since the establishment of political democracy. Theretofore aristocracy spoke in its own name and arrogantly asserted its right to rule; thereafter it fought its battles under the banner of popular rights and even assumed the dress and language of the people. It is not a matter of pure chance that no political party in the United States, however reactionary in fact, has ever dared to adopt the title of *conservative, aristocratic,* or *big business.* The more thoroughly reactionary it has been, the more loudly it has proclaimed its devotion to popular liberty and democratic principles. This fact can be easily documented since the triumph of the "common man" under Andrew Jackson. The movement led by Old Hickory put long pants on the aristocracy. Daniel Webster, though opposed to the principle of universal manhood suffrage in the early years of his career, apologized publicly in an oration delivered at "the Great Mass Meeting" at Saratoga, New York, August 19, 1840, for not having been born in a log cabin, while proudly claiming that honor for his elder brothers and sisters:

Gentlemen, it did not happen to me to be born in a log cabin; but my elder brothers and sisters were born in a log cabin, raised amid the snow-drifts of New Hampshire, at a period so early that, when the smoke first rose from its rude chimney, and curled over the frozen hills, there was no similar evidence of a white man's habitation between it and the settlements on the rivers of Canada. Its remains still exist. I make to it an annual visit. I carry my children to it, to teach them the hardships endured by the generations which have gone before them. I love to dwell on the tender recollections, the kindred ties, the early affections, and the touching narratives and incidents, which mingle with all I know of this primitive family abode. I weep to think that none of those who inhabited it are now among the living; and if ever I am ashamed of it, or if I ever fail in affectionate veneration for him who reared it, and defended it against savage violence and destruction, cherished all the domestic virtues beneath its roof, and, through the fire and blood of a seven years' revolutionary war, shrunk from no danger, no toil, no sacrifice, to serve his country, and to raise his children to a condition better than his own, may my name and the name of my posterity be blotted for ever from the memory of mankind! [6]

Almost a hundred years later the managers of Calvin Coolidge, standard bearer of the few, sedulously cultivated in the mind of the people the idea that he was of humble origin, of simple tastes, fond of pitching hay and milking cows, and a personal embodiment of all the homely virtues. In the summer of 1935, in order to win the agricultural population away from the reform program of Franklin D. Roosevelt, these same forces staged in Springfield, Illinois, home of the "rail splitter" and Great Emancipator, a conference purporting to be a spontaneous uprising of "grass-roots" farmers against the policies of the New Deal. In January, 1936, the American Liberty League, an organization representing the interests of concentrated wealth, held a great banquet in Washington in the cause of "liberty" and engaged as principal speaker a man who had grown to manhood on New York's east side and who thus could be made to symbolize the common people of the present day. The spokesmen of aristocracy have become, of necessity, masters of the ancient art of political deception. And this has been made possible by the great democratic heritage to which the American people are loyal but which they do not adequately understand. Such a condition is ideal for the development of a fascist regime.

Spread of Spectacles and Circuses

During the first seventy-five years of the history of the Republic the American people sustained a high level of political knowledge and understanding. The fact was noted and commented upon by innumerable observers, both native and foreign. "What is most worthy of admiration in the history of America," wrote Fanny Wright in 1820, "is not merely the spirit of liberty which has ever animated her people, but their perfect acquaintance with the science of government, which has ever saved that spirit from preying on itself."[7]

Half a generation later Chevalier noted that "in political affairs, the American multitude has reached a much higher degree of initiation than the European mass."[8] Even those representatives of European aristocracy who traveled widely in the United States during this period, while ridiculing and castigating the crudeness and vulgarity of American life and manners, admitted that the ordinary citizen was remarkably well-informed on civic questions and capable of participating in political discussion. Sir Charles Lyell in 1845 thus characterized the American voter: "If there be one characteristic more than another which advantageously distinguishes three-fourths of the American population, it is the high social, intellectual, and political condition, relatively speaking, of the working classes."[9] It seems that the discussion of political personalities, measures, and theories was one of the major spare-time activities of the people. Wherever two or more citizens were gathered together, whether at the rail fence, along trail or highway, in the crossroads store, around the dining table, at the meeting-house, about the camp-fire, or at the spelling or husking bee, the conversation sooner or later turned to politics. Harsh though the working life of these people was, they seem to have had time and energy for the serious study of civic affairs.

Today the situation is greatly changed. Professor S. E. Morison, in his introduction to *The Key of Libberty* by William Manning, observed that "the appearance of so much political acumen and originality in so abscure a source, would be more astonishing today than at the time Manning lived."[10] With the rise of industrial society the attention of the citizen seems to have shifted to other interests. Although his hours of labor have been greatly reduced and his hours of leisure correspondingly increased, he apparently has less time for politics. Whether by chance or design, whether by the blind operation of the commercial motive in exploiting the free time of the people or by the deliberate attempt to keep the popular mind from dwelling on economic and social questions, the average voter finds his hours away from work crowded with activities of a non-political character. He must witness a baseball game, attend a prize-fight, play a game of bridge, see the latest movie, go to a dance, listen to his favorite episode on the radio, drive as far as possible in one direction and back in his automobile, follow the fortunes of the mythical characters of the funny strip, read the highly colored accounts of current crimes and scandals as given in his daily newspaper, or immerse himself in the trash purveyed in the "pulp-wood" publications. He lives from one sensation to another. The time and energy left for a sober study of social problems and issues, arising in a world immeasurably more complex and confusing than the world of his great grandfather, would seem to be wholly inadequate for the task.

Here is the real opiate of the people—those modern spectacles and circuses which have rendered a large body of voters socially illiterate, politically indifferent, and unfit to rule. The average movie, a large part of the radio programs, and the yellow-journal from first page to last have converted great agencies of popular enlightenment and cultural advancement into instrumentalities for the literal debauching of the electorate. Whatever the underlying motive, the "aristocracy of paper and patronage" has revived a method of rule as old as history itself—a method immortalized by the tyrants of ancient Rome. Indeed they have more than revived it: they have improved upon it and so extended its operations that it reaches into and pervades almost every home, molding the mind of each generation from the cradle to the grave. Occasionally the prinicple of diverting the attention of the people from "dangerous thoughts" has been applied in an extreme and amusing form. On July 24, 1937, Mr. Philip G. Phillips, regional director of the National

Labor Relations Board, charged the Clover Fork Coal Company of Harlan County, Kentucky, with hiring women to perform "strip and tease dances when union meetings were scheduled, for the purpose of enticing its employees from attending such meetings." [11] Though this is a striking use of economic power in politics, it is of course of little importance in the total situation. The real danger to democracy comes from the steady corruption of the political sense and morals of the people through the daily purveying of trash, sensation, distortion, and perversion.

Rise of Chronic Unemployment and Relief

Since the beginnings of the present complex industrial order with its factories, markets, cities, and delicate economic fabric men have known and feared the scourge of unemployment. During periods of crisis the number of working people seeking jobs, and unable to find them, becomes a vast army, reaching in the recent depression the extraordinary figure of between thirteen and sixteen millions. Even in good or ordinary times society has grown accustomed to the phenomenon of "normal unemployment," which amounted to approximately one million before the World War, two millions in the nineteen-twenties, and six millions or more in 1937. In addition the present epoch has witnessed the closing of the door of opportunity to youth on an enormous scale. In 1935 and 1936 it is estimated that there were about six million young people between the ages of sixteen and twenty-four who were neither in school nor at work. Denied entrance to occupations and admission to adult responsibilities they were forced to grow old in years without knowing those experiences which normally bring maturity. Public relief of the destitute, whether young or old, necessary as it may be to meet the breakdown of the economy, can be no substitute for work. The "dole" may serve to perpetuate outworn institutions and to ward off the attacks of hungry mobs, but it also tends to convert free men into slaves.

Here of a certainty is one of the most dangerous threats to political democracy. Having no stake in the existing social order, living in a state of perpetual anxiety, feeling themselves victims of gross injustice, casting off their old loyalties, and losing all sense of rationality the unemployed tend toward a condition of such utter demoralization that they are prepared to sell their souls for security, or even for a promise of security. In the case of youth, longing for life and its opportunities, all of these elements are compounded. Starving men have been known to throw off the teachings of thousands of years of civilized existence and resort to cannibalism. For them to forsake family, friends, and class, not to mention political convictions and principles, is but the first step toward complete disintegration of character. From the ranks of the unemployed the dictator, bent on the violent overthrow of government, has always been able to recruit his armies. In the current epoch of social upheaval they flocked to the standards of Mussolini and Hitler; they provided the means for the final destruction of free institutions in Austria; and they form the rank and file of strike-breakers in America.

The threat to democracy, arising from unemployment, does not come wholly and directly from the unemployed themselves. Their presence in society and their pressure on wage standards create a general condition of insecurity and anxiety. The entire population becomes frightened, regresses to a lower psychological plane, and resorts increasingly to irrational behavior. Such a situation may generate those energies necessary to bring about desirable changes in the social order, but only if the masses of the people have been prepared by education and thought to understand competing proposals and to distinguish between demagogy and honest leadership. The time perhaps is not far distant when circumstances will test the truth or falsehood of the Jeffersonian principle that the fate of free institutions cannot safely be entrusted to the guardianship of "the mobs of great cities." The whole of America today is one vast city and the entire population, regardless of dwelling place, is urban.

Tradition of Violence and Intolerance

In reviewing the disregard for law and the resort to violence in American history from colonial times down to the present James Truslow Adams concludes that "we have one of the most sinister inheritances . . . from which any civilized nation could suffer." [12] Michael Chevalier, when he visited the United States in 1834 and 1835, was greatly perturbed and distressed by the intolerance of the masses, the savagery of mobs, the frequent flouting of the law, and the seeming indifference of government to the violation of rights guaranteed by state and federal constitutions. He thus summarized the administering of "popular justice" to the Catholics in Massachusetts: "When the fanatics of Massachusetts, in their savage intolerance, feel offended by the presence of a Catholic convent, in which the sisters devote themselves to the work of educating young girls without distinction of sect, they plunder it and set it on fire, and the sacred edifice is burnt, in sight of a city with 70,000 inhabitants, without a drop of water being thrown upon the flames, and without its being possible to find a jury that would convict the authors of the cowardly outrage." [13]

While the attack upon the Catholics has subsided with the years, the following narrative of the treatment accorded Negroes seems strangely contemporary: "The destruction of the churches and school-houses of the blacks in New York was looked upon as a show, and the merchants of the city as they passed, paused to take a moment's relaxation from the sight;

the fall of the buildings was greeted with loud cheers. In Baltimore, a numerous crowd applauded the work of demolition without inquiring whose house was pulled down, and the women, in the excitement of the moment, waved their handkerchiefs in the air." [14] And here is an account of the torture of an abolitionist which illuminates the lot of the dissenter or non-conformist in American history but which one hesitates to repeat lest the method itself be revived: "A Virginia newspaper relates that an abolitionist, having fallen into the hands of a Committee of Vigilance, was stript naked, and stretched at his length on his face, when a cat was several times dragged across his bare back by the ruffians. A New York Journal repeats the statement with no other comment than some witticism." [15]

The historical record is literally covered with accounts of mobs, lynching parties, vigilance committees, "friends of law and order," and extra-legal bodies of every description, defying constituted authorities, taking the law into their own hands, and administering "justice" according to their own ideas and wishes. Nearly every racial or national minority, if markedly different in religion or color from the American stock, has felt the brutal hand of private hatred and vengeance—the Indians, the Negroes, the Chinese, the Japanese, the Mexicans, the Irish, the Italians, the Slavs, the Mormons, the Catholics, the Jews, and others. In this cruel and savage exercise of violence constitutional guarantees have been abrogated, printing plants and newspaper offices destroyed, homes, churches, and sections of towns and cities burned and pillaged, and men, women, and children beaten, tarred and feathered, shot, and lynched. In the struggle over Negro slavery, entirely apart from the Civil War, passions flamed on both sides and law was disregarded. In Philadelphia in 1838 a pro-slavery mob burned Pennsylvania Hall, an institution dedicated to the right of free speech. In New York in 1863 a riot burst forth, lasted four days, and destroyed property valued at $1,500,000. Similar riots occurred at the same time in Detroit, Kingston, Newark, and other cities. Much of the violence in American history, to be sure, has had no political significance and is to be traced to the march of the people across the continent in advance of the institutions of government. Yet much of it, notably Shay's Rebellion in Massachusetts in 1787, the Whiskey Insurrection in Pennsylvania in 1794, Dorr's Rebellion in Rhode Island in 1842, and the Civil War, did have political motive. And all of it has doubtless served to predispose the people of the United States to the use of violence in the defense of interests and the attainment of ends.

The major concern here, however, is not with violence having no political purpose or with conflicts over differences now dead and buried, but rather with that struggle between labor and capital during the past seventy-five years in which the great social issues of the present age are involved and in which may be discerned the seeds of a future conflict that may end in the complete destruction of democracy. Since the days of the revolt of the Pennsylvania miners against intolerable working and living conditions under the "Molly-Maguires" in the late sixties and early seventies of the last century to the massacre by South Chicago police of ten striking workmen demonstrating peacefully before the plant of the Republic Steel Corporation on Memorial Day, 1937, this conflict has assumed ever wider proportions, alternating between periods of open warfare and periods of preparation for the next trial of strength. It embraces such places, personalities, incidents, and organizations as the Pinkerton Detective Agency, the riots of 1877, the Knights of Labor, the Haymarket tragedy, the American Federation of Labor, the Homestead Strike, Coxey's army, the "Deb's Rebellion," the Industrial Workers of the World, "Big Bill" Haywood, the socialist movement, the Citizen's Industrial Association,

Pearl L. Bergoff, the dynamiting of The Los Angeles Times building, the Mooney-Billings trial, the United States v. Abrams, the great steel strike of 1919, the Communist Party, the Centralia affair, the Sacco-Vanzetti case, Harlan County, company unions, the Wagner Act, the Committee for Industrial Organization, John L. Lewis, sit-down strikes, Tom Girdler, and Henry Ford.

To assess praise or blame in this struggle which has been going on for generations is not the object of the present study. Yet it must be pointed out that the ranks of labor, though sometimes led by irresponsible apostles of violence and even by racketeers, have been fighting the battles of the common man against tremendous odds. In their demands for redress of grievances they have generally had to face a hostile press, unfriendly courts and judges, and the armed forces of government. The employing class, like every ruling class in history, has always identified its own interests with the common good and regarded itself as the only trustworthy defender of "law and order," being quite ready to defy laws and public officials in preserving the "American system" and guarding the "true interests of society." Its members have provided the means and the occasion for the development of great private detective agencies which usurp the police functions of government, send spies and *agents-provocateur* into factories and labor organizations, foment unrest among the workers, build up huge armies of strike-breakers recruited from the criminal and vicious elements of the big cities, and in case of strike hire out these plug-uglies and underworld characters for the purpose of beating or starving workingmen into submission. Also, as revealed by the investigations of the La Follete Committee, they have in many instances converted their factories into arsenals equipped with the lighter engines of modern warfare—revolvers, rifles, machine guns, and tear gas. Little wonder that they fear and oppose bitterly the sit-down strike.

The fact to be emphasized here, however, is that the tradition of violence in the settlement of questions involving the general interest is deeply rooted in American culture. This tradition has been defended and even encouraged by persons who profess to speak in the name of democracy and the welfare of the masses of the people. Certain elements associated with the labor movement have taught the doctrine that social justice can be achieved only by the sword. This is extremely dangerous doctrine for any faction, but emphatically so for all who are devoted to the advancement of popular welfare and rights. Occasional and spontaneous opposition of violence to violence on the part of farmers or workingmen, particularly where clear constitutional guarantees are violated, may serve the useful and necessary purpose of awakening the public conscience and directing attention to intolerable wrongs; but a general appeal to violence as a method of political change constitutes a popular retreat to the eighteenth century, a voluntary surrender of vantage points won at great cost of blood and treasure.

The case in support of the use of peaceful means in a political democracy is based on practical as well as humanitarian grounds. The recent history of Europe seems to teach that, whereas revolutionary violence may be employed successfully, under extremely favorable circumstances, by the people to overthrow autocracy, since no other method is available, it can be used in a democracy only to the advantage of reaction. Mussolini, Hitler, and General Franco owed no inconsiderable measure of the popular support they received to the threats and acts of violence employed by members and representatives of the laboring classes. The reason for the failure of the sword to uphold and advance the popular interest, especially in modern industrial society with its mechanized modes of warfare and propaganda, are

obvious. The concentration of economic power is so overwhelming that the aristocracy will have a decisive advantage
in any trial of military strength, provided it can count upon
the loyalty of a quarter or a fifth of the population. Such
a measure of loyalty is certain, if the onus for the initiation
of violence can be placed upon democratic elements—an
achievement of no great difficulty when the few exercise a
virtual monopoly over the organs of propaganda. Moreover, being the ostensible defender of orderly processes and
being the apparent victim of extra-legal force, the aristocracy would be in undisputed possession of the full power of
the state. Long before a popular movement can expect to
be sufficiently strong to cross swords with special privilege,
it will be in a position to take over the government by the
ballot and sweep aside all legal barriers to basic reform. The
ultimate triumph of democracy under these circumstances
will depend on its ability, with legality wholly on its side,
to meet any attempt of the few to prevent the transformation of property relationships by an appeal to violence.
Reactionary forces actually fear the ballot far more than the
sword: the latter has ever been their natural weapon. For
this reason they are always delighted when their opponents
advocate violence, even going so far as to put the words of
such advocacy into their mouths. A large element of the
American people are so thoroughly committed to orderly
procedures that their sympathy and loyalty will go to that
party in the controversy which appears to be on the side of
law and order. In the light of all these considerations any
"friend of the people" who counsels resort to the machine
gun may be set down as either a fool or a provocateur. If the
leaders of democracy are unable to win a majority of the
citizens to support vigorously and understandingly a program designed to achieve popular control of economic
power, that program cannot be successful.

System of Checks and Balances

William Manning observed that the "few have a grate advantage over the Many in forming & constructing Constitutions & Laws." By making "them numerous, intricate & as inexplicit as possible" the privileged orders "take to themselves the right of giving them such explanations as suits their interests."[16] If this New England farmer could view the system under which his successors live today, he would find far greater support for his thesis than was discernible in his time. Any candid student of contemporary American government, with its separation of powers, its geographical divisions and subdivisions, its maze of conflicting authorities and jurisdictions, its uncounted volumes of statutes and judicial decisions, must admit that a more "intricate and inexplicit" instrument of collective action would be difficult to conceive. The amending process, moreover, is so beset with hazards and obstacles that the system is often paralyzed when quick and vigorous action is desirable.

The federal constitution which as interpreted by the judges of the supreme court determines the general framework of the American political structure is calculated to make the administration of the public welfare feeble, uncertain, and inefficient. By separating the several branches of government and making them coordinate and independent, it renders unity of purpose and action on the part of the national authority practically impossible, except for brief and undefined periods. Some scholars have attributed this separation of powers to an error of observation by Montesquieu in his study of English political institutions in the eighteenth century. But whatever may be the responsibility of the great French jurist and philosopher, there is evident throughout the debates in the Constitutional Convention a distrust of the people. An effort was consequently made to remove the federal government as far from popular control as possible and keep substantial power in the hands of the holders of large property. Although in the meantime the executive and legislative branches have been made more directly responsible to the many, the judiciary has maintained its independence, assumed un-anticipated prerogatives, and greatly increased its authority. The net result is that the American people live today under a system of government that places an ever mounting strain on the democratic process and creates a condition which might prove favorable to the rise of dictatorship.

This critical situation, as noted in an earlier chapter, is due primarily to the fact that the age is greatly enlarging the burdens of government. For a century now the advance of industrial society has so extended and multiplied the functions of the political state, and particularly of the federal authority, that the very conception of public administration has been transformed. Moreover, the highly dynamic character of this new order founded on science and technology makes delay costly and efficiency imperative in public no less than in private enterprise. Consequently, the incompetence which is now practically compelled by the law tends increasingly to discredit democratic government. The opposition on the part of the aristocracy to the President's proposals to reorganize the federal departments and bureaus suggests an ill-concealed desire to bring political action into disrepute.

But, from the standpoint of the central argument of the present volume the crucial question pertains less to efficiency of administration than to ability to achieve fundamental economic reform through governmental action. The American system of checks and balances is admirably designed to thwart any expression of the popular will, to reverse through the machinery of government victory won at the polls, to enable an aristocracy of riches to rule in spite of the verdict of the ballot. The way it may be employed to such ends is well illustrated in the first year of the second administration of Franklin D. Roosevelt. Elected by an overwhelming majority in November, 1936, he proceeded along lines already laid out and understood by the people to employ the institutions of political democracy to make the economy serve more fully the general interest. But the aristocracy refused to accept defeat. Enlisting the services of newspapers, columnists, commentators, and public relations counselors and marshaling its matchless resources for influencing congressmen and other public officials, it turned the legislature against the executive and set aside the election returns almost as effectively as if it had stuffed the ballot box and placed its own nominee in the White House. Playing upon the traditional jealousies of the executive cherished by legislature and judiciary, charging congressmen sensitive to the expressed will of the electorate with servility to the President, praising its own obedient henchmen for independence of thought and character, promoting with its entire arsenal of propaganda a cult of constitution worship, accusing Mr. Roosevelt of harboring both communist and fascist leanings, cajoling and threatening all who dared to act in the public interest, and predicting in screaming headline and lugubrious editorial the end of liberty in America, it succeeded in paralyzing the machinery of government and brought political action to a standstill. How many times this course can be repeated before large masses of the people will lose faith in the efficacy of political democracy and follow the magic strains of some pied piper of dictatorship cannot be foretold. But the system of checks and balances, of separation of powers, can only be regarded as a serious liability by all who would employ the democratic process in achieving fundamental economic reform.

Failure of Organized Civic Education

In conclusion the fact must be noted that organized civic education in the United States has failed. At any rate, in the presence of the great obstacles already catalogued, it has not succeeded in producing a generation of citizens capable of understanding the present social order and of promoting effectively the general welfare. The school, to be sure, has vastly extended its operations both horizontally and vertically: it has reached out to embrace practically the entire population and has greatly increased the quantity of schooling. The opportunities of secondary and higher education have been provided on a scale hitherto unknown in any age or country. It has taught children to read and write and spell, and to manipulate the fundamental combinations of arithmetic; it has acquainted them with certain facts of geography and history, including the names of cities, presidents, and foreign states; it has given to an increasing number of them a smattering knowledge of ancient and modern foreign languages; it has taught girls to sew and cook, and boys to saw, hammer, and take a gasoline engine apart; it has even explained to them the operation of the electoral college, the duties of the dog-catcher, and the causes of the advancing divorce rate. And yet something vitally essential seems to have been omitted.

While the school has taught children the mechanics of reading, it has not taught them to understand what they read in the newspapers and magazines. While it has acquainted them with many important facts about American history, it has not given them an intelligible picture of the nature of democracy and its changing fortunes during the past several generations. Since the Civil War it has by implication taught succeeding generations that with the emancipation of the slaves a complete democracy was established and that no real threat to free institutions could come from the concentration of economic power. Through the McGuffey Readers and their successors, it continued to teach the maxims of Poor Richard and the Sunday School while the "robber barons," in obedience to wholly different principles, were gaining control of the material resources of the nation. It has burdened the minds of children with endless details of governmental forms and practices, but has failed to give them an understanding of the underlying forces in economy and society. It has required of them "scholarship" of a formal and academic type, but it has not given them practical insight into the social order, nor a sense of responsibility for participating in its democratic guidance. It has taught them to salute the flag and take oaths of loyalty to the constitution, but has prepared them to understand neither. In a word the school, in spite of its many and genuine achievements, has failed to give to the rising generation that penetration into American history, institutions, and society essential to intelligent citizenship. In the words and spelling of William Manning it has failed to give its charges the "knowledge nesecary for a freeman."

REFERENCES

1. William Manning, *The Key of Libberty* (Billerica, Mass., 1922) , 22.

2. "Program of the New York State Economic Council," adopted by Board of Directors, July 20, 1934. *The New York Times* (August 6, 1934).

3. Alexander Hamilton, *The Federalist* (Everyman's Library edition, New York, 1911) , 402.

4. Harvey O'Connor, *Mellon's Millions* (New York, 1933) , 1.

5. F. J. Turner, "Social Forces in American History," *American Historical Review*, (January, 1911) , 227.

6. Daniel Webster, *The Works* (Boston, 1857) , II, 30.

7. Fanny Wright, *Views of Society and Manners in America* (New York, 1821) , 239.

8. Michael Chevalier, *Society, Manners and Politics in the United States* (Boston, 1839) , 430.

9. Sir Charles Lyell, *A Second Visit to the United States of North America* (New York, 1849) , I, 204.

10. *Op. cit.,* xiv.

11. *The New York Times* (July 25, 1937) .

12. James Truslow Adams, "Our Lawless Heritage" in *Our Business Civilization* (New York, 1929) , 117-118.

13. *Op. cit.,* 390.

14. *Ibid.,* 390-391.

15. *Ibid.,* footnote, 387.

16., *Op. cit.,* 21.

CHAPTER *10:*

SOME ASSETS

T HE foregoing catalog of liabilities, incomplete as it is, would seem to remove all hope of employing political processes in reconstructing the economic foundations of American democracy. The list is indeed long and formidable. As one passes in review the obstacles which time and circumstance have placed in the path of popular rule, the thought keeps recurring that the grand experiment with free institutions may be but a brief interlude in the long course of autocratic government which is the normal condition of human society. One wonders whether the undermining of democracy, in both its inner and its outer manifestations, in both its mentality and its social arrangements, has not already proceeded so far that the battle is lost before it is begun; whether the American people may not have missed their opportunity two generations ago when the aristocracy was relatively confined and feeble and the forces of democracy were strong and confident. Such gloomy forebodings may be proved correct; but thus to prejudge the case would paralyze the will and insure defeat. It must not be forgotten that what a people may think of a social situation constitutes a vital part of that situation.

The other side of the ledger is by no means barren of items. The American people possess certain powerful assets which should go far toward canceling the liabilities—greater assets assuredly than any other major nation in the contemporary world can marshal. Comparatively, it is as true today as in the time of Daniel Webster that "no combination of circumstances more favorable to the experiment (of popular government) can ever be expected to occur." The faith in democracy, though dimmed by the social changes of a century, still has its roots in reality and has enormous resources at its disposal. The more important of these resources will be developed under the following ten heads: the liquidation of feudal institutions and mentality, the democratic heritage, the experimental temper of the people, the tradition of "good neighbourship," the contemporary European spectacle, the weaknesses of the aristocracy, the natural and technical resources of the country, the security of the nation from external attack, the high political sense of the population, and the growing body of precise knowledge of man and human affairs.

Liquidation of Feudal Institutions and Mentality

From the standpoint of the utilization of democratic methods in the solution of the difficult problems now facing the American people, the relative absence of feudal institutions and mentality may prove to be an asset of very great, even of decisive, worth. In this respect the United States is to be distinguished from practically every country in the Old World and from most in the New. America was settled at the time of the disintegration of the Medieval system and for the most part by immigrants from countries that had moved farthest on the road toward the modern order. "America was opened after the feudal mischief was spent," wrote Ralph Waldo Emerson in 1878, "and so the people made a good start. We began well. No inquisition here, no kings, no nobles, no dominant church. Here heresy has lost its terrors."[1] John Taylor, commenting on the fact that in Europe the new "aristocracy of paper and patronage" had grown up by the side of the older "aristocracy of the sword," observed that the European nations "are subjected by both, so that their chains are doubly riveted."[2] The significance of the relative absence of feudal influences can best be developed by considering some of the implications of the high level of social mobility, the absence of a state church, and the lack of a military caste.

The fact of social and occupational mobility has already been noted. The conditions attending the conquest of the new continent led to the abandonment of the feudal system of landholding, the opening up of economic opportunity to the individual, the overthrow of aristocratic conceptions of birth, family, rank, and caste, and generally the attainment of the highest level of social mobility known to history. All of this has given a special character to the struggle of classes and interests in the United States. That such a struggle exists and has existed in more or less acute form since colonial times is scarcely a subject for dispute. The fact was recognized as basic to any true understanding of politics by the founding fathers and has been recognized by every realistic student of the history of the Republic. Also it is clearly at the root of the social problem today. On this point Mr. George Gallup, whose American Institute of Public Opinion during the last three years "has interviewed hundreds of thousands of American voters, composing a true cross-section of the population in all walks of life," is in a peculiarly favorable position to comment. He finds that among the "cleavages that exist today in American public opinion" the one that "overshadows all others has to do with wealth. It is the cleavage between the high and low income brackets, the split between the 'haves' and the 'have nots.'" He estimates that "in the 1936 election the upper third of the voting population, economically speaking, was on the Landon side. The middle third was strongly for Roosevelt; the lower third overwhelmingly for Roosevelt." [3]

The present struggle over wages, the control of economic power, the extension of the authority of the state, and the coordination and planning of the economy in the interests of the whole community, is at bottom a conflict of social classes. With the rise of industrial society the overwhelming mass of the population has become dependent for wages, salaries, and the means of livelihood on a minority which has grown smaller as the concentration of title to productive property has advanced. It is this struggle primarily that has led to revolution, appeal to the sword, and rejection of the democratic political process in Russia, Italy, Germany, Spain, and a number of the smaller countries of the Old World. The only debatable question has to do with the form which the conflict is to assume in the United States. And here the special character of the American class structure may play a decisive role.

That the great majority of American citizens can be placed primarily either in the class owning productive property or in the dependent class is capable of statistical demonstration. This seems to be as true for all practical purposes in America as in Europe. Yet it does not follow that the pattern of the struggle on the two continents will necessarily be the same, for there seems to be a powerful moderating factor here which is largely absent on the other side of the Atlantic. While the individual in the United States can ordinarily be shown to belong in the one category or the other, the family *as a rule* cannot. Whatever the future may hold, the American family today is not confined within class boundaries.

While this subject merits far more study than it has received, considerable evidence is at hand to support the conclusion that the members of the larger family—brothers and sisters, parents, uncles and aunts, first cousins, grandparents, and grand-uncles and aunts—are commonly distributed over almost the entire range of occupations and economic circumstances.[4] Even within the smaller family of parents and children, where time has had its opportunity to make differentiation possible, the distribution is impressive. There are doubtless numerous individual, group, and regional exceptions. The above study was confined to families which had lived in America for three generations or more. In the case of recent immigrants the pattern is probably somewhat different. The same may be true of the Negro, of certain other racial and national minorities, of a few families long established in wealth, of backwoods and isolated districts, and possibly of occasional communities in which modern industrialism has founded a quasi-feudal rule. Yet, while the rate of social mobility is certainly declining and while a tendency toward class stratification is discernible, it seems highly probable, in fact almost certain, that in its membership the average American family today, unlike its European counterpart, cuts across class lines and softens class divisions. As Pitirim Sorokin says in summarizing the available data on shifting on the economic ladder, "it is not accurate to depict present economic classes as 'hereditarily rich' or 'hereditarily poor.'" [5] The mentality of the American people today, moreover, is largely a product of all of those leveling factors which accompanied the settlement of the continent.

The bearing of this fact on the future of democracy in America is fairly obvious. The institutions and practices of popular government rest upon the assumption that conflicts of interest arising in society can be adjudicated by some process which stops short of the exercise of physical might. The relative absence of the one-class family would seem to lend strength to this process. Where the class differences of capitalistic society are reinforced by the feudal tradition with its fairly rigid caste lines, its distinct and mutually exclusive orders, its master and servant relationships, its deep-seated conceptions of inferiority and superiority, and its attitudes of servility and arrogance, the ensuing struggle, once it has broken through the crust of tradition, may be expected to scorn every compromise and go to extremes of bitterness and hatred. In such a society each party to the struggle tends to repudiate completely the binding conception of a common humanity and to regard the other as a different order of creation: the masses come to look upon the aristocracy as a race of tyrants, while the latter views the former as dogs and cattle—brutes to be beaten into submission with the lash. That this condition will never appear in America is by no means suggested; but it is not here today. And until it does emerge, the class struggle will probably not be carried to its last extremity. In the meantime because of the relatively classless character of the family and the molding influence of frontier and farm in the past, large elements on both sides will be reluctant to abandon the democratic process. Compromises will be made and in all likelihood an unusually large number of individuals in the privileged orders will forsake allegiance to their class, reject their immediate and narrow economic interests, and throw their influence and talents on the side of the democracy and the general welfare.

The state church, one of the most characteristic institutions of the feudal system, is also lacking in the United States. For this heritage of religious freedom and diversity every friend of democracy should be deeply grateful. Where such a church exists, it almost invariably throws its great power on the side of reaction, applies the sanction of divinity to existing institutions and relationships, holds over the apostles of change the threat of excommunication and eternal damnation, and generally through ties of loyalty stronger than physical chains binds all but the bolder spirits to the conditions which exploit them. "Poor, love your humble state and your work; turn your gaze toward Heaven; there is the true wealth. Only one thing I ask: of the rich, love; of the poor, resignation." [6] So speaks the universal state church in the pastoral letter of a Catholic Archbishop addressed to the working people of Mexico. In the course of time, whatever its original doctrines and professions, the institution acquires wealth and property, the ecclesiastical hierarchy becomes an integral part of the governing authority, and the princes of the church become princes of the temporal order. So it was in France under the Bourbons, so it was in Connecticut under the Dwights, and so it was in Russia under the Romanoffs. Moreover, regardless of its relationship with the state, the strong authoritarian tradition of the church tends to breed in the people a temper which is alien to the spirit and processes of democracy.

In America the state church disappeared entirely in the early part of the nineteenth century. And through the guarantees of religious freedom written into state and federal constitution the United States came to be marked in exceptional measure by numerous and competing creeds and sects. Under such conditions, particularly when combined with a high rate of literacy and the leveling of all geographical barriers, the arbitrary quality of ecclesiastical authority becomes highly attenuated. While certain of the denominations may be expected to support the cause of aristocracy in the current struggle, others will doubtless throw their weight on the side of the people and a single pronouncement in the name of God will be rendered impossible. Where the deity speaks in many and discordant voices the ordinary citizen may be permitted to choose that particular revelation which to him seems most just and reasonable. Also, where all churches must live by popular favor and where mistakes will redound to the advantage of powerful competitors, every sect will incline toward caution and moderation in its declarations of social doctrine. Certainly the American people should thank God every night and morning for the complete absence of anything resembling an established church in the United States. Also they should be ever alert to thwart the political ambitions of any denomination and to block every effort that even suggests the reunion of church and state.

Equally important is the absence of a military caste, proud and arrogant, scornful of peaceful persons and pursuits, confident of its natural right to rule, and ready at all times

either to impose its own will upon the state or to ally itself
with some faction for the protection or promotion of its
special interests. Where such a caste exists, as the historical
record plainly shows, from the time of the Caesars to contemporary Germany, Japan, and Spain, the existence of
democracy is rendered extremely precarious. So the founding fathers, familiar with the role of the professional soldier
in human history and particularly mindful of their experience with English armies during the long struggle for independence, endeavored to write into the fundamental law of
the land provisions which for all time would safeguard the
nation from the depredations of a separate class of warriors.
The Constitution subordinates the military to the civil
authority and guarantees "the right of the people to keep
and bear arms." Moreover, as Michael Chevalier observed,
"one of the fundamental maxims of American politics is, that
the sword and purse should not be united in the same
hands." 7

While the development of a regular army and a professional navy, and the formation of organizations of veterans,
from the Society of the Cincinnati to the American Legion,
have perhaps placed the principle in some danger, during
the century and a half since the founding of the Republic a
tradition making the military subservient to the civil power
has been firmly established. Because of the mechanization of
warfare and the consequent practical nullification of the
constitutional provision regarding the right of the people
to keep and bear arms, the perdurance of democracy in the
United States may well depend on the vitality of this tradition. Although only the event can settle the question, there
is little reason for believing that the armed forces of the
nation would under any imaginable circumstances follow
the precedent of the Spanish military caste and violate their
oath of loyalty to the Constitution. If the American aristocracy, defeated at the polls, should draw the sword in

defense of its privileges, it would doubtless have to reckon with the army. Such at least would seem to be the probability.

The position in the United States of certain of these feudal or quasi-feudal institutions and practices, and particularly the army, was recently summarized by Charles A. Beard:

In America we have no legalized aristocracy, no hangover aristocrary, no legalized clergy, no military caste with its heredi- tary corps of officers, no quasi-hereditary bureaucracy enjoying a privileged position in the state, ready to serve any de facto government, however raised to power; not yet! The politics of our military system is remarkable. Every Congressman, as you know, can name two members from his district for West Point, and every Senator his quota. Thus the potential cadets are scat- tered all over the country, so that under this beautiful system of spoils and patronage we are spared that great enemy of democ- racy, a hereditary military caste—through no efforts of our own but by favor of politics, democratic politics. Now these peculiar features of American life give evidence of a democratic practice that is not to be found in England or on the continent.[8]

Democratic Heritage

In the immediately preceding chapter attention was directed to the dangers resident in the misuse of a great heritage. That such dangers exist must be freely admitted; but they exist only if the heritage is not understood and used by the people. If it is understood, it immediately assumes the rank of the greatest asset of the American nation during the present critical period. If it is fully used, the future can be faced with optimism. The fact must not be overlooked, however, that to make full use of it, with the agencies of propaganda largely in hostile hands, will be ex- tremely difficult. The campaign of obfuscation is already far advanced. The immediate task is to recover a legacy which is in process of being turned against its rightful claimants. The American people have had long experience with

democratic institutions and ideas. Habits, dispositions, and
loyalties thus fashioned through generations and centuries
are not easily cast aside even in moments of great national
stress. The citizens of the United States, moreover, as already
noted in another connection, are peculiarly the children of
one of the truly great epochs in human history—the epoch
that witnessed the birth of the modern spirit. The age which
shaped them was the age which began with the Renaissance
and the Reformation, produced the Enlightenment and the
English and French revolutions, nurtured the growth of
science and the overthrow of authoritarianism in one field
after another, repudiated the dogma of divinity of kings
and institutions, propagated throughout the world the great
ethical conceptions of liberty, equality, and fraternity, com-
municated to mankind the idea of progress and the indefinite perfectability of man and society, saw the writing
of the great documents of the American revolution, and
aroused in ordinary men and women the hope and the conviction that they might be secure and free. The fact should
be emphasized that America was discovered and settled, her
institutions and outlook formed, during this period. More
than any other nation the people of the United States are
the product of all of those influences which marked the
coming of the modern age.

This has given to the American people a conception of the
state which may prove of crucial importance. To them the
state with its manifold institutions is no transcendent entity
ordained by God and destined to be worshiped and obeyed:
it is but an instrument fashioned by their own hands, intended to promote the welfare of ordinary men and women,
dedicated to the development of individuality and character
in its citizens, and subject to modification on the clear and
unequivocal expression of the popular will. These are the
A, B, C's, of American political and social doctrine; and,
while not always clearly understood, they are generally

sensed by the rank and file of the people. The deepest loyalties of the average citizen are not attached to any particular
historic or contemporary party program, political institution, or economic practice; rather are they attached to a
conception of social welfare which is deeper and more
abiding than any set of social arrangements and by which a
given practice or measure is to be judged. In the essential
American political tradition the form must at all times be
sacrificed to the spirit. This philosophy was clearly expressed
by Jefferson in the Declaration of Independence when he
delibately altered the political triad composed by the rising
middle class and changed *property* to *pursuit of happiness*.
Here is the reason that the admonition, often administered
to the critic of the existing social order, "if you don't like
America, you should go back to where you came from," has
a hollow ring. The American system of government and
society requires criticism, the most searching criticism possible, from all loyal sons and daughters. In contrast with
authoritarian states, where thought is monopolized by the
few, here thought is both a right and a duty of the many.
While this fundamental principle of democracy is often
honored in the breach, its authority is generally recognized.

It is relevant to observe that the American people have
already in the course of their history passed from one economic system to another. At the time their nation was founded
they lived under a pre-industrial economy that was neither
feudal nor capitalistic—a simple agrarian order of relatively
self-contained households in which the market played a
secondary role. Consequently, if they know their own past,
they can hardly be expected to fight and die in defense of
the current economic arrangements; particularly if they
become convinced that those arrangements threaten their
democracy and are at the same time the cause of injustice,
misery, and frustration. On the contrary, in such an event,
provided they could gain some release from the cult of an-

cestor worship so sedulously cultivated by the few, they would doubtless demand even profound changes in their economic system. This is the true spirit of American democracy.

At the same time the long experience of the American people with popular government has tended to breed in them that elastic temperament which is essential to the successful operation of democratic institutions. They realize, at least in their more sober moments, that the introduction of sweeping changes into the social structure is not to be undertaken lightly, that even the best of minds cannot penetrate far into the future, and that simple solutions of complex social problems should be met with honest skepticism. Similarly do they know that the peaceful settlement of differences requires its own sacrifices, that the legitimate rights of minorities should be respected, that the possibility of error must ever be recognized, and that a spirit of compromise is preferable to blind loyalty to dogma or doctrine. While this temperament is doubtless less widespread and deeply rooted than might be desired, it is probably sufficiently strong to withstand shocks of considerable severity. Whether it will prove equal to the task of meeting the demands of the coming struggle will depend, on the one hand, on the severity of the struggle and, on the other, on what is done in the meantime to propagate and vitalize the entire democratic tradition.

Experimental Temper of the American People

Closely linked with the democratic heritage is the experimental temper of the American people. Having been nurtured on the rationalism of John Locke, the French Encyclopaedists, and their successors, they have a deep faith in the powers of the human mind. Having broken with the past originally to cross the Atlantic and having broken with it again and again in the settlement and conquest of the continent, they tend to be impatient of the authority of tradition. Having passed with great rapidity through a succession of frontiers, having moved within a century from a simple agrarian order into a most advanced industrial society, having experienced in a few generations the transformation of most of the institutions of family and community, having changed their places of residence, modes of life, and social arrangements often and profoundly in the course of their relatively short history, they have acquired a mentality favorable to experiment and adventure. Although proposed changes in every field have commonly evoked the vocal and spirited opposition of a minority, the opposition as a rule has been overwhelmed. In a word the American people do not fear change as have most of the peoples who have lived on the earth.

More than that, they possess an outlook that welcomes change, that expects improvement from change, that regards change as an omen of good, that looks with hope to the future, that even tends uncritically to think of the new as better than the old. "Nobody," wrote Michael Chevalier of the American, "can conform so easily to new situations and circumstances; he is always ready to adopt new processes and implements, or to change his occupation." [9] This same observer quotes with approval a humorous passage from an unnamed American writer which reveals this characteristic confidence in the future: "We are born in haste; we finish our education on the run; we marry on the wing; we make a fortune at a stroke, and lose it in the same manner, to make and lose it again ten times over, in the twinkling of an eye. Our body is a locomotive, going at the rate of twenty five miles an hour; our soul, a high-pressure engine; our life is like a shooting star, and death overtakes us at last like a flash of lightning." [10] That such optimism reflected the unexampled opportunities for individual advancement, which at least for the time seem to have been checked, does not destroy it as a factor in the present.

Experience with change has bred in the American people a suspicion of prophecies of doom and a readiness to experiment. While this empirical and adventurous temper has thus far been particularly manifest in the realm of the material and mechanical aspects of the culture, yet the extreme popularity of Franklin D. Roosevelt suggests that it is already spreading to the sphere of economic and political arrangements. The worship of the constitution and the supreme court, for example, though carefully promoted, could scarcely long withstand their failure to function effectively. If the ordinary citizen exhibits an overweening loyalty to certain features of the social structure, it is probably because for a long period they have seemed to work unusually well. With the standards of living of the Old World ever in mind he has regarded himself among the favored of the gods. Let him become convinced that his institutions stand in the way of his interests and he will make comparatively short shrift of them. The fact that they are hallowed with antiquity will give to them a wholly illusory support.

The fact that the philosophy of instrumentalism developed in the United States is no accident. When in 1930 the University of Paris bestowed an honorary degree on Professor John Dewey, with whose name this philosophy is most closely identified, the Dean of the Faculty of Letters, in conferring the degree, characterized Doctor Dewey with true insight as "the most profound, most complete expression of American genius." [11] In the domain of practical affairs, where results can be checked, the average American is an instrumentalist by long experience. Paraphrasing Franklin, he does not inquire concerning an institution, *What is it?* but *What can it do?* Indeed he "instinctively" determines the nature of an institution by the manner in which it functions. He grasps quickly and eagerly the observation of Jesus of

Nazareth that the Sabbath was made for man, and not man for the Sabbath. Also he tends to reject those neat systems of social logic, those "high-falutin" ideologies so congenial to the European mind which, while being great achievements of the intellect, tend to lose touch with the living reality, seek to force society into the artificial categories of a scheme of consistent propositions, and serve as false guides in grappling with the actual world in which men toil and struggle. As a consequence, not knowing the ultimate truth, he can escape that slavery to doctrine which has ever been the bane of civilized man and consigned millions to the torture chamber. He is ready to experiment, to judge by consequences, even to compromise. All of which is necessary to the operation of the democratic process.

That this predilection toward change, this practical and experimental temper, this scorn of theoretical knowledge has its dangers in the contemporary situation is obvious. Under the spell of the blind optimism nurtured by their history the American people may rush into strange experiments in economy and government without adequate intellectual preparation. Unfortified by general conceptions they may become the easy victims of some gifted demagogue. And yet it scarcely seems probable that they would ever behave more irrationally than that great people which for the past two centuries has dominated the field of systematic thought and philosophy—the German nation. If a country could be saved by its theorists, the Second Reich certainly would not have succumbed to the mad proposals of Hitler. Perhaps the experimental temper of the American people will prove dangerous only if it is not informed.

Tradition of "Good Neighbourship"

As pointed out in an earlier chapter, the economic individualism of the frontier and the farm which the great majority of the American people practiced for generations was far less rugged and ruthless than many champions of the virtues of calculated selfishness would have the present generation believe. It was tempered in the family group by a spirit of cooperation and mutual helpfulness: it was tempered in the sphere of community relationships by a spirit of "good neighbourship" and simple human kindliness. Isolated and self-sufficient individuals, living by the principle of "each for himself, and the devil take the hindmost," could never have conquered and settled the North American continent. The curbing of egoistic impulses and the pooling of resources and energies were demanded on innumerable occasions. In an economy without money, without extensive division of labor, without a dependent class of slaves, serfs, or wage-earners, voluntary exchange of services, paradoxically, was "compulsory." According to Tocqueville, co-operation was fostered by that very "equality of conditions" which produced the individualism of the many. This equality, "whilst it makes men feel their independence," he wrote, "shows them their own weakness: they are free, but exposed to a thousand accidents; and experience soon teaches them that, although they do not habitually require the assistance of others, a time almost always comes when they cannot do without it." [12]

In the presence of danger or disaster these "individualists" often enforced severe discipline, despising as cowards or loafers all who refused to share the burden of defending the general welfare. For two and a half centuries the settlers along the frontier carried on an intermittent but pitiless struggle with the Indian—one of the most courageous and warlike races ever to face the white man. Frontiersmen of both sexes arranged their dwellings and planned their common life in order to meet the threat of attack from the savages. For the same reason, as they migrated toward the Pacific, whether by trail or waterway, whether through the forests, across the plains, or over the mountains, they advanced in bands and companies more or less well organized and disciplined. Also they combined to protect themselves against the depredations of horse-thieves and bandits, against the ravages of floods, droughts, and pests. Their recognition of the community interest went so far as to deny the rights of private property to fish, game, bee trees, wild nuts and fruit, and within limits even the produce of orchard and garden.

They were always ready to come to the aid of the individual or family in distress, whether friend or stranger. "When an American asks for the co-operation of his fellow-citizens," observes Tocqueville, "it is seldom refused; and I have often seen it afforded spontaneously, and with great good-will. If an accident happens on the highway, everybody hastens to help the sufferer; if some great and sudden calamity befalls a family, the purses of a thousand strangers are at once willingly opened, and small but numerous donations pour in to relieve their distress." [13] And this assistance was usually proffered without a thought of charity or feeling of self-righteousness, it being well understood that no one is immune to the visits of misfortune.

But perhaps the most striking and significant form of cooperation was called forth by those varied tasks and undertakings which tended to exceed the powers of the individual family or which lent themselves peculiarly to group performance. Indeed, these early individualists seem to have found much of their recreation and social life in occupational "festivals" which still survive here and there in vestigial form. Great numbers of activities were made the occasion for community gatherings and cooperative effort. John Bradbury thus describes and interprets this feature of American rural life as he saw it:

It is necessary to remark, that in the early part of the settlement of a country like this, a great number of things occur neces-

sary to be done, which require the united strength of numbers
to effect. In those parts, money cannot purchase for the new
settler the required aid; but that kind and generous feeling
which men have for each other, who are not rendered callous by
the possession of wealth, or the dread of poverty, comes to his
relief: his neighbours, even unsolicited, appoint a day when
as a *frolic*, they shall, for instance, build him a house. On
the morning of the appointed day they assemble, and divide
themselves into parties, to each of which is assigned its respective
duty; one party cuts down the trees, another lops and cuts them
to proper lengths, a third is furnished with horses and oxen, and
drags them to the spot designed for the scite of the house:
another party is employed in making *shingles* to cover the roof,
and at night all the materials are ready upon the spot; and on
the night of the next day, he and his family sleep in their new
habitation. No remuneration is expected, nor would it be
received. It is considered the performance of a duty, and only
lays him under the obligation to discharge the debt by doing the
same to subsequent settlers. But this combination of labour in
numbers, for the benefit of one individual, is not confined to
the new comer only, it occurs frequently in the course of a year
amongst the *old settlers*, with whom it is a continued bond of
amity and social intercourse, and in no part of the world is *good
neighbourship* found in greater perfection than in the western
territory, or in America generally.[14]

Certain interesting details are added in an account by
John Woods, an Englishman who from the vantage point
of an English settlement in Illinois in 1820-21 made a competent study of American life and customs on the frontier.
After describing a "Husking Frolic," he observed that while
the English settlers harvested their corn without recourse to
group action, "the Americans seldom do anything without
having" a frolic:

Thus, they have husking, reaping, rolling frolics, &c. &c.
Among the females, they have picking, sewing, and quilting frolics. Reaping frolics, are parties to reap the whole growth of

wheat, &c. in one day. Rolling frolics, are clearing wood-land, when many trees are cut down, and into lengths, to roll them up together, so as to burn them, and to pile up the brushwood and roots on the trees. I think this one is useful, as one man or his family can do but little in moving a large quantity of heavy timber. Picking cotton, sewing, and quilting frolics, are meetings to pick cotton from the seeds, make clothes, or quilt quilts; in the latter, the American women pride themselves. Whiskey is here too in request, and they generally conclude with a dance.[15]

James B. Ireland, "looking backward through one-hundred years" of life in Kentucky, tells how these group undertakings looked to a participant and explains something of their philosophy:

It was slow, laborious work clearing the land of the heavy timber. In the fall of the year people would raise houses and barns and in the spring every man would have a log rolling. I would lose a week or two at a time in the busiest part of the year helping my neighbors roll logs. Every one had to be neighborly in self defense. If you did not help others, others would not help you. This log rolling was no fun. Men would go early, work hard and late. At dinner time they would gather around the Spring, quench their thirst and wash their blackened hands. The bottle and sugar would be set out. All would take a toddy and sit down to a good dinner which had been cooked in pots and skillets around the fire place or outside under a shed and which the women took great pride in serving. We would be treated to hog jowl, fried eggs, turnip greens, corn bread, fried ham, hot biscuits, butter and butter milk, winding up with half moon fried pies and maple molasses. In order to make one dinner answer two purposes the women would frequently invite their friends the same day to a quilting or wool picking.[16]

Charles A. Beard, in a recent communication to *The New York Times* in which he takes issue with certain statements made by James Truslow Adams in an article printed in the paper the week before, gives vigorous expression to the cooperative and neighborly aspect of the old frontier and farming life. Mr. Adams had said that "on each frontier the same fundamentals were driven home. A man had to depend upon himself. He made his clearing, built his house, and sowed his crops or hunted game. With no police or courts, he was a law unto himself." In responding Mr. Beard writes in part as follows:

The frontier was crude in many ways, no doubt. The English language was badly treated, in a fashion somewhat Elizabethan. But the frontier was far removed from the harsh, materialistic picture which Mr. Adams and his colleagues are fond of giving us.

Now I come down to the individualism business. Neither the man nor the family stood alone, save perhaps in isolated cases. No individual man could build himself a log cabin or make a clearing without help. If he had no near neighbors, his wife took the other end of the cross-cut saw. But generally he had neighbors. They "swapped" work. It was a common thing when a couple was married for the neighbors to gather, cut trees, and build a cabin for them.

The spirit of the frontier as I knew the pioneers was not the spirit of individualism that characterizes the war for trade, jobs and profit in the cities. Pioneers were individuals, of course, and had a strong sense of individual responsibility—perhaps stronger than some of the great bankers in charge of fiduciary trusts in 1928. But pioneers were not striving to get trade or jobs away from the neighboring pioneers. Their profit was the spirit of neighborly helpfulness—in work, in times of adversity, in hours of celebration.[17]

Some may argue that this tradition of "good neighbour-ship" is wholly a thing of the past, that it is dead, that it has left no imprint on the character of the American people. And they may be correct. Perhaps it has been destroyed by the pecuniary standards of capitalism, by the impersonal relationships of the great industrial society, by the deep divisions of interest that shake the contemporary economy. But all of this is mere speculation. Whether the tradition still lives can be ascertained only by appealing to it. If it has in fact disappeared with the conditions from which it sprang, then no appeal can evoke a response. There is evidence, however, that it still possesses some vitality. The predilection of the American people to join organizations, their well-authenticated generosity in the presence of suffering, and their readiness to respond to leadership devoted to the general welfare suggest that it only awaits the direction appropriate to the new age. At any rate those who would make democracy work in the present epoch of close interdependence cannot afford to ignore or repudiate this possible resource from the past. Perhaps the central social task of the age may be defined as the application of the old principle of "good neighborship" to the great neighborhood of today.

Contemporary European Spectacle

The spectacle of contemporary Europe must convince any American that the substitution of the method of violence for the democratic process invariably exacts a heavy, an intolerable, price. The course of events in Spain, as reported in every newspaper, repeats the experience of thousands of years of history. For more than two full years now that country has been ravaged by a civil struggle of unsurpassed bitterness in which the deadly engines of modern warfare have been turned against civil populations and thus have added to the terrors traditionally associated with fratricidal strife. Regardless of which side is finally victorious, the cost of this conflict in material goods, in human life, in maimed bodies and souls will burden the Spanish people for a generation and leave a heritage of hatred that will live on for a century. Even those ambitious and brutalized minds in Spain and Europe which calmly engineered the uprising of July, 1936, can scarcely look with satisfaction on the work of their hands today. Although they may retain no vestige of human conscience and thirst only for power and dominion, they must at least be profoundly dismayed by the heroic and sustained resistance of the Spanish people. In its issue of August 7, 1937, *The New York Times* printed the following tragic comment on the news that the New England Crutch Company of Worner, New Hampshire, had been operating day and night since the outbreak of the Spanish struggle:

> Crutches to Spain! . . . Crutches for Moors maimed in the drive for Madrid, crutches for Spaniards mutilated in the shadow of the ruined glories of the Alcazar, crutches for Frenchmen, Germans, Russians crippled in a senseless slaughter. . . . Crutches to China, where brown men are slaughtering brown men in the land of Li Po, where youths are dying in the dust of centuries. . . . Crutches for a world sick with the throbbing fever of fanaticism, blinded by petty prejudice and false loyalties to false gods, crippled by the personal lust for power, the national lust for empire and for gain. Crutches to Spain! . . . A bitter mockery to the maimed and to those who died for dreams that died, a bitter mockery unless the world vitalize the stuff of shadows and make live its ancient dream of peace.[18]

In those other countries of Europe where civil strife has ended and dictatorships are firmly in the saddle, the spectacle is no less horrifying to the friends of democratic methods and values. These new autocracies, whether launched in the name of the few or the many, of nationalism or internationalism, of capitalism or socialism, have brought profound disillusionment to their well-wishers. Those who hoped that the cooperative commonwealth, the dream of the ages, was at last to be realized in Russia have been no less disappointed than those leaders of business who hoped and believed that Mussolini and Hitler would make the world safe for the rights of private property and free enterprise. The whole experience of revolutionary Europe seems to demonstrate the truth of the ancient maxim that means and ends cannot be separated, that the choice of incompatible means will destroy the ends proclaimed, that the use of undemocratic methods to achieve a more complete democracy will in all probability lead straight to some form of autocracy. Undemocratic procedures form undemocratic attitudes and sentiments which in turn lend support to the indefinite continuation of dictatorial practices. Neither communism nor fascism has set an example which American citizens, whether liberal or conservative, radical or reactionary, would choose to follow.

Of course, it may be contended that men have no choice in the situation—that the advance of industrial civilization has destined every nation of the contemporary world to pass through the holocaust of civil strife and under the iron heel of dictatorship. But this is theology pure and simple: bare assertion incapable of either proof or disproof. Worse than that, it is definitely calculated to close the mind to the peaceful solution of the social problem and to increase the likelihood of strife and dictatorship. Fortunately for the American people, being able now to witness with their own eyes and with a measure of detachment the results which flow from the general and complete suspension of civil liberties, they can know without having to undergo the experience themselves that the method of violence is no quick and sure road to an earthly paradise. With the madhouse of the Old World before them they are able to place a proper value on those liberties for which their fathers fought in the eighteenth and nineteenth centuries. They can see with undimmed vision that an autocracy, regardless of its auspices and announced purposes, is still an autocracy—capricious, brutal, and unpredictable. The maintenance of political freedom in America may have been made easier by its loss in Europe.

Weaknesses of the American Aristocracy

The American "aristocracy of paper and patronage" is far less formidable than superficial appearances or the analysis in Chapter III would indicate. It does, to be sure, hold title to most of the productive property of the country and thus has at its disposal the power that goes with economic resources. Yet, as Tocqueville predicted, it is one of the "most confined and least dangerous" ever to appear in history. In order to be strong and enduring an aristocracy, besides being able to wield overwhelming force when occasion requires, must enjoy two separate but closely related supports: it must have support in fact and support in theory; it must render to society a palpable and unequivocal service and it must rest upon solid and accepted moral foundations. An aristocracy cannot maintain its position indefinitely if it allows itself to be shorn of responsibilities or fails to discharge effectively the responsibilities attached to its position. The feudal lord gradually lost his holdings when he proved himself incapable of defending them and of giving security to his vassals. In a word, an aristocracy must perform according to expectations or perish. Also, it must be confident of its own worth and proud of its achievements. And this confidence and pride must be shared by society. By both of these tests, the practical and the moral, the aristocracy of contemporary America is incomparably more feeble than its predecessors in history.

Clearly the only conceivable social justification of an economic aristocracy is that it will administer honestly, efficiently, and wisely the economic resources of the nation. If it fails to do this, its reason for existence disappears and its position becomes purely parasitical. Measured against such a standard it must be recorded that the American aristocracy built up an enviable reputation both at home and abroad during a period of a century or more. Under its leadership

technology advanced at an unparalleled rate, a modern economic mechanism was flung across the continent, and industry reached an extraordinarily high level of productivity.
American business enterprise became the symbol for efficiency and daring throughout the world. Could any aristocracy have a greater claim on the gratitude of society?

A closer examination, however, reveals deep shadows in
the picture. American economic advance during the past
one-hundred years must certainly be traced largely to the
matchless natural resources of the continent, the restless
energies of the people, and the spirit of an age that had
turned the attention of men to the material conquest of the
earth. The nation, moreover, is only beginning to realize the
price that it will have to pay for the utter disregard of social
welfare with which the few pillaged the natural riches of the
country. The depleted soils, the ravaged forests, the denuded
hills and mountains, the wasted gas, oil, coal and metals, the
alternation of floods and stagnant rivers, the march of the
dust bowl, and the destruction of those forms of animal life
from which a profit could be derived—all these things tell
but part of the story. In addition must be included the steady
importation of strikebreakers from the impoverished villages
of Europe and Asia and the employment of methods legal
and illegal to keep wages down and swell the stream of
profits. With far less sense of responsibility than that of a
slaveowner for his slaves or of a farmer for his horses, this
aristocracy exploited the labor of the people. More than that,
it has thus far shown itself incapable of keeping the economic
system in even fairly continuous and full operation; though
holding power it has evaded responsibility for the general
state of the economy by attributing breakdown to the laws
of nature or the hand of God. In the face of catastrophe it
has refused to expose its own breast to the storm and sought
refuge behind the cloak of government, only to repudiate its
savior as soon as the winds abated. It has thus proved itself

no genuine aristocracy, courageous in the face of danger or
conscious of its obligations, but a predatory band determined
to hold its spoils. Rarely in history has a privileged order
confessed more frankly and naively its incompetence and un-
fitness to rule.

The point should be emphasized that in all probability
the downfall or survival of the current aristocracy will depend largely upon its own actions. It certainly will not be
overthrown because a few poets and philosophers prefer a
democratic social order, nor yet because the great masses of
the people decide to do battle for an abstract idea. Never
have ordinary men and women, molded by the life and institutions of a stratified society, sought to overthrow aristocracy
simply as aristocracy. They have fought individuals and
classes whom by experience they have come to regard as
tyrants or as obstacles to tangible satisfactions. As a rule they
are quite as hostile to social change as any privileged caste.
They love the sense of assurance which accompanies an established regime and are prepared to suffer even grievous
injustice rather than encounter the risks and uncertainties
which always attend social upheaval. There is reason for
believing that all the agitators on earth could not stir to
revolt a people reposing in the arms of a truly enlightened
and benevolent despotism. If the American aristocracy
should abolish unemployment, guarantee material security
to all, release fully the productive energies of technology,
maintain the high living standards patently possible, and
open up ever wider opportunities for cultural advancement,
it could probably rule forever. Its members then would know
the luxury of sleeping on restful beds and could banish completely from their slumbers the twin nightmares of civil
strife and economic democracy.

That the aristocracy will endeavor to perpetuate itself by
taking thought and resolutely providing leadership in the
conduct of the economy seems highly improbable. There is

little in its history that points in this direction, while there is much that points the other way. When Franklin D. Roosevelt offered it the services of his great talents and energies, it abused him as few public men have been abused in American history. When he sought to save it by arousing its members to subordinate immediate for more distant and permanent interests, they turned to sabotage and invective. The temper and capacity of the class were revealed strikingly in the eight-point program adopted by the American Manufacturers Association at its meeting in December, 1937. After eight years of severest economic distress the leaders of American industry could only propose a return to the conditions out of which that distress had emerged. Their program presented no evidence that they had either learned or forgotten anything since 1929. Indeed it is reliably reported that they were restrained from the preparation of a violently vitriolic statement only on the urgent solicitation of conservative congressmen who feared that such a statement would strengthen the position of the President in the popular mind. Lacking the will or inclination to assume social responsibilities at all commensurate with its power, the aristocracy seems to be paving the way for its own demise.

The weakness of the aristocracy is thus seen to be moral as well as material. Among other things it is the victim of the social and economic philosophy under whose doctrines it has risen to power—the philosophy of an extreme individualism which assumes that the general welfare, being the by-product of calculated and steadfast devotion to private and selfish ends, requires no special thought or consideration. Having been molded to a peculiar degree by such anarchistic conceptions, the privileged classes are peculiarly unprepared to provide the necessary leadership in an age of close social integration which demands coordination, planning, and unity of effort, if utter catastrophe is to be avoided and the resources of technology utilized. It must be admitted, how-

ever, that they exhibit a larger measure of social vision and
responsibility than their spiritual counterparts in the lower
ranks, those "little business men" who met in Washington in
January, 1938, exposed their ignorance, expressed their prejudices, and prescribed magic and witchcraft for the ills of
the nation.

In yet another respect the moral foundations of the privileged order in America are feeble and unsubstantial. As observed above, this order has not yet attained the stature of a
mature aristocracy, bound together by the ties of blood, a
distinctive mentality, and a code of honor. Rather is it
largely an aggregation of ordinary persons only recently
emerged from the popular mass by reason of acquisition of
productive property. In spite of their power they are still for
the most part of the people, cherishing substantially the
same values and acknowledging the same loyalties. Moreover, having risen to eminence under the aegis of democracy
and generally attributing their success to the virtues of free
institutions, they are held captive by the mores of the populace. Even if they so desire, they fear openly to declare themselves and defend their special status. From the standpoint of
integrity of soul therefore other aristocracies have stood on
much firmer ground. Believing fully in their right to rule
and being relieved of the necessity of practicing self-deception, they have proudly proclaimed their superiority by
dress, language, manners, insignia, and the practice of virtues "becoming" persons of birth and rank. The contemporary aristocracy, constrained to profess to be what it is not,
and to be what it dare not profess, finds itself in a wholly
anomalous position. This is especially true of its more intelligent and sensitive members who see and feel the incongruity of their situation and may consequently be expected
to break the solidarity of the ranks of the aristocracy in any
contest with the people. Unquestionably great numbers of
them would be without the moral support necessary to sus-

tain a concerted and ruthless war upon the democracy. "The upper classes (*bourgeoisie*)," wrote Michael Chevalier a century ago, "are not here what they are in Europe; while in Europe they rule, here they are ruled. Democracy takes its revenge in America for the unjust contempt with which it has been so long treated in Europe."[19] Although this observation may contain less of truth today than formerly, it reflects a tradition that still possesses vitality.

Natural and Technical Resources of the Country

The matchless natural and technical resources of the country should encourage the peaceful solution of the economic problem. Favored above other nations in the richness, variety, and distribution of their natural resources and possessing the most advanced technology in the world, the American people have reached a point in economic development which opens up for the first time in human history the possibility of relative abundance of goods and services for all. If the engineers are to be believed, if the studies made by competent investigators during the past two decades are to be taken at their face value, economic production could be increased immediately from twenty to one hundred per cent above the highest level yet achieved, provided the social relationships involved could be properly adjusted.[20] The only effective barrier to such a condition of abundance is the absence of the necessary social will. Inherited practices and the vested interests of the aristocracy alone seem to stand in the way.

The possibility of an economy of abundance has profoundly changed the terms of the political equation. Throughout their history men have been faced with a necessary condition of scarcity. Their control over the forces of nature has been severely limited; their rate of reproduction has ever tended to outrun the means of subsistence; their life in almost all ages and places has been marked by unceasing toil and battle with the elements; their lot has been one of insecurity, privation, starvation, pestilence, war. The grim horsemen of the apocalypse have dogged their footsteps since the Garden of Eden and exacted a heavy toll from the strong as well as the weak. Man's hold on existence has always been precarious; his command of the barest necessities of the stomach uncertain. Only by enslaving the mass through the exercise of artifice, fraud, or violence could a few individuals and families achieve a modicum of ease, plenty, or luxury. With an insufficiency of all things needful to living, the human struggle, whether inside or outside tribe or nation, has naturally been carried to its bitter extremity. The stake for which men have fought has been life itself; the penalty of defeat, enslavement or death.

The age now dawning, an age which has been in preparation since the making of the first eolith and which has been approaching with incredible rapidity during the past century in America, alters the entire aspect of human existence. If the people of the United States but succeed in coordinating their efforts, devising appropriate social relationships, and bringing all the forces of technology into the service of the nation, the entire population could be assured economic security, comfort, leisure, and even luxury. Through the harnessing of natural energies and the creation of new materials according to desire men are at last in a position to lift the age-old curse of harsh, stupefying, and unremitting toil. Under such circumstances they would be mad if they should refuse to live cooperatively together and should choose rather to continue the ancient feud over bread and the opportunity to bask in the sunlight. Here is the most powerful argument for the employment of the democratic method in the settlement of disputes—a method which has probably always been dependent on benign life conditions and the consequent moderation of human passion. It seems not unlikely that the spread and success of democracy in America have been made possible by the relative ease of making a living which has attended the settlement and conquest of the continent from early colonial times. If this is so, then the miraculous advances of technology during recent generations should provide for free institutions a foundation far more solid and enduring than that furnished by the natural riches of a comparatively raw and uninhabited land.

Security of the Nation from External Attack

Everything said in this volume implies that democracy is a tender plant capable of growing and flowering only under certain unusual conditions. It thrives in the presence of peace and security, but is easily consumed in the heat of conflict. It is indeed the antithesis of military combat and cannot long survive on the field of Mars. Even in democratic states of long standing the course of free institutions is inevitably interrupted when the eagles of war are loosed. Also no democracy has ever been able to introduce and maintain the spirit of liberty and equality in the army organized to defend its life and institutions. Civilization itself was developed in those places and times where, because of isolation or superior means of defense, a people could devote itself primarily to the cultivation of the arts of peace. Stanley Casson has emphasized the importance of this factor in ancient and prehistoric times. The oldest experiment of civilization in the world, that of the Sumerians, he says, was possible only because this gifted people made two great inventions—the city state and organized warfare.[21] They were able to build around themselves solid and dependable ramparts within whose shelter they could withstand the assaults of barbarians and throw their energies into the advancement of culture. In history defensive warfare has always been one of the indispensable adjuncts of civilization. In the contemporary world, with the recrudescence of barbarism under the banners of fascism and the philosophy of unabashed aggression, security from external attack is one of the essential conditions of the survival of democracy.

From this standpoint the American people occupy an incontestably favored position among the nations of the world —large or small. In the first place, they are separated by two great oceans from the two major sources of aggression in Europe and Asia. While neither the Atlantic nor the Pacific is as wide as it once was, they are both sufficiently broad to protect the country from any sudden and unprovoked attack. In the second place, the United States has no powerful and warlike neighbors on either American continent capable of endangering their security. The three-thousand miles of unfortified boundary line separating the United States from Canada may be taken as a symbol of the spirit of peace which reigns in North America. In the third place, the unrivaled industrial power of the nation, the foundation and source of military strength in the modern world, makes the American people all but impregnable to invasion and conquest. In practically every important field of industrial production the United States occupies first place among the nations, while in consumption of mechanical energy it approximately equals them all. In the fourth place, the great variety of soil, climate, flora, fauna, and minerals found within its borders gives to the country a measure of economic independence which is matched only by the Soviet Union and the British Empire. When all of these things are taken together, along with the spirit and energy of the people, it is apparent that at the present juncture in history no single country and no probable combination of countries could expect to wage a successful war of aggression against the continental possessions of the United States.

These things being so, the American people probably can avoid war if they so desire and if they are prepared to make the necessary sacrifices involving distant possessions and the interests of nationals abroad. They can escape war and all that war carries in its train—material and spiritual impoverishment, destruction of life and resources, the psychology of fear, suspicion, hatred, and desperation, that exaggerated and psychopathic form of patriotism which strips man of his humanity and leaves him a naked savage rejoicing in the brutality and slavery of a military despotism. But actually to achieve escape they will have to do more than pass resolutions; they will have to do more than proclaim their neutrality. As noted in an earlier chapter, they will have to take positive steps in the development of a policy of peace; they will have to control their economy in its international relations and ramifications. Although the American people doubtless learned something from their participation in the last war, it is patent that they did not learn enough to keep them out of the next one. They have not yet learned how private economic interests working on public opinion twenty-four hours in the day and three-hundred-and-sixty-five days in the year gradually break down popular resistance to war and eventually create in the mind of the people an insistent demand for military intervention. The fact remains, however, that the American people alone among the great nations hold almost within their own hands the power to choose between peace and war. This is a tremendous asset in the struggle for democracy.

High Political Sense of the Population

Although certain of the nations of Europe doubtless equal or surpass the American people in the realm of intellectual and artistic achievement of the highest order, it seems probable that the cultural level of the masses in the United States is unusually high. For more than a hundred years the dominant aim of the educational agencies of the country has been the dissemination of knowledge among the people, even though standards of excellence had to be sacrificed in the process. While this practice has called forth much criticism from abroad and even from the intellectual classes at home and while it has not realized the fond hopes of its advocates and progenitors; while the opportunities have been extended quite unevenly to the various regions and population elements; and while an honest and realistic program of civic and political education has never been attempted on a large scale, yet the work of the formal educational agencies combined with the experience of living under institutions which have been relatively free has given the rank and file of the citizens a large measure of political sense and understanding. The fact that they may not be as far advanced in their command of systematic social knowledge and theory as certain European peoples is to be attributed primarily to the ease of life in America and the absence of that impulsion to think which must come in large part from the environment. Given the need, and apparently the need is now being given, the American people can be counted upon to render a very satisfactory account of themselves in the sphere of political discussion, thought, and action. The example set by their fathers in the first seventy-five years of the history of the Republic would seem to justify this conclusion. Let them once become clearly aware that there is something wrong in their democracy and they may be expected to strike their political tents.

Such a generalization is suggested by the recent behavior of the American people. Mr. Gallup, on the basis of his unique experience, concludes that the "public mind is remarkably alive to the issues of the day," that the "typical American is highly articulate on questions of public policy," and that "by and large, the majority of voters seem to have an acute sense of values—a ready ability to distinguish reality from sham." He also states that the "institute has found no evidence" of that "fickleness" which the critics of democracy in all ages have attributed to the people.[22]

Perhaps the most striking vindication of the political sense and independence of the American people was shown in the presidential campaign of 1936, when reactionary elements resorted to every device known to demagogy to discredit Franklin D. Roosevelt and his administration in the eyes of the public. In the prosecution of their attack they possessed, besides almost unlimited funds, the voluntary services of the representatives and agencies of entrenched wealth. According to an analysis of the record of the daily press in the fifteen largest cities of the nation made by *The New Republic,* "approximately 71 percent of the total circulation of the fifteen cities . . . was hostile to Roosevelt." [23] And three-fifths of the circulation favoring the President were in New York City. With almost no newspaper support in the country, with old Democratic papers going over to Mr. Landon, and with the short end of the radio program, Mr. Roosevelt found himself charged daily with the intention of destroying the American form of government and society. It was said that he was following the lead of both Stalin and Hitler, that he proposed to introduce into the United States both fascism and communism, that he intended to regiment both labor and business, that he had nefarious designs on both large and small enterprise, that he desired to destroy both property and liberty. It was a new and manifold edition of Theodore Dwight framed in the hopes and fears, loves and hates of the fourth decade of the twentieth century. In addition employers, according to an old tradition, endeavored to frighten their employees with the threat of insecurity should Roosevelt be reelected.

And what was the response of the American people, lacking a press and without adequate organization, to this unprecedented barrage of accusation, recrimination, misrepresentation and downright falsification? They went to the polls and voted overwhelmingly for the President, placing but two small states in the Landon column—states that have not yet fully emerged from the pre-industrial epoch of American history. Regardless of the merits of Mr. Roosevelt and his program, a subject about which there is much room for debate, the election of 1936 registered one of the greatest victories for democracy ever achieved in the United States. The American people exhibited wholly unexpected powers to resist political propaganda—one of the best possible measures of the political sense and civic competence of a people.

Precise Knowledge of Man and Society

A final asset of great potential worth would seem to be that vast body of precise knowledge of man and society which has been accumulating ever more rapidly during the past several centuries. The existence of this knowledge is one of the distinguishing characteristics of the contemporary world. The ancients, in spite of their very real accomplishments in the realms of social knowledge and thought, knew relatively little about man—his origin, his nature, his history, his life and institutions. The modern age has witnessed the application of the methods of science and the spirit of objective scholarship to almost every phase of the subject. While perhaps only a good beginning has been made, the results already achieved constitute one of the greatest glories of the human mind. The geologists and biologists have disclosed man's place in the natural order, the physiologists and psychologists have explored his physical and mental equipment, the archaeologists and anthropologists have pieced together the early stages of human development, the geographers have revealed the relationships between man and the earth, the historians have given a systematic account of the evolution of cultures and the succession of states and systems, and the economists, political scientists, and sociologists have studied the customs and institutions, processes and structures of human society in all times and places. As a consequence man today knows incomparably more about himself than he ever did in the past.

It may be said also that the body of available knowledge concerning the American people and American society, while deficient at many points, is especially detailed and comprehensive. The temper of the country, probably because of its democratic and practical outlook, has been particularly hospitable to the development of the social sciences. There are probably more teachers and investigators in such fields in the United States than in all other countries combined. And these specialists, together with their students, are pouring a constant stream of findings into the current of social life and thought. Also learned societies, commissions, and committees are engaged perpetually in prosecuting inquiry into the operation of American institutions. In addition governmental agencies during the past generation have subjected to careful and relatively objective study one department of the economic and political life after another. At no time in their history have the American people been in so favorable a position to know themselves. If knowledge is truth and if truth can make men free, a faith that marks the modern spirit and lies at the heart of the entire democratic experiment, they presumably hold in their hands the "key of libberty."

This vast body of precise knowledge of human society in general and of American society in particular, however, is only a *potential* possession of the ordinary citizen. At present it reposes too largely in those books, monographs, and documents which gather dust on the shelves of the libraries, large and small, that literally dot the country. The task of making this knowledge functional, of converting potentiality into actuality, of equipping the American people to deal intelligently with the problems of the age is a central task of both education and democracy. To a consideration of this task the next two chapters will be devoted.

REFERENCES

1. Ralph Waldo Emerson, "The Fortune of the Republic," *Emerson's Complete Works* (Cabot edition, Boston, 1878), XI, 410-411.

2. John Taylor, *An Inquiry into the Principles and Policy of the Government of the United States* (Fredericksburg, 1814), 41-42.

3. George Gallup, "The American Mind: a Test of Democracy," *The New York Times Magazine* (April 24, 1938), 2.

4. Data from students at Teachers College, Columbia University, and Northwestern University. See also Pitirim Sorokin, *Social Mobility* (New York, 1927), Ch. XVII and Ch. XVIII.

5. *Ibid.*, 478.

6. Ernest Gruening, *Mexico and Its Heritage* (New York, 1928), 341.

7. Michael Chevalier, *Soicety, Manners and Politics in the United States* (Boston, 1839), 125.

8. Charles A. Beard, "Democracy and Education in the United States" in *Social Research* (September, 1937), 394-395.

9. *Op. cit.*, 285.

10. *Ibid.*, 286.

11. *The New York Times* (November 9, 1930).

12. Alexis de Tocqueville, *Democracy in America* (New York, 1898), II, 213-214.

13. *Ibid.*, II, 213.

14. John Bradbury, "Travels in the Interior of America, in the Years 1809, 1810, and 1811" in R. G. Thwaites, *Early Western Travels* (Cleveland, 1904), V, 282-283.

15. John Woods, "Two Years' Residence in the Settlement on the English Prairie, in the Illinois Country, United States," in R. G. Thwaites, *Early Western Travels* (Cleveland, 1904), X, 300.

16. *Op. cit.* See also E. C. Jerman, *History and Directory of Ripley County* (Versailles, Ind., 1888), 65-67; Henry S. Nourse, *History of the Town of Harvard, Massachusetts 1732-1893* (Harvard, Mass., 1894), 81, 102; William Cooper Howells, *Recollections of Life in Ohio from 1813 to 1840* (Cincinnati, 1895), 145-151.

17. *The New York Times* (January 23, 1938), Section IV, 9.

18. *The New York Times* (August 7, 1937)

19. *Op. cit.*, 93.

20. See particularly Committee on Elimination of Waste in Industry of the Federated American Enginering Societies, *Waste in Industry*, with foreword by Herbert Hoover (New York, 1921); Harold Loeb, *The Chart of*

Plenty (New York, 1935) ; and E. G. Nourse et al., *America's Capacity to Produce* (Washington, 1936) .

21. Stanley Casson, *Progress and Catastrophe* (New York, 1937) , 80-81.

22. George Gallup, *Op. cit.*, 1-2.

23. *The New Republic*, "The Press and the Public," Special Section (March 17, 1937) , 178.

CHAPTER 11:

EDUCATION AND AMERICAN DEMOCRACY

THE contemporary struggle for democracy in the United States comes to focus in the field of organized education. While the defense and advance of democracy cannot be completely compassed by education, since both social invention and organization of forces are also required, education is fundamental to the entire process. Indeed, even the release of the inventive and organizing energies of the people depends at bottom on the work of education. Understanding of the present status of American democracy, awareness of the problems and hazards ahead, guidance from the lessons of past and present, achievement of a practical program of action, and utilization of the available resources of the heritage all must rest in the last analysis on a comprehensive and relevant program of education. Also, while the greater part of the education of any society is carried on outside the formal agencies specially and exclusively established and conducted for the purpose, the work of the school, including all levels and branches, is central. If the American people are not able to direct this institution to the service of democracy, then clearly they can scarcely hope to oppose successfully the further advance of the aristocracy. Here is the decisive test of the vitality and strength of American democracy in the second quarter of the twentieth century.

American education, moreover, is inextricably involved in the fate of the democratic process. This is due in part to the broad truth that education, being intimately related to the structure and life of the society which it serves, is inevitably affected by every more or less profound change in that society. It is also due to the peculiarly intimate relationship which education has sustained historically to democracy in America.

The former has been one of the most characteristic expressions of the latter. It is not too much to say that, on the one hand, the perpetuation of the democratic process is dependent in no inconsiderable measure on the spirit, program, and activities of the school; and that, on the other, education, as it has been commonly conceived and conducted in the United States, could not survive the destruction of that process. The role of the American school, and particularly the public school, in preserving and making effective democratic procedures and institutions is the theme of this and the following chapter.

In the current battle for democracy American public education faces its supreme test. Largely a child of the liberal spirit with which the birth of popular government in the United States was closely associated, the public school has generally been looked upon as a substantial and effective bulwark of a society of free men. So it was regarded by the founders of the great state systems of education in the middle decades of the last century; and so it has been regarded by ordinary men and women from generation to generation. If the citizens of the Republic, nurtured preponderantly by the public school, should acquiesce, either knowingly or ignorantly, in the destruction of democracy, then the institution itself will seem to have failed. Perhaps this is placing upon organized education a larger burden than it is capable of bearing, but no less has been expected of it by the leaders of American democracy.

If the democratic process is abandoned, if the method of public discussion is replaced by violence, if the bill of rights is abrogated, if rule by popular consent gives way to rule by police power, if dictatorship, stark and ruthless, occupies the seats of government, the conception of education which has generally prevailed in America—the conception of education as a progressive and enlightening force in society—would be utterly destroyed. While that conception has rarely been fully realized in practice, while it has always been opposed by vested interests and powers of obscurantism, while it has been honored as often in the breach as in the observance,[1] it has rarely been openly repudiated and remains today the central idea in the heritage of American education and democracy. Indissolubly linked with this conception are integrity of person, freedom of conscience, scientific method, the spirit of unfettered inquiry, and all those creative forces for whose release courageous men and women in many ages have faced the combined power of church and state armed with inquisition, dungeon, sword, and faggot. If organized education cherishes freedom for itself, its first task is the marshaling of its resources for the purpose of preserving and perfecting a condition of society in which this great liberating tradition may live and flourish. Let the reign of authority return and the school will become a handmaiden of autocratic power, a defender of privilege, a conserver of fixed doctrine, an instrument for sealing the eyes, stopping the ears, stilling the tongue, and darkening the mind of each generation.

The teachers of the country should have a special interest in the future of democracy. Their derivation from the ranks of the people, their relatively disinterested position in society, their freedom from the ties of large properties, their devotion to the spread of knowledge, their tradition of loyalty to the popular welfare, and their whole outlook on life, tend to identify them overwhelmingly with the fortunes of the democratic process. Moreover, the experience of the Old World demonstrates conclusively that they are among the first victims of the rule of modern dictators. A totalitarian regime, resting as it does on the propagation of myths and falsehoods, cannot survive under a condition of free inquiry and thought. Consequently, once it has overcome its adversaries by machine gun and radio, it proceeds inexorably to a ruthless regimentation of the entire intellectual class, giving

particular attention to all who have any responsibility for
informing and molding the minds of the young. The teacher,
if he would retain his position, is required to be a soldier in
the ranks, to surrender his individuality, to make obedience
his highest virtue—to teach doctrines he may not believe, to
affirm as true today what was false yesterday, to applaud that
which he detests, to make the ugly appear beautiful, to live
a life of hypocrisy, to crucify his own soul. He is asked to spy
upon his colleagues and pupils, only to be spied upon by
them in turn. He is compelled to violate the finest traditions
of his calling and to become the slave of a demagogue, a
party, or a body of social doctrine.

Education and Politics

The heart of the problem of the role of education in the
contemporary struggle for democracy is found in the relationship between education and politics. In the absence of a
clear analysis here there is certain to be much confusion regarding such fundamental issues as indoctrination, freedom
of teaching, and the formulation of educational policy. And
there is much confusion among American teachers today. In
the same breath or on a single page an educational leader
may oppose the slightest suggestion of indoctrination, advocate the teaching of democracy in the schools, and demand
the formulation of a highly specific list of objectives. He may
argue that the school is controlled to the last detail of its
program by the economic aristocracy and then proceed to
advise teachers to participate in the radical reconstruction
of society. He may contend that the school is completely free
from external pressures and immediately caution teachers
about the dangers attending the discussion of all controver-
sial subjects. Or he may maintain that the scholar should be
indifferent to the tendencies of the social structure and at

once lament the regimentation of the intellectual life characteristic of dictatorships.

In America today there are three divergent and conflicting conceptions of the relation of education to politics which, though rarely defended in their extreme forms, have a certain vogue. According to the first conception, education is by nature entirely separate from politics. To the extent that the outside world intrudes upon the program of the school the process of education is violated and corrupted; and in the measure that the school enters the arena of contending social forces and purposes it forsakes its peculiar function. The central purpose of the educative process is neither to inform the mind nor to equip it with the powers immediately useful in the contemporary restless and changeful world, but rather to mold it through a mastery of the universal and abiding tools, forms, and categories of human thought and experience. Remote from market-place and forum, above the clash of philosophies and systems, independent of time and circumstance, dedicated to the conservation of eternal values, and governed by its own laws and principles, known and understood only by the initiated, education is regarded as the private possession of teachers, an esoteric art practiced exclusively by pedagogues—austere, timeless, immaculate. At least, it is argued, only such education is good and true: all other kinds are bad and false.

According to the second conception, education is itself an original and positive political force, a child of history and geography and yet a creative factor in the world—local, temporal, and changing, yet having an integrity of its own. While it always reveals the impress of a given society in its purpose, content, and methodology, it need not be bound in any complete sense by the existing balance of social forces. It is at the same time both sensitive to and responsible for the conditions which surround it. Standing outside the conflicts of doctrine and interest, it may nevertheless intervene and tip

the scales to the one side or the other. In some way it escapes
the vicious circle of historical determinism and becomes a
molder of the future. Being a trustworthy road to collective
salvation, as well as to individual success, it is capable of
abolishing crime and corruption, of purifying personal and
public morals, of establishing the reign of peace and justice,
of building a new social order. It is a lever with which man
may move the earth on which he stands, a bootstrap with
which he may lift himself into a better world, a magical substance with which he may free himself of all the ills to which
the flesh is heir. In one form or another this view of education has been held by generation after generation of Americans since the founding of the Republic.

According to the third conception, education is by nature
wholly an instrument of politics, and inevitably so. The
school is not, and never can be, a prime mover in the social
process. Real power lies outside educational institutions in
the changing fortunes of the economic and political struggle.
The school, no less than the police and military arms of society, is part of the legitimate spoils of victory. In a sense the
public school is twice removed from the ultimate source of
power, being a tool of the state, which in turn is a tool of the
dominant class or group in society. This class or group makes
of the educational undertaking whatsoever it will, directing
the program sedulously and effectively toward the end of
guarding and promoting its special interests and purposes.
No part of that program, moreover, from the teaching of
arithmetic in the grades to the organization of research in
the university, is without political significance, fundamentally considered. Entirely lacking independence, education
is a plaything of party, wherever parties are distinguishable,
an expression and organ of state power, a child of time and
place—changing, partisan, earthy—shot through with the
hopes and fears and passions of men. At any rate, whatever
the ideal may be, so the argument runs, such is the reality

which any honest study of history reveals. Whenever and wherever the contrary would seem to be true the explanation is found in the fact that no deep differences divide society and the underlying premises of education, being accepted by all, assume the aspect of eternal and universal verities.

The problem of the relation of education and politics is complicated and made difficult by the fact that each of these three conceptions contains a certain measure of truth. Data from educational and social history could be assembled in support, or at least in partial support, of any one of them. Presumably the relationship under consideration is not fixed, but varies greatly with time and place and social structure. Moreover, it would seem to be an expression of social policy, whether such policy is the product of conscious formulation or the slow growth of tradition, whether founded on law or on custom. The elements of the problem can be seen and grasped only by an analysis of the nature of organized education.

Fundamentally and comprehensively considered education is a process of inducting the young and immature into the life and culture of the group—into its ways of acting, thinking, and feeling, into an appropriation of its material and spiritual possessions—its folkways and mores, its institutions and social arrangements, its skills, knowledges, and appreciations, its arts, sciences, and philosophies. Through this process the individual human being is formed and a particular society perpetuated. Actual educational programs therefore, when taken in their totality, are as varied in detail and pattern as human society.

In the case of *organized* education, which even among the most advanced peoples embraces but a small part of the entire process of tuition and learning, the group, whether tribe, sect, class, or nation, deliberately sets out to control the educational process in the light of more or less carefully formulated purposes and conceptions—to make of young and immature members something which by themselves they would not become. In fashioning the program of organized education the responsible agents of society engage in a positive creative undertaking which involves the continuous selection and rejection of materials, methods, and values. The product, regardless of the efficacy of the tuition, is no more neutral than a work of art or an act of statesmanship. The conduct of education as a collective enterprise, resting upon choice among many possibilities and involving the acceptance of definite patterns of learning and living, constitutes one of the most basic forms of social action. Indeed it *is* society acting. Even though the curriculum of the school should be confined to the contemplation of distant stars or the study of some ancient civilization, it would still represent a positive act on the part of the group concerned and responsible.

Organized education has two phases or aspects which, though closely interwoven, may be distinguished for the purposes of the present discussion. The one may be called technical, the other political. The former is represented in those professional knowledges and powers which are the special possession of persons trained to perform the functions associated with the conduct of education—understanding of the nature of the human organism, with particular reference to the learning process; knowledge of the individual disciplines and activities composing the school program; mastery of the various methods and procedures involved in teaching, management, organization, and administration. While no one of these matters, almost without exception, is wholly lacking in political significance, they represent the areas in which, in any society, educational workers might most appropriately claim a high degree of sovereignty. The intrusion of political forces here might impair the efficient operation of the school and therefore prevent the most complete fulfillment of the purposes which those very forces might wish to impose upon the institution.

The political phase of education embraces all of those broad features of the enterprise which lie somewhat outside the areas of special professional preparation, which are of fairly direct concern to those elements that rule society, and which involve ethical choice, social relations, and conceptions of welfare. It includes such subjects as the extension of educational opportunity, the magnitude and distribution of the tax burden, the general pattern of the program, the relation of the school to the political structure, the social ideas and values to be inculcated, the conceptions of individual and common welfare to be fostered, the goals and purposes to be achieved, and the choices to be made affecting the future substance and pattern of society and culture. It is apparent of course that political considerations, as here understood, are involved more or less in everything that is done in the school, even in the teaching of the so-called "tools of learning," as an examination of the practice of communist and fascist states fully demonstrates. Yet, though the technical and political aspects of education are closely interwoven, the distinction between them is essential for an understanding of the problem which American citizens and teachers face today.

This brings the analysis to the most crucial question involved in the relation between education and politics—perhaps the most crucial question involved in any effort of society to inaugurate and administer a program of organized education. Granted that such a program—positively or negatively, passively or actively—affects in the measure of its power the future of society, in whose hands should the making of relevant choices rest? Here is the question about which the struggle over education revolves today.

Some say that the question answers itself automatically; that it is a matter, not of ethics, but of social mechanics, not

of what should be, but of what is and shall be; that those
make choices who can, and those submit who must. According to this view, power over education naturally and inevitably resides in the hands of persons who, whatever the
institutional forms, do in fact make their collective will effective in society. And since practically every society known
to history has been composed of classes, with one class riding
on the backs of the others, an aristocracy, whether of blood,
of wealth, or of military might, always molds the educational
program to its wishes. Such, so it is said, is the verdict of the
rudiments of social arithmetic. To expect anything else in
the real world of clashing interests and struggle for domi-
nance is to nourish illusions. The only practicable course for
teachers to pursue is either to consult the reigning aristocracy and follow faithfully its behests or to abandon the educational profession and engage in revolutionary activity.

Such an answer to the question, however, is irrelevant. To
the extent that the statement itself is true, it merely enumer-
ates the conditions which any answer must take into account.
That all advanced human societies have contained classes is
admitted. It is further admitted that American society is no
exception to this general rule. In fact the burden of argument in the present volume has pointed to the rise of a
powerful economic aristocracy in the United States as a
characteristic and dominant feature of an industrial civilization founded upon private capitalism. Nevertheless an objective study of the situation reveals little of the simplicity
in social relations which the theory of complete and systematic control of education by a privileged order would seem
to assume. The most that can be said is that a tendency in
this direction, varying in strength from time to time, may
be observed.

As a matter of fact, the seat of absolute power in any society, and particularly in a complex and dynamic society of
the modern type, is difficult to locate. Even contemporary

dictatorships, hard and pitiless though they are, have been compelled to move toward their objectives with a certain measure of circumspection, adjusting their methods and programs to the traditions, the sentiments, the prejudices, and the prevailing social conceptions of the peoples over whom they rule. In America, moreover, as already emphasized, the aristocracy, besides being weakened by insecure moral foundations, is far from united, being divided by interest, outlook, loyalties, and jealousies. Tocqueville observed that the privileged order of industrial society which he saw emerging a century ago, while harsh and powerful, would be more confined and less dangerous than its predecessors. Also the contemporary aristocracy recognizes bounds, set by the political folkways and mores, which it dare not trespass, even though it should desire to do so. The infinite pains which it takes to conceal its purposes under the cloak of revered popular rights, its appeals to the constitution, to the founding fathers, to simple patriotism, show this to be the case. Composing a small minority, its position is always more or less precarious; and holding power at the mercy of the great majority, it is compelled to rule by deceit and indirection, as John Taylor pointed out in the early years of the Republic. The fact that it resorts habitually to cabals, manipulation, secret correspondence, smoke-filled rooms, and clandestine operations is both a condition of its existence and a tribute to the strength of democracy. Then there may be found in American society powerful traditions, deeply rooted in the history of the country, which the aristocracy fears to violate openly, lest it arouse the slumbering suspicions of the masses and consolidate the forces of democracy into a movement of overwhelming might. The American people, perhaps more than any other, as noted in an earlier chapter, are heirs of all the liberalizing and democratizing tendencies of the past several centuries. Doubtless many members of the aristocracy, having been nurtured on this great inheritance, would feel uneasy in conscience if called upon to repudiate its teachings altogether—faith in popular government, in the potentialities of common people, in the wisdom of the free play of reason, in the indefinite perfectability of man and human institutions. Finally, the few do not stand in undisputed possession of the citadels of power. Through both economic and political organizations the many, today as in the past, are in a position to challenge the authority of privilege and vested interest. Mention should also be made of the churches which on certain issues might be expected to oppose complete domination by any group or class. Hitler seems to have encountered more determined and sustained resistance from certain religious denominations than from the trade unions.

All of this, and much more that might be said, would seem to suggest the possibility of the establishment of varied relationships between education and politics. And such is indubitably the case. Historically the relationships have been diverse; today among the various countries of the world the relationships are diverse. Among the totalitarian regimes the school is frankly but an instrument of the class or clique possessing the state, quickly responsive to the changing whims, fortunes, and purposes of the dictatorships and never presuming to inquire into the bases of social structure and political power. In the democratic countries the school enjoys a measure of independence and is expected to deal more fundamentally and comprehensively with the problems of life and society, sensitive to obligations more profound and abiding than loyalty to either persons or parties. Consequently, since there is no clear and universal response to the question as to who should make those choices of a political nature which may be found in any educational program, it remains to outline an answer which is appropriate for American democracy today.

But the point should be emphasized again that the answer

itself constitutes a political choice, the most far-reaching which society ever makes regarding its agencies of organized education—a choice that cannot be made and enforced by teachers. In a word, the determination of the relation of the school to politics, which is also a determination of the conception of the role of the school which shall prevail in a given society, is a political question. If the teachers of the nation should approve unanimously a certain conception of education, they would be powerless to put that conception into operation in the absence of support from the effective forces active in community, state, and nation. And since in a democracy every question of politics is also a question of adult education, the cycle from the one sphere of interest to the other is closed. The present analysis therefore is addressed quite as much to educational laymen as to members of the profession.

In undertaking the formulation of a conception of the relation between the school and politics it is helpful to note that, besides the transmission of technical knowledge and powers indispensable in any modern society, every educational program embraces the apparently logically contradictory processes of molding and enlightenment. A program that emphasizes the former to the entire exclusion of the latter, an actual impossibility in fact, would result, if successful, in an indoctrination of the most extreme type, in the reduction of learning to a mere matter of conditioning, in the absolute fixing of loyalties to social ideas and institutions, and in the development of minds impervious to new conceptions, dominated by servility to authority, and lacking elasticity, resilience and creativeness. Such a view of education is approached historically in the practices of various religious denominations and today in the totalitarian states of Europe and the Orient. On the other hand, a program that endeavors to repudiate the molding process completely, an actual impossibility also, would result, if successful, in the cultural disinheriting of its subjects and in the rearing of a generation without roots in any society or epoch—futile, amorphous, purposeless, lacking in common loyalties, and wholly unfitted for life in this world. Indeed, enlightenment itself can have no substance or meaning apart from personalities formed and created by the molding influences of a given culture and system of social arrangements. Such a conception of education has of course never been practiced, for it would have destroyed immediately the source of its being. The point should be made, however, that there is very little danger that any society will ever overstress the process of enlightenment in its program for rearing the young. Although the importance of this process for human advance has been recognized by thoughtful men and women since the days of the ancient Greeks, the architects of organized education have almost uniformly erred in the other direction, and grievously. The molding process has been so generally and powerfully emphasized that in many minds it has been identified with education. The security of the state and the established order has ever been the dominant motive in the organization and conduct of the work of the school.

If organized education is to reinforce the democratic method in society and serve the purpose of achieving social change with a minimum of disorder, while conserving all democratic values, it must strike a balance between the processes of molding and enlightenment. While, on the one hand, it must not become a thing of the moment and a tool of any political faction or party temporarily occupying the offices of government; on the other hand, it must not be so remote from the present that it would obstruct the road to social advance. In either case, the process of enlightenment would be subordinated to that of molding, and education would compound the hazards which democracy faces today. Without responding to the eddies on the surface of society, it should be sensitive to the deep-flowing social currents and tendencies; without reflecting the passions of the day, it should give expression to the more profound changes in sentiment and outlook; without presuming to shape the entire social process, it should accept its share of responsibility for the reconstruction of society. Elastic but not dispersive, detached but not unconcerned, judicial but not insensitive to social values, education should oppose all forces which threaten the survival and development of democracy. This means that education, employing the recognized methods and tools of scholarship, should proceed to fashion a broad frame of reference for the guiding of its operations.

In order that an education of this type may be promoted, two closely related conditions must be achieved: education must attain a relative measure of independence of the state and escape the domination of the contemporary aristocracy.

If the school is to possess genuine freedom, it must be removed from the immediate supervision of the state and from every other form of authoritative control. The historical record shows that whenever such control has been established honesty and sincerity have been destroyed and education reduced to its formal and mechanical aspects. Great education, like great art, cannot be summoned forth at the crack of a dictator's lash. State power can exact conformity, but it cannot inspire excellence; it can compel order, but it cannot evoke spontaneity; it can arouse fear, but it cannot command thought; it can produce subjects, but it cannot create free men. That the state will shape the broad policies of the school in every modern nation is probably inevitable, even as the church did in an earlier age. But in the measure that it decrees the details of the curriculum, methods of instruction, and elements of social doctrine to be inculcated it moves in the direction of the totalitarian conception of the relation of education to politics. This is so, even though it may presume and appear to enforce liberal prescriptions. The state may destroy old tyrannies and set the conditions under which freedom is possible, but it can neither dispense nor administer liberty.

The question of educational and intellectual freedom in any society depends upon the prevailing conception of the state. If the latter is elevated to the position of a transcendent entity to be worshiped blindly and obeyed implicitly, endowed with absolute prerogatives and assumed to be capable of doing no wrong, the school can have no independence. But if the state with all its organs is conceived merely as an instrument for the promotion of individual and social welfare, limited in authority and subject to every human passion, organized education may with confidence ask for a measure of freedom. Under this second conception, which is essential to the successful operation of the democratic process, the deepest loyalties of school and teacher are attached, not to the state or to any political personality or body, but to the boys and girls in their charge and to the society which they serve. That in some instances individual members of the profession will violate these loyalties in their own interests and that in others they will be persecuted for remaining faithful to them is probable, even certain. Yet such hazards are infinitely preferable to that intellectual and moral straight jacket into which the totalitarian states force their schools.

Perhaps in the present critical period it will prove impossible for schools and teachers to place loyalty to the political state in a secondary position. It may be that the state, or the power back of it, will over-ride the entire liberal tradition and compel the school to do its bidding to the last detail. If this should occur, as many thoughtful people believe it will, organized education can play no positive or creative role in either the preservation of democracy or the reconstruction of society. If the independence of the school is completely destroyed, its function becomes purely instrumental and servile and the faith of the eighteenth century in its ameliorative influence will be shown to have been an illusion. In that

event organized education becomes an agency for impound-
ing the forces of change and driving the social struggle to
extremes of bitterness.

It is also imperative that the school escape the domination
of the contemporary aristocracy. Although this problem is
identical in some measure with that of achieving independence of the state, since political organs may be expected to
fall into the hands of any powerful and privileged group in
society, it manifests certain complexities and peculiarities of
its own. An aristocracy may rule through the direct capture
of the institutions of government, but it is by no means confined to the use of such methods. Possessing overwhelming
economic power and enjoying a virtual monopoly of social
prestige, it is able to influence the conduct of education in
numerous and subtle ways. It can often elevate or degrade
the socially aspiring, make or break reputations, open or close
the doors to preferment, and in general take persons of talent
and ambition up on a high mountain and show them all the
kingdoms of this world. It can also destroy personal integrity
and transmute the idealism and enthusiasm of youth into the
cynicism and complacency of middle age. Clearly, if education is to serve American democracy, it must steadfastly refuse
to enter into any alliance with the "ordirs of the few." For
generations the latter as a class, in spite of magnificent individual exceptions, opposed the extension of educational opportunities to the people; and having failed in this they have
sought with equal tenacity to control the program of the
school. The future of democracy requires that this control
be broken and remain broken.

Responsibility of the Profession

The responsibility for the development and propagation of
a conception of education designed to guard and nourish
democratic values must rest largely on the teaching profes-

sion. That the latter must have the support of the broad masses of the population is of course self-evident. The teachers of the country, constituting but a small minority, cannot themselves wield sufficient authority to make any conception of education prevail. Moreover, even if they had the power arbitrarily to impose their will upon the schools, they would be violating the principles of their calling if they should do so. But they can take the initiative in promoting discussion and arousing popular concern over the work of the school. They can, if they desire, make the problem of education a major public interest.

The end to be sought at the present critical juncture in the history of American democracy is a second great educational awakening. The first began something over a century ago in the more advanced states and eventually achieved throughout the country the "educational ladder" or system of free schools from the kindergarten through the university —an achievement justly hailed as a major contribution to the development of democratic institutions. The popular instinct which led to the establishment of this system was sound, even though at the time the question of the content of an education appropriate to a democracy was given relatively little consideration. The "battle for free schools" rested largely on a naive faith in the general efficacy of a process which required no definition, presumably because its character was fixed in the nature of things. How naive this faith was, is demonstrated today in the eagerness with which dictators turn to education to marshal and organize support for their tyrannies. Democracy, no less than autocracy, must have its own special conception of education. The formulation of this conception should mark the second great educational awakening in the history of the Republic.

The difficulty of the problem has advanced hand in hand with the growing complexity of society and of educational enterprise. The ordinary citizen simply cannot be sufficiently

informed to pass judgment on the details of school policy
and program. There must be delegation of authority and
responsibility. The traditional method of meeting this situation has been the creation by one means or another of a
board of education to represent the public in the school. But
the citizen is quite incapable of making intelligent selections
for this board unless he not only knows the candidates, but
also has a fairly clear conception of the nature of education.
The inadequacy of his equipment in these respects is indicated by the personnel of the typical city board of education
in the United States. A study made by the author approximately ten years ago showed such a board to be composed of
six members, distributed according to occupation as follows:
"One of the six members is a woman, who follows the occupation of housewife. Of the five men, one is a merchant; one,
a lawyer; one, a physician; one, a banker, manufacturer, or
business executive; and one, a salesman, clerk, or laborer." [2]
Other types of boards of education were found to be much
like the city board. Clearly, with such persons in control of
the public school—persons who by association and interest
are for the most part closely identified with the economic
aristocracy—there is small probability that it will conduct a
vigorous program in defense of democratic values. A task of
immediate urgency therefore is the creation of boards of education truly representative of the people. The accomplish-
ment of this task, however, must wait upon the development
of a widespread popular interest in the responsibilities and
possibilities of the public school in the defense and development of democracy. Having no special privileges or vested
interests to defend, the ordinary citizen is in a position to
welcome and support a curriculum intended to promote the
widest possible enlightenment with respect to social institutions and ideas. The teaching profession is under obligation
to open his eyes to this obvious truth.

But the teachers have further obligations in the situation.

They must not only take the initiative in arousing popular interest in the problem of education; they must also exercise a far more effective leadership than hitherto in everything that touches the work of the school. At two points in particular, as suggested above, they must become more articulate and aggressive. They must be prepared to check or, at least, challenge the encroachments of government and the attacks of minorities upon the school. Here are the two chief threats to an intellectually free and honest education and the two major obstacles to the dedication of education to the guarding and promoting of democratic values.

The encroachments of government constitute the first threat to education, and particularly the encroachments of federal government. Because of the increasing complexity of the social structure and the growing integration of the national life, the state is everywhere in the ascendant in the modern world. Although in America this tendency is less manifest in the sphere of education than in certain other areas, even here the trend is unmistakable. Any one who has studied the developments in the authoritarian states of Europe and Asia can only look with misgivings on the emergence of centralized control of education in the United States. And while outward effects might be almost negligible under a liberal administration, the machinery would be set up for the use of the entire system of education of the country for the political regimentation of the national mind. It is a hazardous road to pursue.

Yet this rise of governmental concern is not to be opposed successfully by a policy of pure negation. The need for a more comprehensive and more fully integrated program of education for locality, state, and nation would seem to reside in the very structure of contemporary society. The teaching profession therefore, while opposing the assumption of educational functions by the federal government and insisting upon the perpetuation of the principle of local and state au-

tonomy in the field of control, should proceed boldly to
the task of formulating educational policy for the nation.
Beginnings have already been made, notably by the National
Education Association and the Association of School Administrators in the launching of the Educational Policies Commission; but time does not wait. If the teachers do not proceed
immediately and effectively to meet this situation, they may
find themselves forestalled.

Teachers must also be prepetually on the alert to detect,
expose, and thwart, in so far as they are able, every attempt
by any minority, however powerful and respectable, to dictate
the program of the school. From the standpoint of the threat
to democracy arising out of economic and political conflict,
here is the source of greatest danger. Owing to the fact that
reactionary forces are generally in a favored position at the
beginning of such a conflict, the chances are that the school
will serve their interests and thus embitter and prolong the
struggle. Certainly this was the case, both North and South,
in the middle of the last century when two rival economic
and cultural systems moved toward the settlement of their
differences. Whether they boast an ancestry dating from
Jamestown and Plymouth and carry the sacred banners of
patriotism, or come from the latest immigrant boat preaching
the doctrines of some authoritarian state of contemporary
Europe, all minorities, all pressure groups, must be stoutly
resisted by the profession and compelled to leave the public
school alone. Teachers must always insist that the educational
program be conceived and administered in terms of the general and unfolding interests of the American people. It is perhaps needless to add that whatever the vehicle or instrument,
the only genuine danger today comes from concentrated
power—from the aristocracy of wealth and privilege.

But, it will be argued, all of this is asking the impossible of
teachers. By the quasi-servile tradition which has nurtured
them and the sheltered condition which has generally sur-

rounded them, they are unfit to discharge such heavy responsibilities. And certainly one of the most disheartening facts
of recent years has been the readiness with which the great
majority have submitted to humiliation at the hands of ignorant, illiberal, and rapacious elements. The ordinary American teacher, in both his professional and private life, has been
spied upon and harassed by gossips, busybodies, heresy hunters, self-constituted guardians of public morals, paid agents
of power and privilege, and by anyone who desired to conceal piratical designs on society under the cloak of patriotism
or to gain a reputation for courage and public spirit without
danger to himself. In many communities the teacher is
scarcely allowed to become a well-rounded human being. It
is not surprising that some wit has characterized the teaching
profession as the "third sex."

This is not the whole picture, however. The fact that
teachers have been subjected to organized and systematic
abuse during the past dozen years or so is in itself an evidence
of progress. Under the impact of the depression upon the
schools and the general deepening of the social crisis, individuals and even small groups among them stepped out of
their accustomed role of acquiescence and began to raise
questions about the economic order. The concerted drive
of the so-called patriotic societies to force American education into the totalitarian mold, the relentless campaign of
the less responsible newspapers to destroy freedom in the
schools in the name of freedom of the press, the passage of
laws in twenty-two states requiring all members of the profession to take loyalty oaths, and the frequent dismissal of
teachers for espousing liberal and humane causes indicated
clearly that eductors were developing both a social conscience
and a social consciousness. In a word, these developments
show that the calling is moving toward a new status in society.

The major issue resides in the question of organization.
If the teachers are to participate effectively in the shaping of

educational policy and program—the central thesis in the present argument—they will have to become thoroughly organized. In a world in which organization is the order of the day, in which all influential groups are organized, it would be the height of folly for individual teachers to attempt to shoulder the burdens of the profession. Already, through the National Education Association, the American Federation of Teachers, the Progressive Education Association, the Association of School Administrators, the American Association of University Professors, and other national and local organizations, the teachers have moved a long distance in the right direction. The desired goal will not be reached, however, until the entire membership of the profession from kindergarten to university is gathered into one great body fully equipped to fight the battles of teachers and to represent education in the councils of community, state, and nation. As the process of organization goes forward financial resources should be accumulated, the art of publicity mastered, ability to deal with government officials and bodies acquired, and a procedure for handling all cases involving freedom and tenure developed.

Concerning the primary object of a comprehensive professional organization there should be no misunderstanding. While teachers as individuals and as workers have certain claims on society which should not be denied, while they should be permitted like all other human beings to lead normal lives, it is not assumed here that they have any natural and indefeasible rights in the situation superior to the public interest.

The argument for greater freedom and power for the teacher cannot be based on the principle of protecting and advancing the class interests of the profession, important as those interests may be to the members. The schools are not run to give employment to teachers nor to establish the rule of pedagogues. About this there should be no mistake. The guiding consideration must always be the welfare of children and society. The great ideal of intellectual freedom, so dearly bought and yet so tenuously held in the Western World today, and with which the work of the teacher is closely linked, can rest on no more solid foundation than its general social utility.

Why then should teachers organize, increase their power, and defend one another against attacks of powerful individuals and groups? The answer to this question is to be found in the nature and obligations of education in an industrial society "dedicated to the proposition that all men are created equal." As already observed, the only practicable check on the encroachments of government and the attacks of organized minorities is a powerful body of teachers. But there is another aspect of the problem which merits attention. The process of education, if it goes beyond mechanical training and conditioning, is peculiarly personal and intimate. In a democracy, certainly, the teacher must first of all be a person of dignity, worth, and character—master of himself and an individual of moral stature. To make him a hireling or a lackey of a community bully, a political boss, or an owner of property is to destroy him. Anything that tends to make teachers subservient and slavish should be opposed by every friend of American education. Today, unfortunately, there are altogether too many teachers in the schools who do not dare to speak their minds either inside or outside the classroom. This is the real educational tragedy of a time that requires a generation capable of clear, courageous, and creative thinking. And there are citizens and organizations favoring legislative proposals which would still further crush and dwarf the spirit of the profession. If teachers do not fight back against these forces which strike at their integrity, they are scarcely worthy to serve boys and girls as examples of American democracy.

But, it is contended, teachers may be disloyal to American

institutions: they may introduce subversive doctrines into the classroom. The fact that almost invariably such charges come directly or indirectly from those elements in society which have plunder to conceal or special privileges to protect, from the hereditary and emergent enemies of democracy in the United States, can be disregarded. The fears expressed will be regarded as genuine, as indeed they are in those instances where honest democrats have become victimized by the propaganda of the aristocracy.

It is of course conceivable, and even probable, that an occasional teacher may deliberately and consistently work against the best interests of the democracy. But, if he does, he will be discovered far more quickly and effectively by the profession itself than by any outside official or body. Certainly he will not be exposed by any legal enactment. The teachers of the country, moreover, are more truly "American" than any other important occupational group in the country. Studies show that as a body they are overwhelmingly not only native-born but also descendants of old American stock. There is no intention here of casting reflections on those who trace their lineage to the later migrations or who themselves have come from the other side of the Atlantic; but since the argument is often couched in such phrases it should be met and refuted. Also the teachers come disproportionately from the farms and small communities where the traditional American institutions and values are most deeply rooted. Too, they have been molded in exceptional measure by the schools and other cultural agencies of the country. Even to question their essential loyalty to the general welfare is to raise doubts regarding the worth and significance of historic ideals and modes of life in the United States, to lend support to the most extreme revolutionary doctrines. They are more truly American than those minorities which are so vocal in requiring certificates of loyalty of others— a very un-American procedure. The charges of disloyalty hurled at teachers were recently answered in unequivocal terms by Dr. E. F. Tittle, a distinguished educational layman who has had unusual opportunities to know the members of the profession:

When it comes to pure, unadulterated patriotism there is simply no group of Americans which, actually, has given a better account of itself than the teachers in our public schools. There is no group among us that is more intelligent or better informed or more truly and persistently devoted to the welfare of the nation. We can afford to trust our school teachers to give our children needed information concerning the society in which they live. We cannot afford to let our children grow up ignorant of what is going on in the world.[3]

In assuming the heavy responsibilities for the conduct of public education here outlined the teachers must cultivate and merit the good will and confidence of the people. This they must do, not only in their relations with individuals, but also in their relations with organizations. It was argued in an earlier chapter that the defense of democracy today requires the comprehensive organization of the working people of the country, using the term to include all elements in the population gaining their livelihood primarily by labor of hand or brain. Teachers should constitute an integral part of this nation-wide organization of producers. This does not mean that they should refuse to work with such bodies as the United States Chamber of Commerce, the American Bankers Association, and the National Association of Manufacturers, much less that they should shun individuals representing these interests. But they should recognize that, if democracy is to be defended and its methods employed in the reconstruction of society, the job will have to be done primarily through *popular* organizations. In the very nature of the case a privileged order cannot be counted upon to lead a movement intended to reduce its privileges or impair its status. And if the analysis developed in this volume has any merit whatsoever, the preservation of democratic values requires the conquest by the people of economic power. It would seem therefore that teachers, in their effort to convert the school into an instrument of profound social enlightenment, must seek the solid foundation of broad mass support. Otherwise their program is certain to collapse the moment it shows signs of becoming effective.

REFERENCES

1. For thorough documentation of this point see Howard K. Beale, *Are American Teachers Free?* (New York, 1936).

2. George S. Counts, *The Social Composition of Boards of Education* (Chicago, 1927), 79.

3. Ernest Fremont Tittle, "Education and the Public Welfare," *Educational Trends* (Evanston, Oct.-Nov., 1937), VI, No. 2, 11.

CHAPTER 12:

A PROGRAM FOR PUBLIC EDUCATION

THE fact has been emphasized that no educational program is without bias. Indeed to be without clear and unmistakable bias would mean that it would lack character and individuality, that it would not exist. Like any actual culture or social order, it must have form and substance, pattern and value, aversions and loyalties. This truth is revealed in even the most superficial study of the history of education—in the educational practices of the American people today and yesterday, no less than in those of the primitive Australians, the ancient Chinese, the Russian communists, or the German Nazis. While there are of course common elements in the most diverse educational programs, as there are in the most varied civilizations, there is an appropriate and distinctive education for every order of society. Any denial of this principle represents either an effort to escape the hard choices which life always presents or an attempt to conceal the actual social import of a program under the veil of universality.

The first obligation of American teachers, and of all who would engage in the fashioning of educational policies and programs for the United States today, is to bring into bold relief those underlying assumptions and guiding principles which are to give structure and direction to the work of the school. That this is a hazardous undertaking, not to be entered upon lightly, is obviously true. And yet it is a task that cannot be evaded. It may be shifted to other shoulders or even go unacknowledged; but when the educational program is in operation, a more or less distinct moral and intellectual framework will be discernible to any competent analyst.

The point should be emphasized, moreover, that those who

build this framework are by no means free agents in any complete or abstract sense. They cannot derive their principles from the air or from culturally rootless philosophical speculation; they are bound by the necessities of time and circumstance. Their choices are limited to possibilities; and what is possible depends upon the social heritage, the contemporary situation, and the resources of human thought, will, and purpose. It should be said also that, though choices are conditioned, they are nevertheless genuine, as genuine as any choices that man ever makes in this world. In the historic process, within which education plays its role, men are neither ruled by iron necessity nor wholly freed from the coercions of the natural and cultural environment. The essential practical function of social science is to reveal the limits of choice and to provide the materials essential to rational decision and construction.

A Frame of Reference

This brings the argument to the actual formulation of a suitable frame of reference for American education today. It is proposed that such a frame include two major elements —one an affirmation of a set of values which is deeply rooted in the past of the American people and the Western World; the other a recognition of a necessity which is the dominant emergent reality of contemporary society: the first is the democratic conception of life and human relations; the second the fact of industrial civilization with all its compulsions, possibilities, and conditionalities.

The democratic conception has always occupied a central position, not only in the life of the American people, but also in the frame of reference of public education in the United States. While a precise and full definition of this conception is doubtless impossible, its content has been set forth and expounded on almost every page of this volume, certainly in sufficient detail to be of service in the construction of an educational program. By way of summary it may be said that democracy asserts the worth and dignity of the individual human being and the fundamental moral equality of all men; that it proclaims a faith in mind and reason, in the capabilities of ordinary people, and in the indefinite perfectability of human society. Also democracy believes in material security and independence for all, equality of opportunity for personal growth, reasonable equality of economic condition, general participation in the processes of government, safety of life and liberty of person, access to the sources of relevant knowledge, unfettered exchange of ideas and opinions, freedom of thought and conscience, and rule by majority decision. Democracy repudiates the theory of rank and caste, the doctrine of autocracy and authoritarianism, and the dogma of divinity of persons and institutions. That there are no decisive compulsions in present-day America to continue and develop this great tradition is entirely obvious. Indeed, it has been the burden of the argument of these pages that democracy today is facing an extremely precarious future, that it confronts the threat of disintegration and extinction. If it is to be preserved and fulfilled, positive measures will have to be undertaken. In bringing their faith in this heritage to life through the reconstruction of the program of the public school the teachers of the country will be making one of the great and fateful choices of American social and educational history.

The position of the second element in the educational frame of reference is radically different. Although the sweep of industrial civilization has already profoundly influenced the public school in innumerable ways, the implications of this new and revolutionary factor in history are neither fully understood nor frankly accepted. Yet here it would seem that, broadly speaking, education has no choice in the matter. For better or for worse, not only American, but world, civilization is well into a new stage which is fraught with unmeasured and unpredictable consequences for every department of life and culture. A society is already emerging that is marked by rapid change, fabulous power, and close integration on a vast scale—a society that makes ever fuller use of science and technology in the organization and conduct of its life and economy. There are of course those who cast nostalgic eyes toward the pre-industrial age and long to return to the ways of a hundred, two hundred, or five hundred years ago. But, as pleasing as this may be in contemplation, it is no more than day-dreaming—an emotional and intellectual escape from the maladjustments attending the flux and decay of institutions, from the hard realities, the strains and tensions, the seemingly insoluble problems of the present. Education, if it is to merit the respect of informed minds, must accept this new dispensation. Here is the major necessity that history has thrust upon the school.

The acceptance of this twofold frame of reference places upon public education the task of assisting the American people in their efforts to arrive at a synthesis of democracy and industrialism: to harness the power of technology to the realization of democratic ends, to preserve the integrity of the individual under conditions of organization and collective activity, to achieve both efficiency and popular control in the management of an economic and social mechanism of unprecedented intricacy and complexity, to rely on the method of peaceful change at a time when old arrangements crumble, interests clash, passions run high, anxieties multiply, and the cult of Caesar revives. It is of course not inconceivable that democracy may prove incapable of surviving under the conditions of industrial civilization. The appearance of dictatorships, apparently as a result of the inability of free institutions to deal effectively with the economic problems raised by the spread of technology through the world, has led some to the conclusion that democracy and industrialism are incompatible, that the former cannot survive under conditions created by the latter. Such a defeatist attiude at this stage of history, however, would seem to be the product of either childish disillusionment or wishful thinking. The battle for democracy in the age of industrialism has only begun.

The task of developing the frame of reference proposed is made both difficult and urgent by the fact that organized education and the teaching profession, like the general body of citizens, are bound by a mentality and social orientation formed at a time when American democracy was linked to a pre-industrial economy of small individualistic and family enterprise. Clearly, unless this link is broken, democracy will follow the earlier economy into the graveyard of history and public education will assist in the interment of popular rule. No conception of life can long survive the destruction of its social foundations. It is such considerations that make imperative the inclusion within the frame of reference of the facts of industrial civilization. In so far as organized education is a force in society, the fate of democracy is dependent upon the reconstruction of the social outlook and presuppositions of the school program. Some of the implications of the frame of reference here outlined for American education will now be developed.

Popular Education

From the standpoint of the preservation of free institutions and the successful operation of democratic processes, the program of popular education is primary. However excellent may be the provision for special and higher learning, it cannot serve as a satisfactory substitute for the organized and systematic enlightenment of the masses of the people. Indeed the more thorough the intellectual equipment of the preferred occupational and economic classes, if the general population remains in ignorance, the greater the danger to democracy. History demonstrates conclusively that the welfare of the many cannot safely be entrusted to the mercies of the few, let the latter be ever so well grounded in the arts and sciences. There must be no monopoly of knowledge and understanding, no great cultural gulf dividing the hewers of wood and drawers of water from those who occupy the seats of power in the economic and political order. Popular education, whatever the nature of its agencies, must always be the support and guardian of democracy.

The institution through which this task may be achieved is well established. In the course of their history the American people, borrowing from the practices of the Old World and adding certain inventions of their own, have forged a superb instrument of popular education—the twelve-year common school obliterating the traditional distinctions between elementary and secondary instruction and forming a unified program for inducting the rising generation into the life of industrial society. Although the advance of this institution has proceeded at different rates in different parts of the country, the trend of the past half-century suggests that it is destined to enroll approximately the entire population from six to eighteen years of age. Here, if organized education has any potency, is democracy's opportunity to save itself.

It should be stated explicitly at this point, perhaps, that no attempt will be made to outline a complete program for the twelve-year common school. The concern of the present argument is with a somewhat limited phase of the problem—that phase which patently is related directly and immediately to the crisis in American democracy. While no aspect of the program is wholly without bearing on the question under consideration, attention will be concentrated on two things: the life of the school and the content of the instruction. The first will be disposed of briefly; the second will be treated at greater length.

The foundational training in social attitudes, dispositions, and powers should be provided in the organization and conduct of the life of the school. The principles and values of democracy should be made explicit in the relations of pupils with one another, of pupils with teachers, of teachers with supervisors and administrators—through the sharing of decisions in government, the recognition of the worth of the individual, the propagation of a pervasive spirit of equality and brotherhood. The imperatives of industrial society should be expressed in the softening of the more narrow egoistic impulses and the placing of emphasis on group and cooperative activity, ideas, and sentiments. This does not mean that teachers should relinquish their responsibility for guiding the educative process. Training in democracy is perhaps the most difficult and exacting task ever undertaken by the school, not at all to be confused with permitting children to behave according to their own pleasure. Also the above proposals do not mean that the administrator is to be superseded and his work dissipated through the teaching staff. The closely integrated society of the present, with its countless intricate, complex, and far-flung enterprises, demands ever more efficient administration. The contention here is merely that members of the profession should participate, along with representatives of the community, in the formulation of school policy. As pointed out in the preceding chapter, a teacher whose role is reduced to the taking of orders is a wholly unreliable and incongruous agency for preparing children to live in a democratic society.

The most ideal school life, however, constitutes an entirely inadequate preparation for effective citizenship in an industrial democracy. Such a life can form character and provide those concrete experiences which are essential to any understanding of the vast world in which the individual must live. But the pupil must be led from the school and the surrounding community to the systematic study of the forces and insti-

tutions of the "great society" of which his school and community constitute but a focal point. Particularly must he be
equipped to utilize those agencies, those mechanical exten-
sions of his sensory apparatus, through which he receives reports of events and personalities and upon which he is
increasingly dependent for guidance in the discharge of his
civic obligations—the printed page, the radio, and the movie.
Certainly a central responsibility of popular education is to
insure a widespread mastery of the apparently simple arts of
reading, listening, and looking—a mastery, not only of the
formal aspects, but also of the substance, of these arts. Only
the rare individual today is equipped to respond intelligently, as well as emotionally, to the welter of stimuli which
beat incessantly on the doors of his mind. He reads, he listens,
he looks; all of these things he appears to do proficiently and
with assurance: but he does them without insight or discernment: he is the unwitting victim of the use of symbols from
which all content has been removed. A major function of
organized civic education is, not to abolish the use of these
symbols, but to put meaning into them. The nature of the
problem can be made clear by an illustration. On January 30,
1936, Mr. John J. Raskob sent the following letter to 150,000
persons inviting them to become members of the American
Liberty League:

Beginning life as a poor boy blessed with splendid health, the
finest heritage which a good father and mother can leave any
child, I was able to acquire a good grammar and commercial
school education before starting to work at $5 per week, at the
age of 19 years, to make my way in the world.

It was my good fortune to be born a citizen of the United
States of America—a country whose government is founded on
a Constitution which respects the rights of persons and property as fundamental to every successful form of government
and which teaches the duty of government to encourage and
protect individual and group initiative and enterprise; to foster

'the right to work, earn, save and acquire property and to preserve the ownership and lawful use of property when acquired. These are human rights.

Through the years I have been successful—successful in retaining good health and, through hard work and saving, in acquiring a competence for old age and the care of dependents. As measured in terms of happiness, however, greatest success has come from accomplishments made possible under our form of government, accomplishments impossible under a socialistic, communistic or other form of government which fails to encourage initiative and teaches that all property belongs to the State to be used under such conditions as the government may dictate through bureaus created for the purpose. This constitutes a government of regimentation and bureaucracy and subjects the citizen to the many kinds of tyranny resulting from such political control of our homes and all else vital to our daily existence.

Paraphrasing the words of the Declaration of Independence, when in the course of the life of a nation a radical minority in both great political parties becomes so strongly entrenched in public positions of power and authority as to threaten the destruction of the fine principles on which that government is built, a decent respect to themselves and posterity demands that all liberty loving citizens of that nation stand forth, rally around a common standard and fight for the preservation of those principles which for 150 years have insured liberty and freedom for a people who declare that their creator endowed them with unalienable rights of life, liberty and the pursuit of happiness. In this way only can the children of future generations enjoy the same opportunities to be happy and succeed through working, earning and saving as were enjoyed by the boys and girls of past generations.

Fortunately, we have such a rallying point already created. The American Liberty League, seeking no office or political control, organized more than a year ago, has established a proud record. Thoroughly nonpartisan, it has stood forth, bravely defending our charter of liberty and presenting its findings through a series of pamphlets so carefully prepared that not one statement of fact has been successfully contradicted. Notwith-

standing this, however, its members have been reviled and mis-
quoted, all of which has advertised and promoted the splendid
work the league is doing. The radicals are now beginning to
realize that the American citizen is demanding facts and that
scurrilous attacks on reputable citizens characterize weakness in
their cause.

As a citizen with the responsibilities of the head of a family
of twelve, as a property owner, stockholder and director in
several corporations, I hope you will not think me presumptuous
in calling on you and your friends to unite with others in issuing
a clarion call to all liberty-loving citizens to join the American
Liberty League, National Press Building, Washington, D. C.,
which is doing everything possible to root out the vicious radical
element that threatens the destruction of our government.[1]

That Mr. Raskob was profoundly ignorant of what he was
saying is suggested by the fact that he gave the letter to the
press. But until the ordinary American citizen is able to read
such a document and detect at once its underlying hypocrisy
and callous complacency, its warping of a great and humane
tradition, its manipulation of the historic symbols of American democracy, its defense of privilege in the name of the
general welfare—in a word, until he can brush aside this cloak
of pleasing verbiage and disclose the reality beneath, as Mr.
Elmer Rice, the distinguished playwright, does in the following letter of reply, he will be quite incapable of discharging
his civic obligations and of defending democratic values in
the present age of industrialism:

My dear Mr. Raskob:

I am happy to be one of the 150,000 recipients of your chatty,
personal letter. It is indeed an honor to be included in that
heroic band of "members of stockholders committees, industrialists and leading figures in business and civic life," (New York
Herald-Tribune) to whom you have addressed your clarion
call "to rally to the standard of the American Liberty League"
(New York Herald-Tribune) in defense of the sacred rights of
property.

It was gratifying to learn from your letter that you have acquired "a competence for old age and the care of dependents." I have, of course, heard rumors to that effect, but one scarcely knows what to believe these days, and it is good to learn over your own signature, that you are not a candidate for home relief, an old-age pension or any of the other hateful forms of governmental patronage.

Too, I was greatly interested to learn something of your background and early experiences, which, in many ways, are similar to my own. I, also, had the good fortune to be born a citizen of the United States—as had my parents before me—and, like you, I was obliged, at an early age, to make my own way in the world. You were lucky enough to be able to remain at school until you were nineteen; I had to go to work, at fifteen.

My first job paid me $4.50 per week. At nineteen (when you were beginning at $5) I had already worked my way up to $9. Later, my fortunes, like yours, improved and, like you, I have succeeded for a good many years now, in making a comfortable living (although I must confess that I have never had to face the embarrassing necessity of avoiding an income-tax liability of $600,000 in a single calendar year).

But now I come to an important point of difference between us. It is simply this, Mr. Raskob: my nature is sadly lacking in that happy resiliency which sparkles through every paragraph of your refreshing and stimulating letter. Temperamentally, I am morose and sombre and so I have never been able to shake off the memory of those bitter early years of drudgery and starvation wages. Morbidly, I have continued, throughout the years, to identfy myself with the tens of millions of underpaid, underfed, underprivileged young men and young women, from whose blood and sinew such great fortunes as yours and those of your associates are distilled.

Like you, I am the head of a family and so I understand how comforting to you is the knowledge that your twelve dependents are not in immediate danger of want. But are you not forgetting, Mr. Raskob, that for each of your twelve there are today, in this land of opportunity and plenty, one million unemployed men and women?—human beings with desires, needs and feelings very much like yours, who are denied, through no fault of their own, the bare necessities of life, the bare right to provide for themselves and *their* dependents. Other tens of millions lead a precarious existence, with little or no margin between themselves and actual destitution, never knowing an instant of real security, their pinched lives darkened by the ever-present specters of illness, unemployment and penniless old age. What about their "human rights"?

You are one of the leaders of a great industry which has always been conspicuous for its refusal to grant to its workers their "human rights" to organize for the betterment of their own condition. You and your fellow captains of industry have met the "group initiative and enterprise" of these workers with the clubs of the uniformed forces of law and order and with the bullets of hired assassins. Secure in your economic oligarchy, you have not hesitated to rob men of their employment, without warning; to toss them on the industrial scrap-heap at forty; so much slag in the process of smelting your gold. Your associates in the American Liberty League—the feudal barons of Delaware—are the beneficiaries of organized mass-murder; they have coined their wealth from the bodies that strew the battlefields of the world.

To the hungry, the maimed, the disinherited of this land of ours, your phrases about liberty and freedom must seem as empty as the Empire State Building or the brown derby of the Happy Warrior. Compared to the "freedom" which serves only to entrench a handful of plutocrats in the possession of their dubiously-acquired wealth, the "tyranny" of a form of government which guaranteed, to all its citizens, economic security and a minimum of decent living would be a blessing, indeed.

Literature is not your trade, Mr. Raskob, and so we must not condemn you for the ineptness of your "paraphrase" of the Declaration of Independence. But permit me to counsel you to read further in that splendid document. In the very paragraph which you "paraphrase" you will find these words which require no paraphrase: "Whenever any government becomes destructive of these ends, it is the right of the people to alter or abolish it and to institute a new government, laying its foundations on such principles and organizing its powers in such form, as to them shall seem most likely to effect their safety and happiness."

When the people of this country see fit to exercise that right, the industrial magnates and the captains of finance will go the way of all the despots and oppressors, whose inordinate lust of wealth and power has blackened and reddened the pages of human history.

And so, my dear Mr. Raskob, I decline with thanks your friendly invitation to join the American Liberty League. I prefer to take my stand with that "vicious radical element" which clamors for a new social order, based not upon the preservation of the property rights of the predatory few, but upon the satisfaction of the human needs of all.[2]

In order to read, listen, and look with understanding the masses of the American people must possess knowledge. While knowledge by itself may be inert and academic, when linked with interest, as it inevitably is in the social process, it is power. William Manning was not far wrong when he placed major responsibility for past failures of free government on popular ignorance. At the close of his analysis he concludes that if free men would but exercise their rights of suffrage intelligently nothing more would be required. "Therefore," he says, "the ondly Remidi is knowledge." But this knowledge must be pertinent to the purposes postulated in the premises. In his own words it must be the "knowledge nesecary for a freeman."

While Manning's categories would provide inadequate guidance for the construction of a program of civic instruction in the schools today, they reveal a much deeper sense of the realities of the social situation than is to be found in any curriculum that has come to the writer's attention. They recognize as fundamental the obvious truth that knowledge, if it is to function in this world, must be relevant to the interests to be served. They also recognize the equally obvious truth that interests are in conflict and that all interests cannot be served by the same knowledge. If knowledge is to be useful in the preservation and development of democratic values, in equipping the masses of the people to protect themselves against the encroachments and exploitations of a privileged "ordir of men," it must be selected and organized with this end in view. No contemporary curriculum-maker in the public schools of America has ever worked from these obvious truths—truths which were apparent to this unschooled New England farmer, unable to spell and deficient in grammar, who "neaver was 50 Miles from whare (he) was born in no direction," and who lived *before* the "horse and buggy days" in the age of ox-carts, candlelight, quill pens, homespun, and wooden-ware.

In the spirit of William Manning it is here proposed that the public school, for the purpose of preparing men and women to defend their freedom in the present age, and without trying "to deceive or misleed" them, proceed to provide knowledge under the following eight heads: the nature and history of man, the story of American democracy, the rise of industrial civilization, the present structure of American society, the contradictions and conflicts of the contemporary world, the social ideas, philosophies, and programs now in competition, the agencies and methods of propaganda in current use, and the purposes and potentialities of American democracy. It is perhaps needless to add that all of this knowledge should be presented without passion or rancour, without any effort to arouse class or national hatreds, objectively and in accordance with the highest standards of scholarship. Each of these eight categories will now be briefly developed.

First, the school should give a broad account of the nature and history of man: his place in the natural order, his relation to the rest of creation, his special traits and powers, his great antiquity, his long struggle for mastery in the animal kingdom, his wanderings and migrations, and his differentiation into races and peoples; his inventions and discoveries, his development of the practical arts, his advances in hunting, agriculture, and industry, his founding of social institutions, and his building of states and empires; his search for truth, justice, and beauty, his creation of art, religion, science, and philosophy, his efforts to surmount the inherent tragedy of existence, to master his earthly infirmities, to re-make the world in the image of his own longings. There should be included also a record of the wars of classes, sects, and peoples, of the triumphs of despots and madmen, of the struggles against tyranny and oppression, of the succession of social systems, of victory and defeat, of progress and catastrophe. Within the limits of the time available, the whole story should be told, not glossing over those manifestations of stupidity and cruelty which place man beneath the brute, nor failing to give due emphasis to those heroic and sublime episodes and achievements which give him the stature of the gods, those tender and selfless acts and sentiments which make him akin to the angels. This basic part of the program of civic training might close with a thoroughly realistic study of the present map of the world—the distribution of natural resources and populations, the diverse races and patterns of culture, the boundaries of nations and relations of peoples, and all of those forces and factors that drive mankind to war. While the task here outlined is admittedly an impossible one, the school can be satisfied with nothing less than the ideal of conserving and transmitting to young and old the entire legacy to which they are the legitimate heirs. Only in the measure that this ideal is realized can the living gain wisdom from the experience of the dead, place a proper evaluation on the worth of their heritage, and view contemporary events and tasks in rational perspective. Such a general account should provide the basic intellectual fabric in which special and distinctive patterns may be woven.

Second, the school should tell the story of American democracy, tracing its origins back through the centuries of Western and world history and charting its course and fortunes from generation to generation on this side of the Atlantic. It is peculiarly necessary that this heritage be viewed and studied in its varied aspects, economic, social, and cultural, as well as political. The account should include the disintegration of feudal institutions and outlooks, the leveling influence of the frontier, the establishment of the pre-industrial agrarian economy, the overthrow of the system of Negro slavery, the immigration of the underprivileged and oppressed of other lands, and the rise of organizations of working people. It should embrace the spread of the ideas of the Enlightenment, the War of Independence, the founding of the Republic, the struggle for popular control of the several branches of government, and the extension of civic and political rights to women. It should not overlook the separation of state and church, the development of public education, the growth of humanitarian conceptions, and the repudiation of authoritarianism in various fields. On the other hand, the forces and trends tending to undermine, destroy, and halt the march of American democracy should be examined—the passing of the frontier and agrarian economy, the perpetuation of autocratic, aristocratic, and authoritarian ideas and practices, the development of commercial, industrial, and finance capitalism, the concentration of economic power in fewer and fewer hands, the emergence of the contemporary aristocracy, and the current attack upon democracy at home and abroad. Special attention should also be devoted to the failures of political democracy, the interruptions and qualifications of democratic processes in American history, and the conditions leading to the complete abandonment of free institutions in various countries of the world.

Third, the school should trace with great care the rise of industrial society, beginning with the earliest application of measurement to the economy, but emphasizing the train of events following the onset of the so-called "industrial revolution" in England in the eighteenth century. It should show how science and its offspring technology, operating within the matrix of capitalistic institutions, have gradually and ever more rapidly transformed the economy and the underlying conditions of life—bringing in new forms of production and exchange, increasing the role of capital goods, making labor an appendage of the machine, adding invention to invention and discovery to discovery, harnessing the inanimate forces of nature, creating novel materials and processes, rendering obsolescent occupational skills and knowledges, changing the modes and instruments of warfare, extending the range and speed of communication, widening the reach of the market, introducing the phenomena of mass production, breaking down family and community boundaries, destroying the independence of farm and locality, integrating society on an ever vaster scale, producing new class divisions, interests, and conflicts, modifying traditional conceptions of property, reducing the role of economic competition, fostering cooperation and organization, placing a premium on planning and control, putting new burdens on government, revolutionizing the modes of recreation, accelerating the tempo of life, altering the relations of nations, compounding economic crisis and catastrophe, ushering in an age of potential plenty, creating social maladjustments of unprecedented number, intensity, and variety, and generally thrusting men into a world inconceivably extended, intricate, complicated, impersonal, and overpowering. So revolutionary and pervasive are these new forces that they are giving their name to the emergent epoch in human history.

Fourth, the school should give a bold and clear analysis of the present structure of American society. The major object of this analysis would be to reveal the emerging pattern of classes, to locate the actual seats of political power, to examine the services and rewards of the various population elements, and to disclose "the differend interest (s) that influence all ordirs of men." Facts would necessarily be assembled on distribution of wealth and income, on the relations of the diverse economic groups to the tools of production, on the sentiments, loyalties, and traditions of these different groups, and on the extent of fundamental community of interest among them. Special attention would be given to that small "aristocracy of paper and patronage" which, because of its strategic position in the economic and social system, has generally been able to dominate, not only the economy, but also government, the press, the radio, the movie, the school, and even the church. Its connections with the several departments or divisions of the common life, through the manifold devices of control developed with the advance of industrialism, would be traced in detail. And all of this would be viewed in historical perspective and in relation to the practices, institutions, and doctrines of private capitalism or rugged individualism operating in the closely integrated economy of the industrial age—the dogma of the economic man, the conception of a natural economic order, the rationale of gain-seeking, the money, market, and price system, the institution of private property in the tools of production, the theory of enterprise, the laws of inheritance, the sanctity of contracts, and the doctrines of *laissez faire*. Attention would be addressed to the problem of discovering just how democratic American society is today.

Fifth, the school should introduce its pupils to the more crucial contradictions and conflicts which grow out of the maladjustments in the culture and the social structure and which shake contemporary society to its foundations. There would seem to be contradictions between the historic individualism of capitalistic enterprise and the close integration of industrial economy; between the private ownership and the social operation of the tools of production; between the planlessness, irrationality, and uncertainty of competitive undertakings and the planfulness, rationality, and precision of technology; between the inherited conception of natural economic law and the necessity of social control; between the tradition of democracy and the fact of a financial aristocracy; between the doctrines of nationalism and the trend toward a world economic order. Out of these contradictions arise conflicts between classes and between nations which threaten to destroy civilized society and throw mankind back for a long period into a state of material privation, political tyranny, and cultural barbarism. Some of the consequences already apparent are insecurity and scarcity in an age of possible security and abundance; incoordination of the factors of production and consumption; periodic panics, crises, and depressions; planned and unplanned restriction of productive forces; waste of natural, technical, and human resources; suppression of invention and perversion of science; isolation, subordination, and commercialization of art; fear of parenthood and "invention of sterility"; suppression of popular rights and liberties; struggles for markets and raw materials; spread of a philosophy of open aggression; armament races, mounting debts, wars and rumors of wars—potential catastrophe and perhaps a return of the dark ages. All of these things should be faced and studied in the public school.

Sixth, the school should pass in honest and critical review the various social ideas, philosophies, and programs which are competing for survival and mastery in the world. This would include, not only the whole body of social, economic, and political tradition upon which the present order may be said to rest, but also the doctrines and practices associated with communism, fascism, socialism, syndicalism, the cooperative movement and any current "new deal." In no case should an effort be made to enforce a narrow indoctrination upon the minds of the younger generation. On the other hand, as pointed out earlier in the present chapter, the approach to these rival systems would not be lacking in bias and orientation. Every one of them would be appraised in terms of democratic values and the necessities of industrial civilization—in terms of the achievement of the composite goal of economic efficiency, material security, personal freedom, cultural diversity, popular intelligence, majority rule, and peaceful change. Doubtless from some of them useful ideas and suggestions would be derived, but the expectation would be that the American road to the future would as a whole be *sui generis*, conditioned and shaped by the peculiar history, circumstances, loyalties, and opportunities of the people of the United States.

Seventh, the school should acquaint the rising generation as thoroughly and completely as possible with the actual agencies and methods of propaganda. The successful employment of the democratic method in the present critical times rests, as already emphasized, in no small measure on making the ordinary citizen propaganda-conscious, -intelligent, and -wise. To the extent that this is not achieved public opinion, the foundation of political democracy, will be corrupted and the elaborate superstructure of free institutions will crumble and fall. Whether the object of the propagandist is to sell a new tooth paste, elect a candidate to public office, propagate a body of political doctrine, or clothe a pirate in the garb of a saint, the citizen should be equipped to unmask his motives and purposes. In its pursuit of this objective the school should proceed systematically and comprehensively. The role of propaganda as an instrument of government and social control should be included in the historical account, with particular reference to critical periods in the American past and the practices of the contemporary dictatorships. The entire network of agencies operating in the United States today should be studied individually, collectively, and comparatively. For example, a number of newspapers should be compared, their methods examined, their fundamental interests disclosed, their policies and purposes laid bare, their connections with the economic, political, and social order revealed.

The student should be led to know the great dailies and periodicals, news-gathering services, broadcasting companies, moving picture producers, advertising agencies, and public relations counselors. He should become familiar with the devices employed to becloud thought and obscure truth—the use of symbols, the calling of names, the manipulation of loyalties, the appeal to prejudice, the suppression and distortion of fact. Employing the community, national, and world laboratory the school should provide exercises in the detection of propaganda. In general a systematic effort would be made to equip the younger generation to employ the method and spirit of science in facing the social problems and tasks of the contemporary world.

Eighth, the school should develop a challenging conception of the purposes and potentialities of democracy in the United States and the world today. Certainly, the fulfillment of the early nineteenth century promise of American life requires of youth more than an informed and critical understanding of past and present, an ability to detect propaganda and unmask hypocrisy; it requires an active and creative attitude, a living and heroic spirit, a positive orientation toward the future, a sense of social responsibility, an eagerness to improve society, a faith in democratic values and processes. And this is also what youth requires. Whatever may be said of older folk, young men and women do not live by bread alone. Particularly in an age of shifting loyalties like the present, do they ask for some course of action through which their lives may be made significant. This fact has been recognized and acted upon by the leaders of men through the centuries. Consider the following appeal addressed by Garibaldi on July 3, 1849, to troops assembled in the Square of St. Peter's, after all hope of defending Rome against the besieging French army was gone: "Soldiers! I leave Rome. Let him who wishes to continue the war against the foreign enemy, come with me. I can offer you neither honor nor gold; I offer you only hunger, thirst, weary marches, battles, and death. Let him who loves the fatherland follow me!"[3] Nearly four thousand men responded to the challenge and followed Garibaldi across central Italy, cutting their way through the French and Austrian armies and finally gaining the shelter of the Sabine mountains.

That the dictators of the contemporary world have invariably employed this method with success in the overthrow of free institutions and the establishment of totalitarian regimes is a matter of record. With songs on their lips and exaltation in their hearts the youth of the countries involved have trampled on the "prostrate form of the Goddess of Liberty," firmly believing themselves to be engaged in building a better world. Many friends of democracy, viewing this terrifying and nauseating spectacle, have concluded that any appeal to youth is undesirable, that such an appeal is itself undemocratic and illiberal. These persons overlook the historic fact that democracy did not enter the world under the aegis of neutrality but through the militant assertion of a set of values. If these values are to continue to live amid the clash of conflicting systems, they will again have to receive the enthusiastic support of youth and be applied effectively to the conditions of industrial civilization. This would seem to mean that the school should seek to enlist the energies and talents of the rising generation in the realization of a program conceived in the spirit of that outlined in Chapter VIII of the present volume—a program designed in the light of contemporary scholarship in the social sciences for the purpose of making the democratic process effective. But it should go further and outline in broad perspective a society which, utilizing the resources of technology, would bring security and relative material abundance to all and at the same time strive to realize ever higher conceptions of justice and beauty. It would address squarely to boys and girls, to young men and women, the challenge of reviving and achieving that vision of a good society—good for even the humblest citizen—which was the possession of the American people in the early years of their history.

The Higher Learning

While a well-conceived and competently administered program of popular education is essential to the preservation of American democracy, the full realization of the potentialities of a society of free men and women, particularly in the industrial age, requires an equally appropriate and excellent system of higher learning. Only as the accumulated knowledge, thought, and wisdom of the race are brought into the service of democratic values and purposes can democracy attain its highest expression. Indeed, in a period like the present when autocratic and authoritarian doctrines are on the offensive throughout the world, the very survival of popular government may depend upon the instruction and the research conducted by the colleges and universities. Fortunately here, as in the field of popular education, the American people are well supplied with institutions many of which are intimately associated historically with the rise of democracy in the United States. But in order that they may meet most effectively the challenge of dictatorship and class rule, certain changes and developments would seem to be imperative. The eight propositions elaborated below, though admittedly only a partial attack upon the problem, should stimulate discussion and provide a modicum of guidance.

First, all economic and social barriers to the higher learning, in both its special and its general aspects, should be removed. This of course constitutes the repudiation of a centuries-old tradition. Today in America, as numerous observations and studies have shown, the advantages of college and university education are severely limited by financial considerations. The great majority of the ablest young men and

women of the country, despite the growth of state institutions, are practically denied admission to the upper levels of
the system, while many persons of mediocre powers, because
of parental assistance, may be found even in the graduate
schools. Since the thesis of Jefferson that the greatest resource
of any society resides in the gifts, talents, and character of its
people is scarcely debatable, calculated and systematic provision for the fullest possible utilization of this human
endowment would seem to be the essence of social wisdom.
Moreover, the most characteristic ideal of American democracy, that of equality of opportunity, points in the same
direction. Also the danger to free institutions of anything
suggesting a class monopoly of the higher learning is obvious.
Clearly the utilization of the human endowment, the equali-
zation of opportunity, and the breaking of a class monopoly
of the higher learning all require the establishment of liberal
maintenance grants to enable gifted young men and women
to attend the colleges and universities of the country.

Second, the conception of the higher learning as essentially
an individual right should be abandoned. In an age when
it was generally assumed that the common good would be
advanced if the individual would only pursue his own
interest with industry and devotion, this conception may
have enjoyed both intellectual and moral support. But
today when the bankruptcy of such comforting doctrines is
revealed in the facts of ordinary life a radically new orientation is required. No longer can the higher learning be
regarded primarily as a means of individual self-aggrandize-
ment, as a road to economic ease and social respectability, as
an avenue of escape from the hard, disagreeable, and poorly
paid occupations, as a sanction for the exploitation of the less
fortunate and more helpless members of society. There is
something grotesquely incongruous in the dedication of great
resources of physical equipment and instructional talent to
the production of bond salesmen and stock brokers, public

relations counselors for buccaneers and racketeers, shrewd and erudite lawyers to assist powerful corporations in the circumvention of the law. In the upper divisions of the educational system individual opportunity must be linked with social responsibility. More concretely, the colleges and universities should direct their energies increasingly to the preparation of young men and women to provide leadership and technical assistance for all popular movements—farmer associations, labor organizations, consumer cooperatives, and political parties. Also, in view of the growth of governmental functions in the past and the probable extension of such functions in the future, they should encourage able students to look with favor upon careers in the public service.

Third, the conception of the higher learning as a badge of aristocracy should be uprooted. Although this conception is far weaker in America than in those countries of Europe where class lines are fairly stable and openly acknowledged, it is by no means absent. Also, although it is particularly noticeable in certain of the old and heavily endowed colleges of the East, it is easily discernible in the more recently established public institutions of the West. In varying measure the members of the aristocracy and the upper middle class everywhere look upon the college as a place where their children, thoroughly insulated from the world of human suffering, may spend four or five pleasant years, romp and play together, make pretensions of serious study, and cultivate notions of superiority. To the sons and daughters of the lower social ranks the college curriculum is a highly elaborated ceremonial for inducting them into the aristocracy, enabling them to form associations with the "right people," to acquire the proper manners, modes of dress and speech, and social attitudes and outlook, to gain that body of prejudices, aversions, and loyalties, that smattering of knowledge of history, language, literature, art and science known as "culture" and essential to the conduct of intercourse and conversation in the "best circles." That this conception is but one strand in the higher learning in America and that it is contradicted by other strands is admitted. But the slightest vestige of this aristocratic heritage has no place in a democratic society.

Fourth, the general aspects of the higher learning should always be conceived in their concrete, cultural, and temporal relations. Every great education in history, though it may have been stimulated by the discovery of ancient truth, has been bound to the living concerns of its own epoch. Education, higher no less than lower, has decayed and become formalized whenever it has sought to copy some celebrated pattern of the past. The most general branches of learning possess vitality only if the life-blood of some actual society courses through their veins. To make any part of education universal and timeless, to remove it from dependence on a living culture, to identify it with the esoteric practices of an academic priesthood, to convert it into a sacred and transcendent art not subject to the judgments of the flesh, is to banish it from the world of humankind. This of course does not mean that the higher learning should be narrowly practical, nor that it should deal only with the immediate and the ephemeral. As a matter of fact, American democracy, if it would survive and justify itself before the bar of history, must leave no doors of learning unopened, must prosecute inquiry into the most remote and profound regions of nature, history, and mind, must bring the greatest possible resources of intellect to bear upon the tasks of generalization, interpretation, and synthesis. But all such undertakings, whether in the sphere of original research or in that of instruction, must start from and return to the earth on which men dwell. Never should they be permitted to lose touch with life and become purely "disciplinary."

Fifth, the special aspects of the higher learning should always be conceived in their general relations. If the divorce of general studies from the world of practical affairs leads to formalism, futility, and parasitism, the divorce of special studies from the world of ideas and thought leads to caprice, irresponsibility, and servitude. Without some understanding of the social implications of his calling the technical or professional worker, whether engineer, physician, lawyer, clergyman, teacher, or scientist, is in danger of employing his special knowledge either in the support of some prejudice or in the service of some predatory interest or end. However good his will, being incapable of making rational discrimination among the possibilities, he sells himself in the market place, becomes the tool of another's purposes, and loses his status as a free man. No person, having received special training at the hands of society, can evade the obligations attending the employment of that training. At any rate, in a democracy a technician must always regard himself as more than a technician: he is also a citizen and accountable to society as a whole for the use he makes of his talents. One of the most encouraging signs of the time is the fact that members of the professions, apparently in increasing numbers, are coming to realize that they cannot be indifferent to the social consequences of what they do. The program of training should recognize this tendency and make provision for those general studies through which the specialist may perceive the social implications of his specialty.

Sixth, the higher learning should identify itself fully and without reservation with all those liberating forces and movements which have marked the advance of the modern era, which have challenged authoritarianism in both church and state, which have aroused the hopes of ordinary men and women, which have promoted faith in the powers of human mind and will, and which make man the measure of all things—the humanism of the Renaissance, the individualism of the Reformation, the liberalism of the Enlightenment, the democracy of the English, American, and French revolutions, the humanitarianism of the nineteenth century, the idealism of the socialist and cooperative movements, the audacity and heroism of the organization of working people, the power and promise of technology, and above all the method and spirit of science. To those who may argue that any such commitment on the part of the higher learning may bind it to a partial world view and destroy its universality and catholicity, the reply can be made that in so doing it is only defending itself. Let the principle of authority re-establish itself in human society and the glorious tradition of freedom of inquiry and thought, the life-blood of learning in all ages and climes, will be mocked and destroyed. Respecting this question there can be no compromise.

Seventh, the higher learning should assume leadership in the earnest and systematic study of the tasks, problems, and resources of American democracy. Every college and university in the country, except those perhaps which are dedicated to some highly specialized purpose, should accept this as a major responsibility. On the one hand, the emergent tasks and problems should be critically and constructively explored; while, on the other, the life and history of the people should be thoroughly searched for material and spiritual resources which may be utilized in the preservation and development of free institutions. A central need in this connection is the discovery of those social conditions and arrangements which are essential to the existence and growth of personal freedom and security. If the practitioners of the higher learning are unable to answer such questions as these, they will be the first victims of their failure; they will learn after the event how fragile are the foundations of democracy. And their failure will write a fitting epitaph over the grave of man's faith in the liberating power and beneficence of his own intelligence.

Eighth, the control and conduct of the higher learning should be liberalized and democratized. At present, as stated directly and by implication again and again in the present volume, power over the colleges and universities is placed to a dangerous degree in the hands of the privileged orders. If these institutions are to serve most fully the interests of the people, if they are to be free to examine fearlessly the bases and prospects of American democracy, membership on their boards of control, whether serving under private or public auspices, should be composed largely of persons representing immediately popular causes, movements, and sympathies. To expect bankers, corporation officials, owners of great properties, and their habitual associates and servitors in the professions to favor the liberation of the higher learning is to ask too much of human nature. Even though boards so constituted may refrain generally from positive acts of censorship and dismissal of instructors, they will invariably impose their outlook by methods of indirection—by appointing "safe professors," by withholding promotions, by manipulating the budget, by sending out invitations to tea, by employing their vast resources of social prestige and respectability. Moreover, whatever the composition of the board, its power should be limited by both statute and tradition. In the sphere of the higher learning, even more than in the area of popular education, the principle should be established that the loyalty of the teacher or investigator is to society rather than the state or any creature of the state. At the same time, lest college and university faculties become insensitive to the needs of society, always a real danger, some provision should be made for subjecting them and their work to continuous and systematic public review and criticism. Also, if they are to merit and enjoy general confidence, they must assume the responsibilities of self-discipline, devise ways and means of removing incompetents, and develop a defensible philosophy of their relation to society.

The Teacher

The role here assigned to organized education in the rising battle for democracy in America requires a teacher of large intellectual and moral stature—a teacher who is more than a technician, more than a skillful practitioner of the art of pedagogy. He should indeed be a thorough master of his craft; but he should also know to what larger ends his craftsmanship is directed. He should be a scholar who has command of the knowledge of his specialty, a citizen who takes a responsible part in the life of the community, a democrat who identifies himself with the interests and fortunes of the many, a patriot who is deeply concerned over the future of his country and his people, a friend of mankind who cherishes the values of world peace and human brotherhood, a poet who feels the tragedy, the pathos, the glorious hopes of the time, a wise counselor of the young who knows the conditions and problems of living in the present confused and challenging epoch. He should also be an active member of his profession, ready to devote time and energy to the general advancement of the cause of public education and enlightenment.

This is not to say that the schools and colleges of the country have not had teachers of this type. They have had many of them, but they need many more. The number may be increased perhaps by providing a more generous program of preparation—a program that will go beyond the techniques of the classroom and place large emphasis on the social, cultural, and philosophical foundations of education—a program systematically designed to develop a person of liberal and humane outlook. But more important than the mode of training are the conditions under which the teacher lives and works. Anything that enlarges the opportunities and responsibilities of the calling will inevitably enlarge the intellectual and moral stature of the individual teacher. For such opportunities and responsibilities the members of the profession should struggle without ceasing. And in this struggle they should have the support of all citizens who would have the schools serve the cause of American democracy more effectively.

REFERENCES

1. *The New York Times* (February 1, 1936).
2. *New Masses* (February 18, 1936), 15.
3. Giuseppe Guerzoni, *Garibaldi* (Firenze, 1882), I, 331.

CHAPTER *13:*

AMERICAN DEMOCRACY TOMORROW

The several parts of the argument may now be brought together. Nurtured on a great ethical tradition of Western and Anglo-Saxon civilization, influenced by all the humanizing and liberalizing movements of the modern age, and shaped by the extraordinary conditions attending the conquest and settlement of a new continent of fabulous natural wealth, there developed in North America during the seventeenth, eighteenth, and nineteenth centuries a society which was deeply permeated by the spirit of democracy and ardently devoted to the guarding and extension of popular rights. Here, far removed from the social patterns and sanctions of the Old World, serfs and slaves broke the shackles of law and custom, persons of humble origin looked their "betters" in the face and were unafraid, ordinary men and women became unusually secure and free, and the life of common people assumed a measure of dignity and nobility.

The foundation of this democratic society was the freehold farmer and the relatively self-contained rural household. With his own land beneath his feet, with a rifle in his experienced hands, with the essential tools of production in his house and barn, with the skills and knowledges of the practical arts in the possession of himself and his family, he was able individually and collectively to challenge the authority of the past and of all privileged orders. He repudiated the doctrines of "classification, caste, and legitimacy," proclaimed the ideal of human equality, overthrew the principle of monarchy, separated church and state, abolished entail and primogeniture, launched a bold experiment in popular government, and even endeavored to storm the citadels of knowledge and learning. Taken in its entirety, this record of the

348

American farmer, supported by the working people of towns and cities and by occasional representatives of the "aristocracy of wealth and talents," constitutes the mightiest achievement of history in the democratization of life.

Today, in spite of its almost uninterrupted advance on the political front, American democracy is in peril. The growth of capitalistic enterprise, the spread of pecuniary institutions, and the rise of technology have gradually, and ever more rapidly, undermined the economic foundations of popular security and liberty. The freehold farmer has been reduced to a narrow minority, while the self-contained rural household has disappeared altogether. That general equality of condition, which Tocqueville and other foreign observers noted, has given way to a condition of great inequality. The fact is that the few have conquered economic power and that the many have lost control over the means of livelihood. On the one hand, is a great commercial, financial, and manufacturing aristocracy; on the other, the overwhelming majority of the people—dependent, insecure, and bound. Apparently, moreover, that high social mobility, that ease of movement from one economic level to another, which has always characterized American society, is declining. Rarely, if ever, in history has the social structure of a country been transformed so profoundly and so quickly by relatively peaceful means. And for the most part this transformation has taken place beyond the knowledge and intention of any individuals or groups of citizens.

As a consequence of this peaceful social revolution American democracy is now in an extremely precarious condition—more precarious than at any time since the days of Jefferson. If it is to survive at all, its material foundations will have to be restored, popular control of economic power achieved. A continuation of the trend toward concentration of wealth of the past three generations, or even a stabilization of the present situation, could only mean the actual, if not the formal, civic disfranchisement and intellectual regimentation of the masses of the people, the inauguration of a regime of industrial feudalism. The crisis confronting free institutions is greatly heightened by the fact that the pattern of democracy in the age of technology remains to be created: retreat into the past is impossible, consolidation of present positions means certain defeat, and advance in any direction is fraught with hazard and uncertainty. Clearly the period immediately ahead will be marked by exploration, invention, and experimentation, provided of course the American people possess the genius and the will to achieve a synthesis of democracy, liberalism, and industrialism—a synthesis of popular sovereignty, personal liberty, and economic efficiency.

The struggle to overthrow the "aristocracy of paper and patronage" is on: for decades it has been gathering strength: sooner or later it will be carried to some conclusion. In what manner and by what methods this struggle will be conducted is perhaps the most urgent question now facing the nation. It does not suffice to say that America is a political democracy and that the verdict of the ballot will therefore prevail. In the contemporary world popular governments have apparently been destroyed at the polls. The very point at issue, moreover, is whether a powerful economic aristocracy can be subdued by the democratic process. Nor does it illuminate the problem to proclaim the dogma of class violence and announce with utter finality that no privileged order ever surrenders its privileges without resort to the sword. This also is to beg the question, and even to close the road to peaceful settlement of differences. That the emergent struggle will be conducted at times with great bitterness, that it will involve defamation and assassination of personal character, that it will be marked by violation of constitutional guarantees, that it will be attended by intermittent and sporadic bloodshed—all of this is already in the record. But whether it will lead finally to organized violence and civil war may well depend on the energy, the devotion, and the wisdom of the friends of free institutions in the United States—on their ability to learn from experience, to define the problem, to formulate a program of action, to discover, appraise, and marshal the apparent and latent, the actual and potential resources of American democracy.

The general pattern of the struggle ahead is probably revealed in the history of the American people and the experience of contemporary Europe. As the freehold farmers under Jefferson fought for political rights, the governing aristocracy responded with a well-organized campaign of misrepresentation and with a resort to state power to halt the popular advance, only recoiling from recourse to the sword to maintain its hereditary position. In Russia a revolutionary party, assisted by the demoralization resulting from a long and exhausting war, overthrew the thoroughly corrupt and unenlightened regime of the tsars, socialized natural resources and tools of production, and maintained itself in power by establishing a rigorous dictatorship in the name of the proletariat and poor peasantry. In Italy and Germany great historic labor movements advocating the democratization of the economy, divided by sectarian quarrels and preaching in some instances the doctrines of violence and the totalitarian revolution, were met and overwhelmed by counter movements from the right sustained by the middle classes and dedicated to national unity. In Spain a democratically constituted government, opposing at the same time John Taylor's three aristocracies—the aristocracies of "superstition," "motto and blazon," and "paper and patronage"—was attacked by its own army, supported by the armed forces of the two great fascist states of Europe and the might of the Roman Catholic Church. All of this experience, and much more that might be added, indicates that a privileged order regards its privileges as sacred rights, that any popular advance will be met by the most determined resistance, that attacks upon the system of property relations are peculiarly hazardous, that the social foundations of the democratic process are extremely precarious, that the appeal to the sword in the age of technology gives the few an advantage over the many, that a wholesale repudiation of inherited institutions and values can only bring discredit and disaster to the popular cause, that division in the ranks of democracy paves the way for the triumph of aristocracy, and that the separation of means and ends is always fraught with peril.

The experience of modern industrial nations shows that the employment of the institutions of political democracy in the profound reconstruction of the economy is hazardous and can scarcely be successful in the absence of a carefully considered program of action. It is proposed here that such a program should embrace at least the following nine points. First, and most basic of all, is a deep and abiding faith on the part of the friends of democracy in the values and the efficacy of the democratic process. Weakness here can only mean disaster. Second, in the words of William Manning, is the dissemination of knowledge among the masses of the people—knowledge necessary for a free man—knowledge relevant to the understanding and defense of the popular interest. Third, and perhaps necessary to achieve the second, is the comprehensive organization of the many. Avoiding sectarian disputes and eschewing revolutionary dogmas born of Old World conditions, the people should organize as producers, consumers, and citizens. Fourth, is the quick and effective execution of popular mandates by government. If elections, won at the polls, are lost in the political machinery, faith in democratic institutions will be destroyed. Fifth, the essence of government, is the maintenance by the constituted authorities of a complete monopoly of military and police power. Relaxation of the watch here, as the experience of Europe shows, may mean the triumph of dictatorship. Sixth, the essence of the democratic process, is the guaranteeing of the civil liberties without prejudice to all elements of the population—security of person and freedom of conscience, speech, press, assemblage, and petition. Seventh, is the systematic exposure of all major campaigns of political propaganda—their sources, methods, and objectives. Eighth, is the conservation of the democratic temper, the exercise of moderation and tolerance, the display of a sense of humor, proportion, and fairness in the political struggle. Ninth, and last, and possibly the most difficult and decisive of all, is the avoidance of war.

In the realization of this program the American people are cursed with heavy liabilities as they are blessed with substantial assets. Among the former are the concentration of economic power in few hands which makes possible the manipulation of public opinion and public officials; the complexities of industrial society which place all but insuperable burdens of understanding on the ordinary citizen; the heterogeneity of the population which invites the unscrupulous political leader to rise to power through the exploitation of racial, national, and religious prejudices; the legacy of economic individualism which renders difficult any cooperative or collective approach to the economic problem; and the symbols and loyalties of a great national heritage which, when not understood, close the eyes and ears of the people to the realities of their own time. Other liabilities are the spread of spectacles and circuses which undermine political sense and integrity; the rise of chronic unemployment and relief which destroys independence of spirit and demoralizes individual character; the long tradition of violence and intolerance which predisposes the American people to abandon democratic procedures; the system of checks and balances which periodically paralyzes the action of government; and a timid and unrealistic program of organized civic education which has closed the minds of the people to the seriousness of their situation.

On the other side of the ledger are certain assets which may give the American people a great advantage over the peoples of the Old World. First and foremost, long ago they liquidated the institutions and mentality of feudalism, always an invitation for the return of authoritarianism and despotism—the stratification of classes, the state church, the military caste, and the master-servant relationship. On the positive side is the long experience with free institutions, the democratic heritage itself which, if understood and utilized, should constitute a priceless, perhaps a decisive, asset. Closely related to this heritage are the high political sense and the experimental temper of the American people which may be expected to protect them against demagogy, ancestor worship, and the more extreme forms of utopianism. The tradition of "good neighbourship," of cooperation and group action, developed by the simple and hard life of frontier and farm, may still possess sufficient vitality to facilitate the curbing of egoistic tendencies and the organization of the economy in the community interest. Also the contemporary European spectacle should cause the American people to hesitate long before abandoning their tradition of political freedom; the American aristocracy, owing to its comparatively feeble moral and intellectual foundations, should prove to be exceptionally vulnerable; the natural and technical resources of the country, making possible an economy of relative abundance for all, should moderate somewhat the acerbities of the social struggle; and the comparative security of the nation from external attack should provide an unparalleled opportunity for the application of reason to the settlement of domestic issues. Finally, the great and growing body of precise knowledge of human society in general and of American society in particular provides an unprecedentedly solid foundation for the successful operation of democratic institutions.

Regardless of the fullness of the analysis, however, the outcome of any effort to employ the democratic process in the reconstruction of the economy remains unpredictable. To attempt to strike a balance between the foregoing liabilities and assets would be both fruitless and unscientific. The potential strength of no one of the factors listed can be accurately gauged. Indeed, to speak of gauging it, apart from the persons in which it will live and the circumstances by which it will be molded, is to talk nonsense. There exists no calculus for striking the kind of balance suggested. And, owing to the dynamic and dialectical character of the social process, the very act of drawing up an account might set off a chain of events which would profoundly alter that account. The object of the above analysis, moreover, is not to reveal, but to help make the future: to place in the hands of the social architect *authentic* materials with which he may recreate the world. The analysis will also serve a useful purpose if it succeeds in directing the attention of the friends of American democracy to the extraordinary riches of their heritage.

The most critical uncertainty probably resides in the vitality of the democratic tradition. How vital this tradition is in the United States cannot be known in advance of the tests to which it may be subjected. Perhaps the American people are tired of democracy; perhaps they have lost their love of political freedom; perhaps they long to lose themselves in the arms of some overpowering authority; perhaps they thirst for the return of tyranny. It is possible that the energies of American democracy have already been dissipated by the bribes of the aristocracy and the regimenting influence of industrial capitalism. Also, how severe may be the tests applied to popular institutions in the United States cannot be foreseen. But whatever the event may prove, it is assumed here that democracy is still a living and creative force in American society. To make a contrary assumption would be tantamount to surrendering before the battle.

Although the American people may be fully committed to democratic values, they are by no means adequately equipped to guard and apply those values in the current age. Their stock of social ideas is largely traditional; their knowledge of industrial society is superficial and fragmentary; their understanding of their situation is still in its most elementary stages. For several generations they have been coasting on the thought and achievements of their ancestors. They have little grasp of the nature of the crisis confronting them. They are beginning to sense vaguely that there is something very wrong with the world, but they are confused and troubled, inclined to cast nostalgic eyes toward the past rather than to press resolutely forward to new frontiers. In a word, they are approaching a mood which would respond readily to the appeal of fascism.

The correction of this condition is largely the responsibility of education broadly conceived. It requires the awakening of interest in the fate of free institutions, the stimulation of political discussion, and the dissemination of social knowledge and understanding. From one standpoint, to be sure, the development of a democratic society in the industrial age is a task of social invention and engineering. Since no historic pattern is available, some new design must be fashioned. But in the deepest sense, in a democracy at any rate, this too is an educational problem. If new paths are to be found and new arrangements devised, the fullest possible release of the creative energies of the American people is desirable. Social invention and engineering, moreover, must have the criticism and support of an informed and discriminating body of citizens. The expert, the man of genius, indispensable as he is, must be checked and guided, understood and appraised, punished and rewarded by the populace.

It is not enough, however, to say that the task is essentially educational in nature. If such were the case, there would be little or no problem; for the American people have developed the most extensive system of schools in the world and they support this vast educational enterprise with unexampled generosity. But education is not an unchanged and universal substance which is always and everywhere the same. On the contrary, when taken in its entire pattern, it assumes a distinctive character in every society and epoch, responding to changing purposes and conditions of life. If it is to serve the peculiar ends of American democracy today, it must be appropriately conceived and conducted. This is interpreted in the present volume to mean that, among other things, it must achieve a high degree of independence of the coercive power of the aristocracy and the state, accept the values of democracy and the necessities of industrial civilization, explore as thoroughly as possible the historical and scientific foundations of the contemporary world, turn the attention of the rising generation to the tasks of the emergent age, and organize its own life in harmony with the democratic conception of society.

It should of course be remembered that the power of the school is severely limited, that life is the great educator. Through their occupations, their recreations, their social and civic activities, their countless associations with their fellows, their changing fortunes and circumstances, the American people are being educated today for the tasks and responsibilities of tomorrow. When their institutions begin to work badly they are driven to serious reflection upon the nature and purpose of the inherited social structure. The World War, the revolutions in other countries, the devastating impact of the great depression, the successive measures of the Roosevelt administration, have compelled many a sluggish mind to ponder, to question, and to seek knowledge. That the general climate of opinion has become much more favorable to the critical study of the economic aspects of democracy during the past generation is apparent on every hand. A striking bit of evidence is found in the reception accorded Gustavus Myers' scholarly *History of the Great American Fortunes* when it was first published in 1909. Before publication the work encountered the general hostility of publishers; after publication, the general hostility of reviewers and commentators. The burden of the criticism, moreover, was not that the facts had been distorted or falsified, but rather that the subject itself was taboo. In the preface to the 1936 Modern Library edition of the book the author thus reports the change in the attitude of the reading public:

For years this book had what might be called an underground circulation. That is to say, it was barred by colleges, ignored by publicists, received no notice, and was altogether left to an uncertain fate. But as time went on colleges and universities and public libraries found that they had to have it, professors used and quoted it, public reference to it became more and more frequent, it was used on the floor of Congress, and there came a new generation of reviewers who . . . found contents and treatment conform to their views and liking, and gave the book increased prominence.[1]

The issue can be left to the mercies and caprice of unorganized education, however, only at the risk of continued drift and possible further undermining of the supports of democracy. The question of time may prove to be crucial. On the one hand, if the existing property relationships should become stabilized over a sufficiently long period, the economic aristocracy might establish itself so firmly in both law and custom that it could not be dislodged; on the other hand, if deep crises should return and engender a revolutionary temper before the social intelligence of the great body of citizens is adequate to deal rationally with the situation, the country might pass easily, quickly, and wholly unwittingly under some form of dictatorship. In either case the urgency of a comprehensive program of organized education, conceived boldly in terms of the present social realities and designed specifically to meet the current challenge to democracy is altogether patent. The fate of free institutions in the United States may hang on the insight, courage, devotion, and practical genius of those who shape the programs and policies of that great hope of eighteenth and nineteenth century democracy—the system of free public education.

In concluding this long analysis of the prospects of American democracy the need for concerted and informed action on the part of the friends of popular interest and welfare should be vigorously stressed. The present age, like all critical and transitional ages in history, is confused, fluid, and dynamic, marked by conflicting forces and tendencies, by growing strains and tensions. Old loyalties are losing their binding power; new allegiances are in process of formation; the younger generation in particular is restless under the precepts of the past. Also, as pointed out in practically every chapter of this volume, the cultural heritage of the American people is not uniformly friendly to the democratic tradition. It embraces many elements and factors which are deeply hostile to that tradition, many historic strands which are favorable to the resurgence and triumph of aristocratic and autocratic principles. The future is consequently full of uncertainty; the years ahead hold numerous possibilities; society may conceivably move in any one of many directions. Which of the possibilities is to become actual will doubtless be determined by the strength of the forces which each can and will muster. Whether American democracy is to survive tomorrow rests fundamentally upon the action taken by the friends of American democracy today. And the fate of world democracy may well be decided in the United States. Let the experiment with free institutions fail here, and men and women in all lands will lose faith in the possibility of organizing a society of, by, and for the many. It may be said today, as it was said by Washington, that the destiny of free institutions is "justly considered as *deeply*, perhaps as *finally* staked, on the experiment intrusted to the hands of the American people."

REFERENCES

1. Gustavus Myers, *History of the Great American Fortunes* (Modern Library edition, New York, 1936), 23.

Index